D1569627

Music
and the
Macintosh

Geary Yelton

MIDI AMERICA, INC.
Atlanta, Georgia

Published by MIDI America, Inc.
941 Heritage Hills
Atlanta, Georgia 30033

Printed and bound in the United States of America.

Library of Congress Cataloging-in-Publication Data

Yelton, Geary.
    Music and the Macintosh / Geary Yelton.
        p.   cm.
    ISBN 0-9623397-6-8 : $16.95
    1. Music–Data processing.   2. Computer sound processing.
3. Macintosh (Computer)   4. MIDI (Standard)   I. Title.
MT723. Y44   1989
780'.285' 4165–dc20   89-91706
                                                                    CIP
                                                                    MN

Table of Contents

Acknowledgments

I wish to express my thanks to the following people and companies for their contributions to this book:

Skip Cook, Pam Cook, and Mark Purser of MIDI America; Mark Lange, Chuck Trocino, Tim Carroll, and all the guys at Micro Music; Jane Brann, proofreader; Tim Tully, Craig Anderton, Vanessa Else, Peter Hirschfield, and Steve Oppenheimer of *Electronic Musician*; Keith Sharp, Mark Lentczner, John Worthington, Richard Long, and Debbie Miani of Apple Computer; Dave Oppenheim, Chris Halaby, Keith Borman, Doug Wyatt, Paul de Benedictis, Aron Nelson, M3 Sweatt, Benjamin Austin, and John Jordan of Opcode Systems; John Mavraides of Mark of the Unicorn; Susan Alvaro, Geoff Brown, Greg Jalbert, and Robb Manning of Resonate; David Zicarelli, Joel Chadabe, Laurie Bishop, and Tony Widoff of Intelligent Music; Peter Gotcher, Mark Jeffries, and John Atcheson of Digidesign; Bill Southworth of Southworth Systems; Jeff Evans of Ar Nova; Terry Wetton of Music Software Plus; Anastasia Lanier, Jeannie Ditter, and Greg Rule of Passport Systems; Stacy Mitchell of Great Wave Software; Farallon Computing; Lenore Mamer of Coda; Marsha Vdorin of Blank Software; Craig O'Donnell; Paul Lehrman; Earnie Earnest of the MIDI Crisis Center; the staff of New Age Sight & Sound; Eddie Horst; Max Carl of .38 Special; Doug Kraul; Gary Osteen; Wendy Carlos of Serendip; Earl Cook, Russ Coffman, and Ralph Ricketts of the Atlanta Desktop Publishers Association; Ben Bradley, Biff Dyches, Curtis Bryant, Howard Davis, and Ron Anderson of the Atlanta Macintosh Users Group; Charles Knox and Bernadette Smith of Georgia State University; special thanks to Skip and Pam for making it possible to finish this project, and for creative isolation on their sailboat; to my Mom and Dad; and to Marisa, Suzanne, Michele, Tommy, David, Chris, Walt, Don, Susan, Wally, Linda, Jena, Joan, Jenny, and Jennifer, and all my friends and family for their love, faith, and encouragement.

My apologies to those whose products didn't make it into the first edition. If it runs on a Macintosh and it makes music, expect to see it in the next revision of *Music and the Macintosh*.

This book is dedicated to the spirit of David Statham.

Photo credits: back cover by Biff Dyches; page 11, courtesy of Music Software Plus; page 13, courtesy of Blank Software; pages 184, 185, and 186, courtesy of Apple Computer; page 191, courtesy of Opcode Systems; p. 96, courtesy of Yamaha; p. 101, courtesy of Roland Corp. Book design, layout, illustrations, and cover by Geary Yelton, using Letraset's Ready,Set,Go!™, Ann Arbor Softworks FullPaint™, Aldus Freehand™, and no clip art.

Macintosh, Mac II, IIcx, IIci, SE, SE/30, Plus, LaserWriter, ImageWriter, HFS, Hierarchical File System, ADB, QuickDraw, Apple Desktop Bus, AppleTalk, MacroMaker, F/DAM, Font/Desk Accessory Mover, Key Caps, MacPaint, Finder, and MultiFinder are registered trademarks of Apple Computer; PostScript and Sonata are registered trademarks of Adobe Systems; DeskWriter is a trademark of Hewlett-Packard; MacRecorder, SoundEdit, and HyperSound are trademarks of Farallon Computing; Studio Session and SoundCap are trademarks of Impulse; Deluxe Music, Deluxe Music Construction Set, DMCS, and Deluxe Recorder are trademarks of Electronic Arts; ConcertWare+, ConcertWare+ MIDI, Music Player, MIDI Player, Music Writer, MIDI Writer, and InstrumentMaker are trademarks of Great Software; Performer and Professional Composer are trademarks of Mark of the Unicorn; Pro 4, Master Tracks Pro, Master Tracks Jr, MIDI Transport, NoteWriter II, and QuickScrawl are trademarks of Passport Systems; Music Publisher is a trademark of Repertoire; Vision, EasyVision, MIDIKeys, Studio 3, Studio Plus Two, Timecode Machine, Lib/Ed, Patch Factory, MouseKeys, Shade Two, LazyKeys, PatchLib, and Cue are trademarks of Opcode Systems; Finale, Finale PowerPlus, HyperScribe, Perceive, MiniDrawWave, MiniDesignWave, and Sound Machine are trademarks of Coda Music Software; Practica Musica is a trademark of Ars Nova; Listen is a trademark of Imaja; Guitar Wizard, Chord Wizard, Scale Wizard, Fretboard Wizard, and Improvisation Wizard are trademarks of Baudville; MidiPaint and JamBox are trademarks of Southworth Music Systems; Sound Designer, Softsynth, Smartsynth, Turbosynth, Sound Accelerator, AD IN, Sound Tools, and Q-Sheet are trademarks of Digidesign; Alchemy and Sound File are trademarks of Blank Software; M, Jam Factory, UpBeat, and OvalTunes are trademarks of Intelligent Music; Dyaxis is a trademark of IMS; QuicKeys is a trademark of CE Software; Bernoulli is a trademark of Iomega; MacFace is a trademark of Sonus; DX7, DX7II, DX7S, TX7, TX81Z, TX802, TX816, TF1, DX11, DX21, DX27, and DX100 are tradmarks of Yamaha Corp.; linear arithmetic, LA synthesis, CM-32L, CM-64, D-10, D-550, and D-50 are trademarks of Roland Corp.; CZ-101, VZ-1, interactive phase distortion, and iPD are trademarks of Casio; K1, K4, and K5 are trademarks of Kawai; M1 and M3 are trademarks of Korg; DE 4X9 is a trademark of Bohm; Synclavier is a trademark of New England Digital; Emulator, Proteus, and Emax are trademarks of E-mu Systems; MIDI Crisis Center is a trademark of Rock Technologies.

The Macintosh at Home, on Stage, and in the Studio

Electronic media pervade our environment. Perhaps without realizing, you've been hearing synthesizers on the radio since the Beatles' *Abbey Road*. These days, it's safe to say, most songs at the top of the pop charts have some sort of electronic instrumentation. The same goes for music in television commercials, kid's cartoons, popular movies, industrial training films — in fact, most of the music that surrounds us in the civilized world is electronic in nature. Pick out any pop song at random, and there's a pretty good chance that a computer was involved in its creation — and chances are good that it was an Apple Macintosh. Desktop computers have revolutionized the recording industry and transformed the sound of popular music, and the Macintosh has led the way.

In the past several years, computers have crept into our leisure lives and into our careers. They've become familiar, even commonplace to millions of men, women, boys, and girls. Of all the computers that people find useful, the Macintosh has sparked the imaginations of some of the brightest, most creative programmers, composers, and musicians. If you have a Mac and an inclination toward music, you're a very lucky person.

Macs are making music in home recording studios, in basements, kitchens, and bedrooms. They're showing up onstage in bars and lounges, creating a bigger sound than a small combo could otherwise muster. For major recording acts performing live, Macs playing MIDI instruments make it possible to reproduce onstage what they labored so long in the recording studio to create originally.

Musical Macintosh software includes everything from the most entertaining musical toys to the most highly advanced studio tools. Almost anything musical you can do with a desktop computer, you can do with a Macintosh. Notate and play your favorite tunes using a variety of instrumental sounds emanating from the Mac itself, or with a few MIDI instruments, conduct and record an entire electronic orchestra.

All you need to connect the Mac to even the most sophisticated synthesizer technology is a standard communications link called the Musical Instrument Digital Interface, better known as MIDI. MIDI is built into practically every electronic musical instrument made, from cheap little synthesizers and studio-quality drum machines to half-million dollar digital music workstations.

The marriage of MIDI and the Macintosh has brought about the realization of some wonderful possibilities. No longer do you have to hire a roomful of musicians to flesh out your musical dreams. Do it all yourself, in the comfort and privacy of your own personal space. Mac software can propel you into musical realms you may have never imagined. The desktop computer, much like the tape recording studio in the 1970s, is evolving into a full-fledged musical instrument in its own right. Among music professionals, the Mac is without a doubt the most desirable computer.

Of course, you don't have to run out and buy a bunch of external hardware to enjoy the Mac's musical capabilities. It can make musical sounds with or without MIDI instruments. All you need is software. Now, perhaps you're wondering how to get started making music with your computer. Maybe you've outgrown stand-alone music applications, and you're thinking about buying your first MIDI gear. On the other hand, composing and recording music with the Macintosh may be something you do every day. Whatever your experience or level of interest, this book is here to speed you along the path of Macintosh musicianship.

The evolution of desktop computer music

We're living in an age of digital arts. Writing, printing, design, animation, entertainment, and most especially music, have been radically changed by computers and the things they do with software and associated hardware. Just as musicians have always relied on the conventions of music notation and performance, today's musician embraces the computer.

It shouldn't be surprising that musicians have developed a fascination for modern office appliances. Throughout history, music has harnessed the available tools of technology, from handmade goatskin drums to pianos made by robots. In times past, craftsmen forged musical instruments of wood, brass, steel, and animal tissues, but in recent years, they depend on aluminum, plastic, glass, and silicon.

Musical instruments have always been machines. Without human hands to give them shape and purpose, even the most traditional instruments don't occur in nature. They are mechanical contrivances. They've always followed the evolutionary path of machines. The primitive wooden pipe evolved into the recorder, which spawned the modern flute. Medieval lutes gradually became classical guitars, then steel-string guitars, and then electric guitars. Music boxes begat nickelodeons, which eventually led to MIDI sequencers. Music always harnesses whatever technology is at hand. It's only natural that computers and their offspring are taking such an active part in the music of our age.

Electronic music has been with us since the beginning of the 20th century. In the last ninety years, the stuff of electronic music has progressed from singing carbon arc lamps to very large scale integrated circuits. After decades of experimental infancy, electronic music has firmly established itself in the mainstream of popular culture.

In the late 1960s, synthesizers with musical keyboards were manufactured and marketed to a wide audience for the first time. Over the 1970s, monophonic Minimoogs grew into polyphonic Prophets.

By the early 1980s, most synthesizers contained microprocessors as the core of their control systems. By the end of the decade, most of them made sounds synthesized by microprocessors.

The development of personal computers has paralleled the growth of keyboard synthesizers. It was only a matter of time until musical instruments mated with home computers to form computer-based synthesizer workstations that would revolutionize the creation, execution, and preservation of musical expression. By harnessing the power of MIDI, one small computer can control every sound coming from any number of synthesizers, samplers, piano modules, drum machines, effects processors, and mixing consoles. Computers are great for organizing things, and what is music but the meaningful organization of sound? With some software, a MIDI interface, and a MIDI-equipped instrument, any Mac user can explore the outer limits of music technology.

Where did synthesizers come from?

Synthesizers, in one form or another, have been around since at least the 1940s — maybe even longer, depending on your definition of synthesizer. One definition is that it's a user-definable musical instrument that generates sound electronically. It can sound like lots of different things, from bells and whistles to cellos and timpani, with thunderclaps and electric pianos thrown in for good measure. Some synthesizers make only a few useful sounds, while others let you design a huge library of sounds from scratch. One type of synthesizer, a sampler, can literally sound like absolutely anything, because it plays back any sound you record, at any pitch.

When Robert Moog and a few others first fashioned musical instruments from electronic lab equipment in the mid-1960s, no one could have predicted the impact these instuments would have on the future of popular music. Synthesizers first caught the public ear when Moog's instruments appeared on popular records by Walter Carlos, the Beatles, the Monkees, and others. Rock music, always searching for the latest sensation, quickly incorporated synthesizers. The analog synth sound of the 1970s laid the foundation for many hit records. Recognizing their educational potential, university music departments bought powerful (at the time) modular synthesizers, putting electronic music into the hands of classically-trained musicians and students.

In the last few years, new techniques in digital synthesis have made an incredible palette of new sounds affordable to anyone who wants to jump on the synthesizer bandwagon.

What's MIDI, and what can it do for me?

Only a decade ago, one could hardly have predicted the important studio tools that computer music software would provide. Even when Japanese and American representatives of the synthesizer industry first met to hammer out a digital standard for musical communication, no one knew how radically the combined crafts of composition, performance, and recording would change. By agreeing on the MIDI standard, they paved the way for computer control of large-scale electronic ensembles.

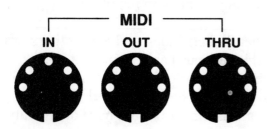

Before MIDI, synthesizers could send note information to other synthesizers, *if* they were compatible, and they often weren't. If they were, with the proper connections, playing a note on one synth sent a signal to another synth, making it play the same note. In the late 1970s and early 1980s, rather primitive digital sequencers could record the pitches and quantized rhythms in musical performances, although playback was often criticized as stiff and mechanical. To avoid incompatibility, your sequencer should have been made by the company that made the synthesizers you were using. With equipment made by different manufacturers, there were problems. Then MIDI came to the rescue by making everything compatible.

It all began in 1982, when American synthesizer maker Dave Smith suggested that competing manufacturers get together to agree on a hardware standard for their instruments. He called it the Universal Synthesizer Interface. The next year, talks between his company and a handful of other synthesizer makers led to the development of the MIDI 1.0 Specification. For electronic musical instruments, that document was a declaration of interdependence. Since then, virtually every respectable electronic instrument has either conformed to the MIDI standard or been rendered obsolete.

The development of MIDI sought to standardize musical signals so that any synth or sequencer could play any other synth, no matter who built it. Though MIDI's original goal was to play two or more instruments from a single keyboard, it quickly developed into a digital language that allows an abundance of other musically useful data to be communicated.

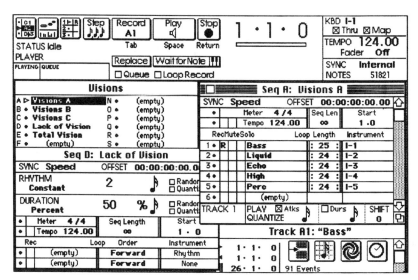

MIDI software lets you invent and experiment with music that might otherwise be beyond your grasp. Use your computer to compose songs, record live performances, transcribe and print scores, create and store thousands of sounds, and give yourself an education in ear training. Whether you're a casual hobbyist or a seasoned professional with a lifetime of chops behind you, the computer offers a whole new palette of creative resources.

Thanks to MIDI, with a little practice and patience, every nuance of a multitrack performance can be edited and polished with a personal computer. MIDI also makes it possible to control synthesizers and related instruments with specialized guitars, violins, drums, saxophones, and other new and traditional instruments.

Because the microprocessors in MIDI instruments all speak the language of MIDI, MIDI is the conduit through which musical information flows between instruments, forming a computer network for creating and performing music. With a MIDI interface and MIDI software, the microprocessor in an Apple Macintosh also speaks the language of MIDI.

With a Mac and MIDI sequencer software, you can record a song into computer memory as you play a synthesizer, then record more tracks as you listen to your recording. You can edit your performance, changing key, tempo, meter, and dozens of other parameters. You can try out new parts, experiment with harmonies, rhythms, and countermelodies, recording an almost unlimited number of overdubs that play back as a complete arrangement.

The Mac's musical advantages

With its ease of use, clear graphics, real portability, and sheer computing power, the compact Macintosh has a lot of potential for music. This platinum plastic box of glass, aluminum, and electrical circuitry has a combination of qualities that make it a hit with musicians and other creative individuals. When it was first introduced, the Mac's memory was lean and software was scarce. It has since evolved into more powerful incarnations, and now that brilliant software is abundant, those qualities are still the core of more than one man's infatuation with the Macintosh.

Any member of the compact line of Macs (128K, 512K, Plus, SE, or SE/30) is a self-contained package — a central processing unit, video monitor, sound generator, and disk drive all rolled into one. Compact Macs are more portable than other desktop computers. With a mouse and a keyboard, the whole thing still weighs under 20 pounds. It doesn't need a lot of separate components, making it rather rugged and dependable. It's ideal for carrying back and forth from home to office, stage to studio, or room to room.

The Macintosh is also renowned for its outstanding graphics. True, most Mac monitors are monochrome, but the black-on-white of the Mac's display is a good metaphor for writing and drawing on paper. The clarity and selection of typestyles, its bit-mapped graphics, and its 72 dots-per-inch screen resolution make it more readable and more pleasant to stare at than the green- or amber-on-black displays of other monochrome computer monitors. While it's true that color on the Mac is too expensive for many users, if you're dealing with music, text, numbers, or most printed graphics, color is a luxury you can live without.

The heart of the Macintosh is its Motorola 68000-series microprocessor, giving it the ability to communicate and carry on its internal processing in 16- and 32-bit words. The Mac Plus and SE contain the same 68000 that fueled the original Mac 128 and 512. The Mac II is based on the more advanced, fully 32-bit 68020 processor, and the IIx, IIcx, II ci, and SE/30 have the even more powerful 68030. What does that mean to you? It means there's power under the hood, power to quickly accomplish any variety of musical tasks, making the Mac so simple, even a musician can handle it.

The Mac's intuitive interface is what makes it so easy to use. Once you've learned your way around one program, learning other programs is easier, because there's a common logic to the way you use them. Every Mac application has a menu bar at the top of the screen, with pull-down menus you access with a mouse. Most Mac applications let you "select" words or images by "clicking and dragging" across them. The Mac's interface feels so natural and is so easily learned that other computer makers have adopted similar icon- and mouse-based interfaces.

Going well beyond beeps and bongs, the Mac can synthesize, sample, and play back sounds digitally. Though the compact Mac's on-board, 8-bit sound generator has less than half the audio accuracy of a compact disc, the SE/30 and the modular Macs, including the Mac II, IIcx, IIci, and IIx, feature stereo sound with twice the frequency response of the compact series.

Even with all the inherent advantages of the computer itself, the real key to its musical success has been its outstanding software. Every kind of music software is available, from simple scoring programs that play four-part harmonies to advanced digital signal processing applications. With Apple's MIDI Management Tools and MultiFinder, different music applications with a common MIDI driver can share musical information in real time.

Teamed with a PostScript laser printer, Mac software lets you score, edit, and print exquisite sheet music, bypassing the traditional music engraver. It's no longer necessary to hire a copyist to transcribe dozens of instrumental parts by hand, a process which is often the most expensive part of creating an orchestral composition. There's even software that automatically transcribes whatever music you play into the computer via MIDI — notes, rhythms, tempo changes, and all. With such capabilities, the future of music should be an amazing one, and you can bet that the Macintosh will lead the way.

Musical and Acoustical Rudiments

To fully comprehend some of the concepts with which

we're dealing in this book, it helps to have a good understanding of sound and music. There are several qualities that distinguish one musical sound from another. Among these are pitch, loudness, duration, and timbre. Changing these parameters turns sound into music.

When sound is converted into electrical impulses, or originates from electrical impulses, the current's frequency is the number of times that it alternates in one second. Current is converted into sound by applying it to a loudspeaker, which vibrates in response to the electrical impulses.

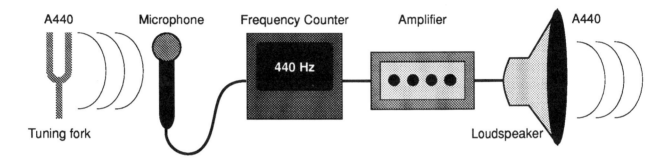

Pitch and frequency

Most of us are bombarded by sounds all day long, from meaningless traffic noises to meaningful conversation. Do you have a clear idea of what causes sound? Sound occurs when vibrations in the air, periodic flutuations in barometric pressure, are set off by the vibrations of an object. That object could be a piano string, a loudspeaker, a vocal cord, or anything capable of rapid movement. An individual vibration is called a *wave* or *cycle*, and the rate of vibration, or *frequency*, determines the sound's *pitch*. Pitch is the quality of sound that determines how high or how low it's perceived on a musical scale. Frequency is measured in *Hertz* (Hz), and since Hertz describes the actual number of times that something vibrates every second, it's also known as cycles per second. One thousand cycles per second is called a kiloHertz (kHz).

Every pitch is named by one of the first seven letters of the alphabet, letters A through G, sometimes with a sharp (♯) or flat (♭) before or after it. Sharp and flat describe a pitch's relationship to the closest pitch with the exact letter name; sharp is just slightly higher and flat is slightly lower. Sharps, flats, naturals, double-sharps, and double-flats are called *accidentals*. Because there are only seven letters to describe pitch, but 88 pitches on the average piano keyboard, pitch is further divided into ranges. A number defining a pitch's range may accompany its letter name, like A#2. A pitch may be described by its relationship to the middle C, like A# below middle C. Of course, computer people have their own way of doing things, so MIDI describes pitch by 128 numbers ranging from 0 to 127, so that middle C is note number 60.

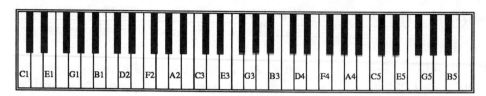

The relationship between pitches is described by their *interval*. An interval is the distance between two pitches, given an interval name like a minor third (m3) or a perfect fifth (P5). A *half-step*, also called a *semitone*, is the interval between a pitch and the next pitch higher or lower, the pitch with the closest frequency. The difference between C and C# is a half-step. Two half steps make a *whole step*, sometimes called a whole tone. An interval of 12 half steps is called an *octave*. Pitches in an octave have the same letter name, so that an octave above A3 is A4, and an octave below A3 is A2. Octaves have a frequency ratio of 2:1; an octave above any tone is twice its frequency, and an octave below is half its frequency.

represents a range of just over an octave, a wider range of pitch is represented on a *grand staff*, two parallel staves connected by a brace. The distance between the top line and the bottom space on a grand staff is less than three octaves. Notes that fall above, below, and between staves are placed on or below *ledger lines* to indicate their pitch.

In Western music, an octave is divided into twelve evenly-spaced pitches. In series, all twelve pitches are called a *chromatic scale*, made up entirely of half-steps. Most music is based on major and minor scales, which divide an octave into eight divisions, made up of both half steps and whole steps. The *key signature* is determined by the scale, and is represented by a configuration of sharps or flats on the left side of the staff.

In written music, musical sounds or tones are represented by notes. A note's pitch determines its position on a musical *staff*. A staff is a convention of five parallel, horizontal lines and the four spaces between them, on which music symbols are placed to indicate pitch, duration, dynamics, and other musical information. Each line or space represents a pitch. Because a staff only

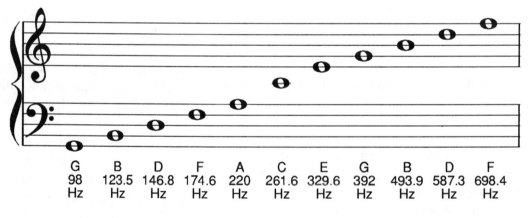

G	B	D	F	A	C	E	G	B	D	F
98 Hz	123.5 Hz	146.8 Hz	174.6 Hz	220 Hz	261.6 Hz	329.6 Hz	392 Hz	493.9 Hz	587.3 Hz	698.4 Hz

Pitches that occur on a line or a staff with a sharp or a flat are modified by that accidental. A natural cancels out another accidental.

Loudness and duration

A sound's loudness is determined by its *amplitude*, or the intensity of its vibration. A loud sound has a high amplitude, and a soft sound has a low amplitude. The loudness of a vibrating source depends on the amount of air it displaces, which depends on how hard it vibrates. If an audio signal is in electrical form, the strength of its current determines its amplitude. Individual cycles have a constantly changing *instantaneous amplitude*.

Duration is simply how long a sound lasts. Written music is divided into *measures*. Most music divides measures into four beats, with each beat having a quarter note's duration. The *time signature*, or *meter*, of such music is 4/4 or common time. The top number in a time signature represents the number of beats in a measure, and the bottom number indicates the duration of a beat. Other common meters include 2/4 (two quarter notes' duration in a measure), 3/4 (three quarter notes per measure), and 6/8 (six eighth notes per measure). The patterns formed by the durations of sounds and silences are what we call *rhythm*.

Rhythm is divided like a ruler. On a ruler, an inch is divided into half inches, halves into quarters, quarters into eighths, and so on. In common (4/4) time, the duration of a note that lasts for a whole measure is a whole note, which is divided into half notes, quarter notes, eighth notes, 16th notes, 32nd notes, 64th notes, 128th notes, and occasionally beyond. If no sound occurs for a note's duration, it's called a *rest*. Like notes, there are whole rests, half rests, quarter rest, eighth rests, etc.

Each of these note values can also be divided by odd numbers into durations that have come to be called *tuplets*. The most common tuplet is three notes with the total duration of two, called a *triplet*. Five notes in the place of four is called a quintuplet, seven in the place of four is a septuplet, etc. Some music software can't handle durations smaller than 32nd notes or tuplets smaller than triplets or quintuplets.

Timbre and harmonic spectra

It's hard to identify a musical instrument simply by the pitch, loudness, or duration of its sounds. The pitch of a note played by a bassoon may be too low to be played by a flute, but that's not how the human ear tells the difference between bassoon and flute.

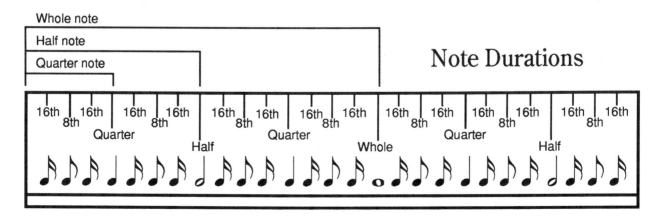

Every musical sound has its own *timbre* (pronounced tam'-br) or tone color. Differences in timbre make it possible to distinguish one instrument from another. Most instruments produce sounds in which the timbre is always changing slightly, but you can still tell what kind of instrument is producing the sound. A sound's timbre is determined by its *waveform*, or the shape of each wave. The waveform, and hence the timbre, depends on the sound's *harmonic content* or *spectrum*.

Any musical tone contains a complex combination of simple waves, each wave different in frequency and amplitude. If they're mathematically related, these waves are called *harmonics*. The frequencies and relative amplitudes of a sound's harmonics determine its harmonic content. An individual harmonic is a *sine wave*, the simplest building block of musical sound. A tone's pitch is determined by its first harmonic, called the *fundamental frequency*. The fundamental usually has the lowest frequency and the greatest amplitude of all the harmonics in a tone. Strictly speaking, other harmonics are exact multiples of the fundamental frequency. Two times the fundamental is the second harmonic, three times the fundamental is the third harmonic, and so on. The mathematical relationship among

harmonics is called the *natural harmonic series*. Most instrumental sounds contain *overtones* or *partials* which aren't exact multiples, but they're often referred to as harmonics anyway.

Basic waveforms and synthesis

Because the variety of sounds in the world is so much greater than the number of instruments, the number of possible waveforms is practically infinite. There are, however, a few basic waveforms that are very useful in electronic music. Analog synthesizers generate sounds by selectively removing harmonics from harmonically complex, basic waveforms, in a process called *subtractive synthesis*. Certain other instruments produce complex sounds by combining individual harmonics in a process called *additive synthesis*. Some synthesizers generate sounds by applying modulating frequencies to individual harmonics, also resulting in new harmonic spectra. This process is *frequency modulation (FM) synthesis*. All these types of synthesis, and quite a few others, can be accomplished by Macintosh software.

Subtractive synthesizers, commonly called analog synthesizers, have *oscillators*, which generate a number of basic waveforms. These often include sawtooth waves, triangle waves, and pulse waves, named for their shapes, which can be visually monitored on an oscilloscope. *Sawtooth* waves, sometimes called ramp waves, contain all the harmonics of the natural harmonic series in specific proportions. The second harmonic is one-half the amplitude of the first, the third amplitude is one-third the fundamental's amplitude,

Pitch	A	A	E	A	C#	E
Frequency	110	220	330	440	550	660
Harmonic No.	1	2	3	4	5	6

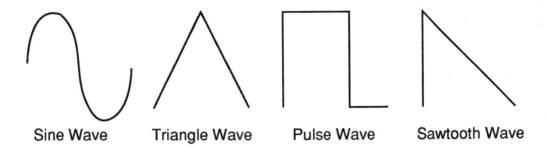

Sine Wave   Triangle Wave   Pulse Wave   Sawtooth Wave

the fourth is one-fourth, and so on. A *triangle* wave, also called a delta wave, consists of odd-numbered harmonics only. Its harmonics are relatively weak, but are nonetheless present.

A *pulse* wave, also known as a rectangular wave, has a variable shape. Changing its *pulse width* alters its harmonic content. In a single pulse wave, the instantaneous amplitude is either up or down, either on or off. The pulse width, or duty cycle, is the proportion of the wave that's on. It can be expressed as either a percentage or a fraction. Different pulse widths yield different harmonic spectra. If the pulse width is exactly half of a complete cycle, its pulse width is 50% or 1/2. This is called a *square* wave. A square wave has only odd harmonics, and the overtones are stronger than overtones in a sawtooth wave.

Shaping sound

When you make a sound, it may take a moment to reach its full intensity. This moment is called that sound's *attack*. The attack often tells us more about how an instrument is

played than any other parameter. Harmonics called *transients* may be heard only during an instrumental sound's attack. When the sound ends, it may take a moment to die away completely, or it may stop suddenly. This drop in amplitude is called its *decay*. The attack and decay, along with amplitude variations in between, make up the sound's *envelope*. An envelope lasts for the duration of the sound.

Electronic instruments and computers generate envelopes in a number of stages with a function called an *envelope generator*. An envelope generator shapes electronic sounds. The most common envelope generator is an *ADSR*, which stands for attack, decay, sustain, and release. If the attack is the time it takes a sound to peak, the *initial decay* is the time it takes to drop to a steady level, called the *sustain*. In synthesized sounds, the sustain level is maintained until the note ends. At that

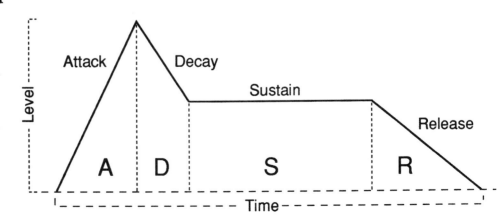

point, its amplitude drops back to zero at the rate of its *release*. The attack, decay, and release stages are specified as lengths of time, and the sustain is a level of amplitude. Some synthesized envelopes can get a lot more complicated, with multiple levels and rates between them.

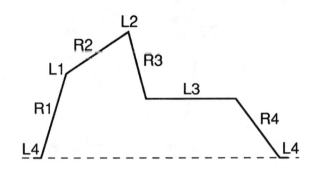

Digitized Sound:
Turning Samples into Songs

Digitizing sound, also known as audio sampling, is an

obvious application for a computer as powerful (and as fun) as the Macintosh. The fidelity of a Mac is — how shall I put this? — pretty good. It's good enough for fooling around, but obviously not good enough for serious audio recording. Just because the Mac's sound generator is digital doesn't mean it's high fidelity, despite what some stereo salesmen may believe. Though your compact Mac may sound like a cheap clock radio with a two-inch speaker, the amazing tricks it can do with sampled sounds are both entertaining and educational.

Straight out of the box, the Macintosh can't hear a thing. To sprout ears, so to speak, it needs both sampling software and a sound digitizer, like the **MacRecorder** from Farallon Computing or the **SoundCap** audio digitizer from Impulse. These analog-to-digital converters turn live sound or electrical audio signals into numbers that the computer can understand and store. Once sounds are converted to numbers, they can be edited and manipulated in many interesting ways. To change those numbers back into sound, the Mac SE, Plus, and older Macs have an onboard, 8-bit, digital-to-analog converter. The Mac II and the SE/30 have a stereo, 16-bit DAC. The computer's ROM contains the know-how to produce and reproduce digitally-generated sound with this circuit.

You need specialized software to record and play back digitized sounds. A vast library of pre-digitized sound files for the Mac is available on electronic bulletin boards and from user's groups all over the world. Just as you don't need a digital

recorder to play compact disks on your home stereo, you don't really need audio digitizer hardware to enjoy digitally recorded sound on your computer, as long as you have software that plays samples.

One type of audio software lets you record, then meticulously edit sound, sonically shaping it any number of ways: make it louder, mix it with other sounds, add special effects, and so on. Applications like **SoundEdit** and SoundCap fall into this category. These programs save sounds in different formats: as instrument files, sound resources, or normal sound files. Playing with sound editing software can teach you quite a lot about the nature of acoustical physics, if you're curious about such things.

```
        🗁 Sounds
┌──────────────────────────────┐
│ 🗋 I was a child...         ⇧ │
│ 🗋 It Won't Die....           │
│ 🗋 Just about enough of you   │
│ 🗋 Knights who say NI         │
│ 🗋 machine that goes ping     │
│ 🗋 PeeWee's Secret Word       │
│ 🗋 Princ Leia                 │
│ 🗋 Rocket J. Squirrel         │
│ 🗋 senseless waste         ⇩ │
└──────────────────────────────┘
  ◉ File              ○ Resource
```

Another type of software only plays digitized sounds as individual events. Such software may let you substitute a sound file for the Mac's system beep, or create a startup sound, so every time you turn on your computer, it crows like a rooster or plays part of the theme from your favorite movie. Programs like **Studio Session** and **Jam Session** play sound files in a musical context, as instruments in a song.

MacRecorder

MacRecorder, from Farallon Computing, is a plastic box about the size of an electric razor. It contains a circuit to convert analog audio signals into digital signals that a computer can digest. MacRecorder plugs into the Macintosh via the modem or printer ports. It features a built-in electrocet condenser microphone, mic and line input minijacks, and a knob for setting input level. MacRecorder's job is getting sound into the computer, where it can be manipulated in the digital domain. With two of them, you can record in stereo. To play back in stereo, of course, requires a Macintosh II with external speakers.

Playing sound files with SoundEdit

SoundEdit is the software side of MacRecorder. When you open a file or record something new, SoundEdit displays a two-dimensional representation of that sound, called a *waveform*. (In case you've forgotten, a waveform is a sound's graphic shape, displaying intensity on its vertical axis plotted against time across its horizontal axis.) This waveform is drawn with either dots or lines depending on the settings in the Display Options dialog box, accessed from the Settings menu.

With **SoundEdit**, playing digitized sound couldn't be easier. Open up the sound file, then click on the speaker icon. If the sound plays an octave too high or an octave too low, that means the sampling rate for playback is different than the one used for recording. To fix it, choose Set Pitches from the Settings Menu, which summons two onscreen keyboards. Middle C is highlighted on the top keyboard. If the sound plays too high, click the C below middle C to correct it. If it's too low, click the C above middle C, then click OK. To play only a portion of the sound file, click and drag across part of the waveform to select it, then click the speaker icon.

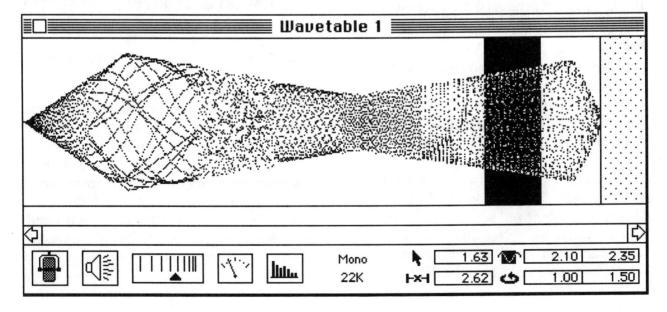

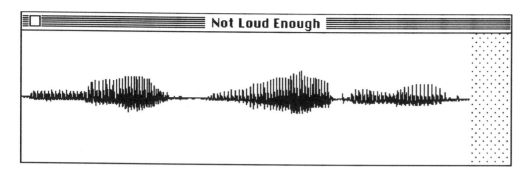

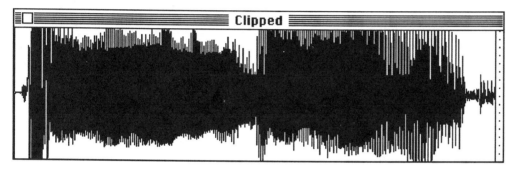

waveform isn't high enough to fill the screen at its peaks, then quantization noise can occur, so you need to turn the volume up. When you have a good level, click on the input level icon again to turn it off.

Now click on the microphone icon and when a meter that looks like a thermometer appears, start talking. That's the time gauge; when it reaches the top, your time is up. When you're finished, click the icon again to stop, or if you have a Mac II or an SE, just moving the mouse stops recording. The waveform is displayed in the window, and clicking the speaker icon plays back what you've recorded. The icon just to the right of the speaker icon lets you zoom in on part of the waveform by dragging the triangle to the left, or zoom out by dragging it to the right.

A number of options are available for recording with SoundEdit. Below the waveform display, in the center, you're told the sample rate and whether the sound is stereo or monaural. If you double-click this spot or choose Recording Options from the Settings menu, a dialog box appears to select the sample rate, the serial port, mono or stereo, and to turn file compression on or off.

Recording with SoundEdit

To record a sound, connect MacRecorder to the Mac's modem port. If you intend to record something from a tape recorder or CD player, connect the source's output to MacRecorder's line input with the appropriate cable. If you're using an external microphone, connect it to the mic input. To use MacRecorder's internal microphone, just hold it near your sound source.

To record your voice, for instance, open the SoundEdit application, or choose New from the file menu if SoundEdit is already open. Before recording, you may want to change a few settings. Click on the input level icon, then speak into the condenser mic to see if you should turn the volume up or down. Your speech is displayed almost instantaneously. If the waveform completely fills the window, or if the peaks extend beyond the window's boundaries, turn down the input volume. If the

There are four possible *sample rates*: approximately 22 kHz (kiloHertz), 11 kHz, 7.3 kHz, and 5.5 kHz. Halving your sample rate cuts the sound quality and frequency range in half, but it doubles the amount of recording time. For each megabyte of RAM, you can record up to three minutes at the lowest rate, but less than 45 seconds at the highest, depending on how much memory is already being used. For the best quality, stick to the highest rate. If you need more time, lower the rate or compress the sample.

If the 8:1 Compression button is clicked, anything you record uses only one-eighth the memory it normally would, and the sound quality is considerably degraded. Though the time indicator doesn't appear for compressed recording, you can record up to six minutes per megabyte. Compression only works in mono mode at a rate of 22 kHz, and you can't add special effects to compressed sounds.

The *playback frequency* can be changed by choosing Set Pitches from the Settings menu. This command displays two onscreen musical keyboards. By clicking a key, you indicate how much a sound is transposed when it's recorded or played

back. This capability is especially useful if the sound is to be used as an instrumental voice in a program like Studio Session.

Digital synthesis

You don't have to record anything to create interesting sounds with SoundEdit. Alternative sound sources include noise generation, tone generation, and FM synthesis, all accessed from the Effects menu. After the raw sounds are synthesized, you can use envelopes and other effects to shape them and make them musically useful, if that's your goal. These features turn your computer into a fairly sophisticated digital synthesizer as well as a sampler.

The *noise generator* creates white noise at full amplitude for any duration you specify. The tone generator synthesizes a sine wave, a square wave, or a triangle wave at a specified frequency, amplitude, and duration.

FM (*frequency modulation*) synthesis uses one tone to change the frequency of another, resulting in new harmonic structures. The *carrier* frequency is the tone's pitch. If the modulating frequency is low, it causes the carrier to waver. If it's high, it creates new harmonics. The deviation frequency is the modulation depth, or how much the modulating frequency affects the carrier. While a thorough discussion of FM synthesis is beyond the scope of this book, suffice it to say some pretty interesting, if unpredictable, sounds can be created by this method.

Editing sounds

Digitized sounds can be edited like text in a word processor. They can be selected, copied, cut, pasted, looped, echoed, filtered, flanged, reversed, mixed with other sounds, and otherwise altered beyond recognition. Portions of a waveform can be labeled by simply selecting them, then typing a name which appears below the selection. Labeling is useful for marking individual words in a sentence, for example.

Options. If nothing is selected, the first number shows where the insertion point is located. If part of the sound is looped, the bottom right numbers reflect where the loop begins and ends.

Loopback repeats part of the sound as long as you hold down the mouse button on the speaker icon. For sustained sounds, looping can conserve memory by reducing sampling time. It's especially useful for notes of long duration in

Choosing Edit Label in the Edit menu calls up a dialog box to change the start and end points, as well as the text you've typed. When you want to reselect the same portion, just click on its name.

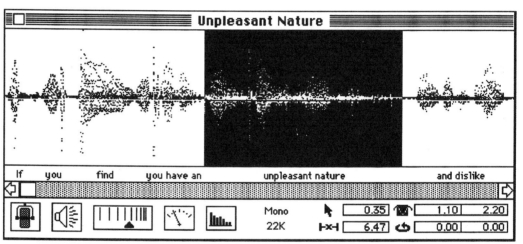

SoundEdit includes other conveniences for very precisely selecting portions of samples. Six numbers appear in "report" boxes in the lower right-hand corner of the SoundEdit window. The first number displays the position of the cursor within the waveform in samples, seconds, or fractions of a second, depending on the Display Options in the Settings menu. Below that is an indication of the length of the entire waveform. When a portion is selected, the top numbers to the right identify where the selection begins and either where it ends or its length, depending on the setting of Display

instrument files. Smooth loops can be tricky, though, and may require lots of patience. To make a loop, select the portion you want repeated, then choose Set Loopback (command-L) from the Settings menu. To remove a loop, the command becomes No Loopback if nothing is selected. If you forget to label a loop by typing in a name when it's selected, you can re-select it by entering its start and end points (or length) in the selection report boxes.

The Effects menu generates variations of a sound or a selected portion. Use this menu to make a sound louder or softer, to filter it or turn it backwards (facilitating the creation of mock satanic messages for heavy metal records), to add echo or flanging effects, to shape the pitch or loudness contour, or to create new sounds altogether.

When you select a sound and then choose *Echo* from the Effects menu, you're presented with a dialog box to specify echo parameters. Echo delay is the length of time between echoes, and echo strength is the loudness of the echo relative to the loudness of the original sound. If echo strength is less than 100%, each successive echo is softer; if greater than 100%, each successive echo is louder. In your selection, you must also include the portion where the echo is to be sustained. If you want it to ring out after the original sound, be sure to leave some dead air or paste in silence at the end before you apply the echo. Otherwise, the echo stops at the sound file's end.

The *bender* is used to change a sound's pitch by means of a "pitch envelope". If the dark line in the bender window is straight, the pitch is exactly as recorded. If it bends upward, the pitch rises; if downward, it

falls. You can create handles to shape the envelope by clicking and dragging anywhere on the dark line, causing pitch to rise and fall with the line's change in direction. You can go as high as two octaves above the sampled pitch, or two octaves below.

The *Envelope* effect dynamically changes a sound's loudness contour. It's most useful for drastically modifying sampled sounds or giving shape to synthesized sounds. When you select Envelope, you summon a dialog box displaying the entire waveform and a dark line like the one in the bender dialog box. Clicking on the line creates a handle, which can be moved up or down to make the sound louder or softer. Remove handles by dragging them out of the window. Clicking on 2X makes the sound twice as loud, or you can make it even louder by typing in a larger number, but then it's likely to be overdriven and clip (distort).

A few other Effects commands are at your disposal. *Filter* works like a graphic equalizer, with cut and boost for five frequency bands. To change a selection's

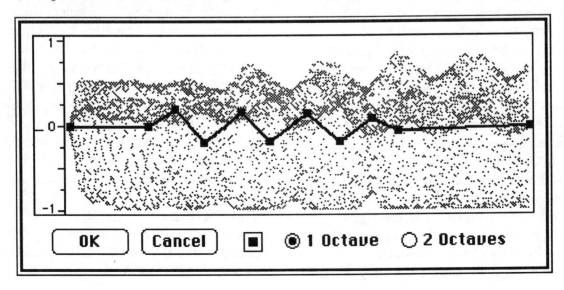

response curve, click and drag the sliders to the desired positions and click OK. The *Smooth* effect is a simple lowpass filter, removing high frequencies from a selection. The *Flanger* effect changes a selection's phase over time, resulting in a familiar swishing sound popular a few years ago.

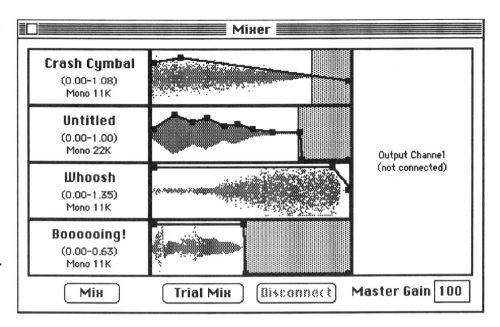

Mixing sounds

SoundEdit lets you *mix* as many as four sound files to create a new sound file. Begin by opening the first sound you want to combine with others. If you want only a fragment of the sound in the mix, select that part. To select the whole sound, use command-A or double-click in the sound's window. Then choose "Set Mixer Input" (command-M) from the Settings menu. Open another sound, select the portion you want in the mix, and again, set the mixer input. Repeat this procedure for each sound you want mixed into the final composite. Each sound file must be open for it to appear in the Mixer window.

All the input waveforms are displayed in the Mixer window. In each waveform, there's a dark horizontal line to shape the way it changes in intensity before mixing it with other sounds. Clicking and dragging the dark line creates handles for shaping loudness. Move these handles to draw the desired envelopes. Clicking Trial Mix lets

you audition it before actually creating a new sound file. When you choose Mix, the composite waveform appears in an untitled window. If the new sound clips, trash it, then lower the master gain in the Mixer window and mix it again. When you're satisfied with the way it sounds, save it and give it a name.

Digitizing instrument files

If you have a MacRecorder or the SoundCap digitizer, your Mac can record real musical instruments and convert them into instrument files, for use as instrumental voices in Studio Session. If you don't have access to a variety of musical instruments, you can always record your dog, your doorbell, or perhaps your own voice, then treat those sounds as if they were musical instruments. Imagine recording a series of pops and clicks from your mouth, then using those sounds as melodic material for Beethoven's Ninth Symphony, or orchestrating a musical arrangement of household noises.

Instrumental sounds aren't hard to find if you know where to look. If you can isolate a single note on a record or tape, you can record it as an instrument file. If you have a sampling instrument, like a keyboard sampler, you can probably connect its output to the audio digitizer's input using a cord with a phone plug at one end and a mini plug at the other. Then it's a simple matter of playing a note on the sampler and recording it with the Mac.

Another source of sounds is a CD sampler library. This is a collection of individual tones from a large variety of instruments, ranging from woodwinds and strings to drums and electric guitar. Just pop a CD into your compact disc player, connect its output to the digitizer's input, find the track with the sound you want, and record it into the Mac.

Long sound files may refuse to load into Studio Session because of memory limitations. If the tone from your source is longer than you need, it's not always necessary to record its entire length. You can always record only the first part, then shape the sound file with the envelope effect, creating your own decay at the end. Since the human mind often identifies an instrument by its harmonic transients in the first few milliseconds, be sure to record an instrumental tone's complete attack portion. Another alternative is to cut out the middle portion, but matching up the end of the first part with the beginning of the last part can be very tricky. For sustained tones, you may want to create a loop within the instrument file to save memory. Finding smooth loop points with sound editing software may be extremely difficult unless you use professional software like Alchemy or Sound Designer.

Studio Session expects instrument files to be recorded at 11 kHz. If you have a good sound recorded at a higher sampling rate, you can always change its playback rate with your sample editing software. If you don't, it plays back an octave lower than recorded. When you save a sound file with SoundEdit, be sure to specify that it's being saved as an instrument. If the sampling rate is anything other than 11 kHz, the program offers to automatically compensate by adjusting the pitch. Compressed files can't be saved as instruments.

After you digitize a sound and you'd like to use it in a song, open Studio Session's Editor and choose Add Instruments from the Windows menu. When you select the new sound, it appears in the Instruments window. Then you can position it on the staff and use it like any other instrument. If the pitch isn't what you expected, go back into your sound editing program and make the necessary changes. With a collection of original sounds and a customized phrase library, you can develop your own musical vocabulary!

Studio Session

Studio Session, from Impulse, organizes digitized musical sounds into complete songs. The Macintosh plays Studio Session songs through its sound circuits, without the need for external instruments, with up to 6-voice polyphony. Two applications make up Studio Session. One is the **Editor**, in which you compose and arrange music. In many ways, it works just like a word processor, only for sound instead of text. The other application is the **Player**, which presents the onscreen image of a cassette recorder for loading and playing music. There's also a collection of instrumental sounds that were digitized with SoundCap. A folder full of ready-to-play standards and original compositions is included, along with a library of musical phrases.

Using more-or-less standard music notation, you can enter, save, and play entire pieces of music yourself. Phrases can be strung together to create songs, and you can assemble your own phrase library. Think of it as a Mac sound processor that works like a word processor. If you have Studio Session, an audio digitizer, and sound editing software, you can sample your own sounds and orchestrate them into six-part harmonies.

Player

The Player looks just like a portable cassette player, but with six tracks. The Play button plays the song, the Stop button

stops it, and so on. Clicking the Power button quits the application. A digital multitrack player has certain advantages over its analog stereo counterpart. Not only can you load new songs and change the volume, you can change the tempo without changing pitch, solo individual tracks, and selectively turn tracks on and off.

When you open a Studio Session song file, its title appears on the cassette label. If *Player* has any trouble finding a song file or an instrument file, it prompts you to insert the needed disk. When you click Play, the cassette hubs begin to turn and music spills out of the Mac. It's not very loud music, so an external speaker is practically essential, especially if your Mac has a cooling fan. If you click the Stop button, clicking Play again continues playback. Rew and FF work just like rewind and fast forward on a real tape recorder.

If there's a disk in the internal drive, the Eject button ejects it. The Search button is used to open song files, just like the Open command from the File menu. In keeping with the tape machine metaphor, the Memory button can be clicked during playback to mark a point where you wish to return when you click Rewind. The location is stored in RAM until you either click Stop, then the 3-digit Counter button, or double-click the Memory button.

As a song plays, six output meters across the top of the screen move to register activity on each track. Instrument names appear next to the track numbers, and change if the instruments on the tracks change. On-off buttons turn individual tracks on and off. Solo buttons let you listen to the tracks one at a time.

Composing with Editor

The Editor displays a grand staff for composing in the *Staff window*. There are six such Staff windows, one for each of six tracks. You can only work on one track in one Staff window at a time. Each track plays one Mac voice, up to a total of six. A tool box contains a music note tool, an eraser, and a transposing tool. The *music note tool* accesses a palette of notes, rests, dots, and other basic music symbols. By default, when the cursor is near the staff, its function (erase, bend, insert, or replace) and pitch position are displayed in two small boxes above the tool palette. The row of spaced dots directly below the staff and just above the scroll bar is the range selector bar, used to select music. Behind the Staff window, there are windows containing a *phrase library* and a list of instruments, and below, Play and Stop buttons with On and Off switches for all six tracks.

To enter music, first click the music note tool, then the desired symbol on the note palette, then the location you want to place a symbol on the staff. The insertion point moves to wherever you click, and the symbol snaps to the nearest line or space within the staff. Unless you specify otherwise, bar lines are automatically inserted when a measure's rhythm is filled up. Since you can't insert chords on a single track, individual notes of a chord must be placed on separate tracks.

If you make a mistake, just click the eraser and then the symbol to be erased. You can also delete notes, rests, and other symbols by backspacing from the insertion point, or click and drag within the range selector bar, then cut or backspace. To change a

</>
</>

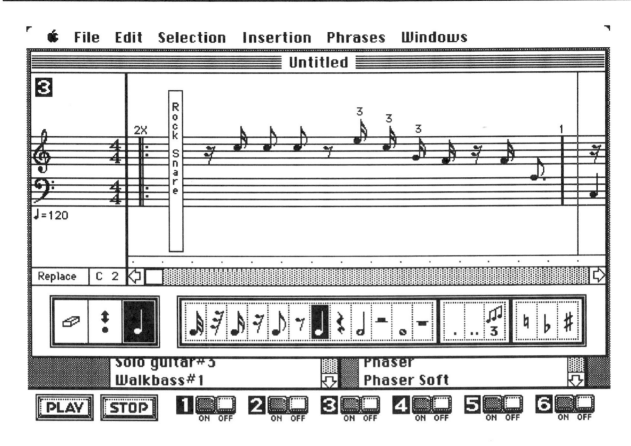

note's rhythmic value, select the note with the proper duration from the palette, then click directly on the note to be replaced. Select the note bender tool to transpose pitch. Place the tool's dot above or below the pitch you want transposed, and the new pitch appears under the dot. Placing the dot over a note and dragging it up or down transposes it half a step. Dragging to the left or right decreases and increases a note's duration. Notes can also be transposed chromatically or by octaves from the Selection menu.

Music can be edited further with the *Selection menu*. When you click and drag across the range selector bar, the music directly above it is highlighted, enabling the choices in the Selection menu which are otherwise grayed out. Single measures are selected by double-clicking in the range

selector bar. When two or more notes are selected, they can be tied or slurred with the Tie command (command-T). Tying notes of the same pitch joins them into a single note of longer duration, and slurring pitches plays them with a single attack, without retriggering the instrumental voice. Reselecting the command removes ties or slurs.

Repeat symbols saves you from having to notate repeating parts in succession. Repeats are preferable to copy and paste because the score is shorter and the file size is smaller than music with repeated parts pasted in. Select the music you want repeated and choose Repeat... (command-R), then type the number of repeats in the dialog box. To change the number, select a repeated part and choose Change Repeats.

The *Insertion menu* is used to place key signatures, time signatures, bar lines, alternate endings, tempo changes, etc., at the insertion point anywhere in the score. Double-clicking on the Tempo display calls up a dialog box to set the initial tempo, with a default value of 120 quarter notes per minute.

The track number is shown in the upper left corner of the Staff window. To display the second track, choose Edit Track 2 from the Edit menu, or hold the Command key and press the number 2 key. All six tracks are accessed from the Edit menu or from command key equivalents. To see three tracks at the same time, open the *Overview* window from the Windows menu. Scroll down to view the other three. To limit the number of tracks shown, select the tracks with Configure Overview in the Windows menu. Individual tracks may only be edited in the Staff window, and not in Overview.

The score can be printed out at any time, but it's not the best looking music you ever saw come out of a Macintosh. The song title and page number are printed in a box at the top of each page. Only tracks that are turned on in the Overview are printed, making it possible to extract parts for individual players.

Phrase Libraries

Musical phrases can be assembled into complete songs. A database of phrases called a phrase library is included with Studio Session and shows up as a list in its own window. To build a song from phrases, position your insertion point, then shift-click on the name of a phrase, or select it and choose Insert Phrase (command-P) from the Insertion menu. Insert another phrase, then another, on as many tracks as needed until your composition is finished.

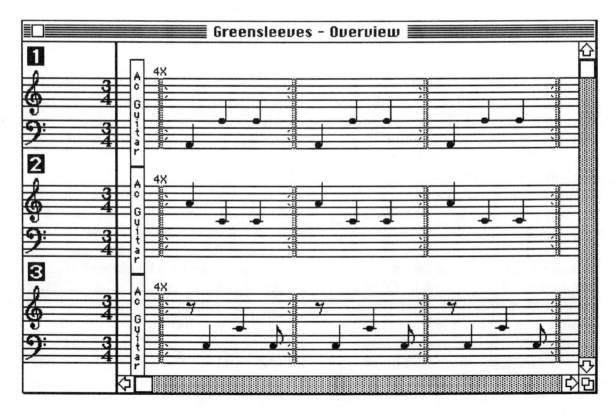

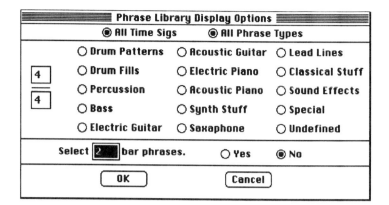

The phrases listed in the phrase library window can be narrowed down to a user-defined classification, time signature, and number of bars. A classification type might have a name like Piano Blues Progressions or Guitar Solos or Sounds of Nature. If you're looking for a 4-bar drum fill in 4/4 time, for example, choose Set Display Options… from the Phrase menu or click the corresponding buttons in the phrase library window. Only phrases that meet the specified conditions are displayed, so there's no need to sift through phrase types you don't need, searching for just the right one. Of course, if you insist, you can also set the options to display all phrase types in all time signatures.

You can create and save your own customized library or multiple libraries of musical phrases. Choose Create Phrase Library in the Phrase menu and give the library a name. To add a phrase, select some music and choose Save As A Phrase from the Selection menu (not the Phrases menu). The Phrase Saving Options window appears so you can type the phrase's name, classify its type, and note its time signature and number of bars. Edit Phrase Info in the Phrase menu also calls up the Phrase Saving Options window. The command Customize Option Names… in the Phrases menu summons the Phrase Customization Window to change the names of the fifteen possible classifications. Custom phrase libraries are opened with Change Phrase Library from the Phrases menu.

Instruments and playback

Before you can play a song, you have to specify which *instruments* play on what tracks. Place the cursor ahead of the notes, then choose Show Instruments from the Windows menu. This brings the Instruments list to the forefront, making it the active window. Select an instrument to insert by shift-clicking on its name. Alternately, you can select an instrument name and choose Insert Instrument from the Insertion menu (command-I). A box with the instrument's name appears just behind the insertion point.

Instruments can be replaced, either one at a time on single tracks, or globally throughout an entire score, just like words can be replaced in a word processor. To exchange one instrument for another on a single track, select Change Instrument from the Edit menu. This command calls up a window to find any instrument and change it to another.

Some instruments are looped and others aren't. If an unlooped instrument plays a note of long duration, it may drop out before the note is finished. This is to be expected in the case of percussion, plucked strings, and the like. Many instruments are looped, and play for the full duration of long notes. A list of instruments can be found in the Studio Session manual, with information about each instrument's pitch, suggested pitch range, and whether it's looped or unlooped.

Studio Session™ Music System
Editor version 1.2u ©1986 by Bogas Productions
Written by Ed Bogas, Steve Capps, Neil Cormia, Ty Roberts
Digital Imagery by Marge Boots
Sound Advice from Tom Hedges, Mark Zimmer

When instruments and notes are both in place, you can listen to your work by clicking the Play button. Unlike Studio Session's Player, the instruments don't load into memory until you actually click Play, so there's always a delay the first time you play something from the Editor. The program searches the disk for the instruments it needs and if it can't find

something, it prompts you to insert the proper disk.

The effect of clicking Stop depends on the settings in the User Interface Options dialog box, accessed from the Configure Editor command in the desk accessory menu. By default, the cursor moves to the position where the music stops playing. If you enable Play from insertion point, you can play a score, stop and edit mistakes, then continue playing from where it left off. The Repeat Play option loops back to the beginning when the end is reached. If you select a part, then click Play, only that part is played, which means that if Repeat Play is turned on, a selected part can be played over and over.

A much sillier way to play back Studio Session songs is to choose *About Editor...* from the desk accessories menu. Six big eighth notes with cartoon faces and hands begin to sing. As the song plays, each character is animated in sync to a corresponding track.

Your composition can be made to play with a jazzy feel by selecting an even number of notes and choosing Swing (command-S) from the Selection menu. This option lengthens some notes and shortens others, with the letters L and S above each note to indicate if they're long or short. Be sure that an even number of notes with the same rhythmic value is selected, or unwanted beats may be added to each measure. If you like to dabble in experimental music, however, try selecting all tracks for an entire song and see what happens when it plays back.

Composition and Scoring Software

Deluxe Music

Deluxe Music, also known as Deluxe Music Construction Set or DMCS, has something to offer both the musical beginner and the veteran musician. Published by Electronic Arts, this affordable music notation program plays back four voices from the Macintosh and up to 32 voices from MIDI instruments. A veritable plethora of DMCS song files are available from electronic bulletin boards and users' groups, so you don't even need to know anything about writing music to enjoy Deluxe Music. As a composer's tool, it fulfills most of the requirements for transcribing and listening to your songs performed by a computer. If you have a

MIDI instrument and an interface, Deluxe Music can unlock an entire world of electronic music for you. If you have Opcode's Vision, Sequencer 2.6, or EA's Deluxe Recorder, you can not only transcribe sequences with Deluxe Music, you can convert any standard MIDI Files to sequencer files, and then to DMCS scores.

Notes, rests, dynamics, and other symbols are entered by combinations of pointing and clicking, typing on the Mac keyboard, and optionally, playing a MIDI instrument. Because you can play music as soon as you enter it, you have immediate aural feedback as you compose or transcribe music. All the

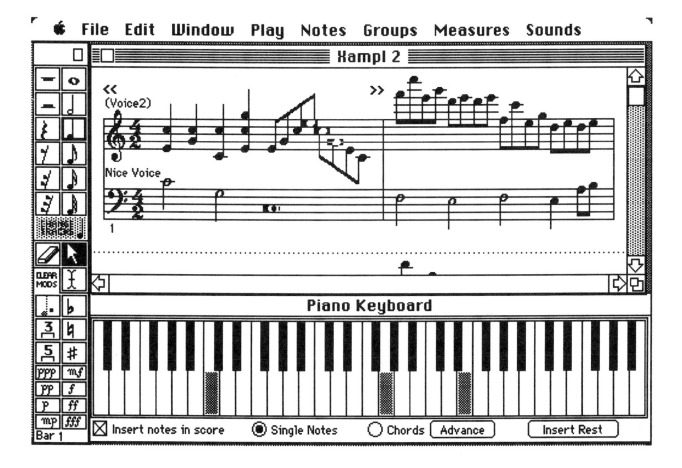

symbols used in most music are available, including fretboard notation for guitar and other fretted instruments. Deluxe Music uses the Adobe music font Sonata, and the display version is included for dot matrix printing and onscreen display. If you have the PostScript version of Sonata, you can produce high-quality laser manuscripts a lot less expensively than other scoring programs. To use Deluxe Music, your System also needs the DMCS ScreenFont and DMCS GuitarFret installed. The screen font contains the symbols in the note palette, the cursors, and grayed-out notes.

Setting up the score

If the default formatting isn't to your liking, you can customize the staff and page layout with the *Score Setup* dialog box, summoned from the Window menu. The default system is a grand staff with up to two measures shown across the screen, and subsequent measures shown below. The default tempo is 90 beats per minute. To change any of these settings, you must open the Score Setup box from the Window

menu. You can add or delete any number of staves in a system, braced or bracketed, with treble, bass, alto, or tenor clefs. Change the number of measures displayed horizontally with Bars Per Line, or by turning off Paged Score, scroll horizontally rather than vertically to see more measures. If you check 2 Tracks per Staff, up to two separate parts or voices can be written on each staff. Also in Score Setup, you can change the distance between staves or make room for a title at the top by changing the Space above staff or Space below staff values with scroll bars.

Also by default, the time signature is 4/4 and the key signature is C major (all white keys on the piano). Meter and key changes can be inserted at the beginning of any measure by positioning the insertion point and choosing a command from the Measures menu. Tempo changes occur at the beginning of any measure by setting Beats Per Min in the Score Setup, then putting the insertion point in the measure and choosing Set Tempo from Measures.

Entering and editing music

The *note palette* resides on the left side of the Deluxe Music screen. It contains notes and rests from a whole to a 32nd, three accidentals, eight dynamic markings, tools to dot notes and group triplets and quintuplets, a text insertion cursor, an eraser, and an arrow cursor. To place a note

---

Score Setup

Bars Per Line ◁▭▷ 3	☒ Paged Score
Beats Per Min ◁▭▷ 90	☒ 2 Tracks per Staff
Score Width ◁▭▷ 441	[Set To Window Width]
Volume ◁▭▷ 7	[Set To Printer Width]
	[Set Margins]

Choose Staff Number ◁▭▷ 1   ☐ Two Way Ties

● Treble Clef   ○ Tenor Clef   ☒ Staff Sound On   ☐ Hide Instruments
○ Bass Clef   ○ Alto Clef   ☐ Hide Staff   ☐ Hide Key/Clef

[Add Staff]   Space above staff ◁▭▷ 16

[Delete Staff]   Space below staff ◁▭▷ 18

☐ Split Bar Lines ☐ Brace Staff ☐ Top Bracket ☐ Bottom Bracket
● Normal   ○ Play 1 Octave High   ○ Play 1 Octave Low

on a staff, click its icon in the palette, then position the cursor over the staff in the Score window and click again. Clicking the icon chooses its rhythm, and where you place it on the staff chooses its pitch. You can also enter pitch from the onscreen piano keyboard, or if you're set up for it, from a MIDI instrument.

Another way to enter rhythm is by pressing keys on the computer keyboard, which selects the appropriate icon on the note palette (see chart). Note durations may be changed by number keys or letter keys, in conjunction with the shift key to enter rests. You can also change a note's duration by dragging it to the left or right with the arrow cursor. Dragging to the left decreases its rhythmic value, and dragging to the right increases its value. Dragging up or down changes its pitch diatonically. A sharp, flat, or natural is entered by clicking it, then the note value, then placing it on the staff. Dots, triplets, and quintuplets are selected the same way: first the modifier, then the note, then the staff. Once a note is in place, you can also change its pitch by selecting an accidental

and placing it immediately to its left, or by transposing it with the Notes menu. Rhythm can be changed by selecting a duration and then option-clicking a note.

Below the Score window, there's an onscreen *piano keyboard* which serves two or three purposes. If you select Player Piano from the Play menu, keys will by highlighted in gray as their associated notes play. If Insert notes in score is checked, clicking on these keys can be used for entering pitch, with rhythm entered from the note palette or the Mac keyboard. If Insert notes in score is turned off, the piano keyboard can be used for reference if you want to hear something before you enter it.

No matter what your mode of input, click the *Chords button* in the piano keyboard window to enter a chord, and Advance when you're ready to enter the next chord. For chords with notes of different duration, check 2 Tracks Per Staff in the Score Setup. To delete a note from a chord, drag it on top of another note in the chord.

If you're using MIDI to enter pitch, you can also enter duration by holding down the note you play. The selected note determines the minimum duration. Let's say you've selected a 32nd note in the note palette. If you play a middle C on your MIDI keyboard, a 32nd note C materializes

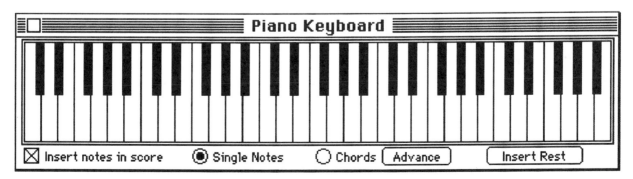

at the insertion point. If, however, you continue to hold down the key, that 32nd note turns to a dotted 32nd, then a 16th, then a dotted 16th, then an eighth, then a dotted eighth, then a quarter, and so on. The longer you hold down that key, the longer its duration grows. Like most MIDI programs, Deluxe Music has a MIDI Setup Dialog. If you click its Change Input Delay button, you're given a chance to change how rapidly the note scrolls through different durations when you hold a note.

As you enter music, the insertion point advances until the current measure's duration is complete, then advances to the next measure. When you begin a new measure, the next blank measure is automatically inserted. If you enter a note or a rest with a duration too long for the current measure, it's grayed out and won't be played during playback. If you click in a measure that's already full and try to add more notes, they'll be grayed out too.

Eight *dynamic markings* from triple forte to triple piano can be entered anywhere on the score from the note palette or key equivalents. Notes positioned to the right of such a marking play back at the level indicated. Gradual changes in loudness can be entered by selecting the beginning and ending notes and choosing Crescendo or Decrescendo from the Groups menu. Loudness is raised or lowered relative to the current dynamic level; if there's no dynamic marking, triple forte is assumed.

Lyrics and other text can be entered by selecting the text cursor, then clicking and dragging absolutely anywhere on the score, and then typing. A small text box appears, which can be resized by clicking and dragging its lower right handle, and

moved with its upper left handle. The text cursor has a tiny crossbar through the I-beam for grabbing the handles. When the text cursor is chosen, the Sounds menu turns into a Fonts menu. If you choose Fonts, a dialog box gives you a choice of installed font sizes. There's no need to click and drag across text to change its font or size; just click it with the text cursor to select it.

The *DMCS GuitarFont* makes it possible to actually type chord symbols for guitars and other fretted instruments above the measures. Create a square text box and select GuitarFont from the Fonts menu. For the lowest string at the nut, type shift-1. Then type shift-2 for the middle strings and shift-3 when you get to the highest string. Press return and type the second fret for each string, then the third, and so on. To mark a fret that should be fingered, click and drag over it, then type shift-4 for the low string, shift-5 for the middle strings, or shift-6 for the high string. Name chords by typing numbers and upper case letters.

To move a barline horizontally, just click on it and drag to its new location. All the notes in the measures on either side of the bar line readjust their spacing automatically. To quickly move from one part of the score to another, command-G summons a dialog box to enter the measure number, just like Go To Measure… in the Edit menu.

To change anything about notes on a staff, they must be selected. When you select a music symbol by placing the arrow cursor over it and clicking it, the symbol is reversed from black to outlined white.

Select a range of symbols by clicking and dragging over them or by clicking the first and shift-clicking the last. Select an entire staff by shift-clicking its first and last notes. To select notes in multiple staves in a system, click the first note in the highest staff and shift-click or drag to the last note in the lowest staff.

Any number of notes or chords, measures, or staves can be selected and *transposed* by half steps or octaves from the Notes menu. You can also transpose with Set Key Signature from the Measures menu. If you change the key signature in any measure, you're given three choices: 1) don't transpose, which only adds accidentals, if necessary, and doesn't modulate the melody; 2) transpose up; and 3) transpose down. To transpose without changing the key signature, click no key change. If you cut something from a treble staff and paste it into a bass staff, or vice versa, the notes are spontaneously transposed.

Instruments

For playing scores, Deluxe Music includes a collection of preset instrumental voices synthesized by the Macintosh. Any instrumental voice can be assigned to any measure in any staff. All the music on a staff following an instrument change plays back using that instrument's voice until it sees another instrument change. If the music on the top staff starts out playing flute, and turns into a twisted bow tie at the eighth measure, and then into a thumbazoon at the twenty-fourth, it's because instrument changes occur in measures 1, 8, and 24. The sound changes from one instrument to another, just like sending patch changes from a sequencer to a synthesizer as a sequence plays.

On the right side of the menu bar, there's a Sounds menu. Add voices to the list by choosing Load Instrument... and picking one from the file dialog box. Then, to assign an instrument to a staff, select Set Instrument from the Measures menu, or type command-semicolon. The selected instrument has a check mark beside it. That's the one that gets assigned to the measure with the insertion point. By the way, every instrument you add to the Sounds menu uses up some of the computer's memory, and since sounds are saved with the song file, it increases the file size too. Remove the ones you don't need by selecting an instrument in the Sounds menu and choosing Remove Instrument. Selecting Erase Instrument from the Measures menu deletes the voice assignments for that measure in all staves.

The sound of each instrument can be further altered by selecting some notes and choosing Set Play Style... from the Notes menu or typing command-Y. This action conjures up a dialog box with a list of variations such as legato, staccato, vibrato, tremolo, etc. Pick a style, and the selected notes play with whatever variation you choose. The style number is displayed beneath each note if you turn on Show Play Styles in the same menu. If you choose

```
┌─────────────────────────────────────────────┐
│  Set play style for Big Bells                 │
│  ⦿ 1 - normal              ┌─────────────┐    │
│  ○ 2 - staccato            │     OK      │    │
│  ○ 3 - legato              └─────────────┘    │
│  ○ 4 - uibrato slow        ┌─────────────┐    │
│  ○ 5 - uibrato -fast       │   Cancel    │    │
│  ○ 6 - low                 └─────────────┘    │
│  ○ 7 - legato/uibrato                         │
│  ○ 8 - slow attack                            │
│  ○ 9 - tremolo                                │
│  ○ 10 - low/uibrato                           │
└─────────────────────────────────────────────┘
```

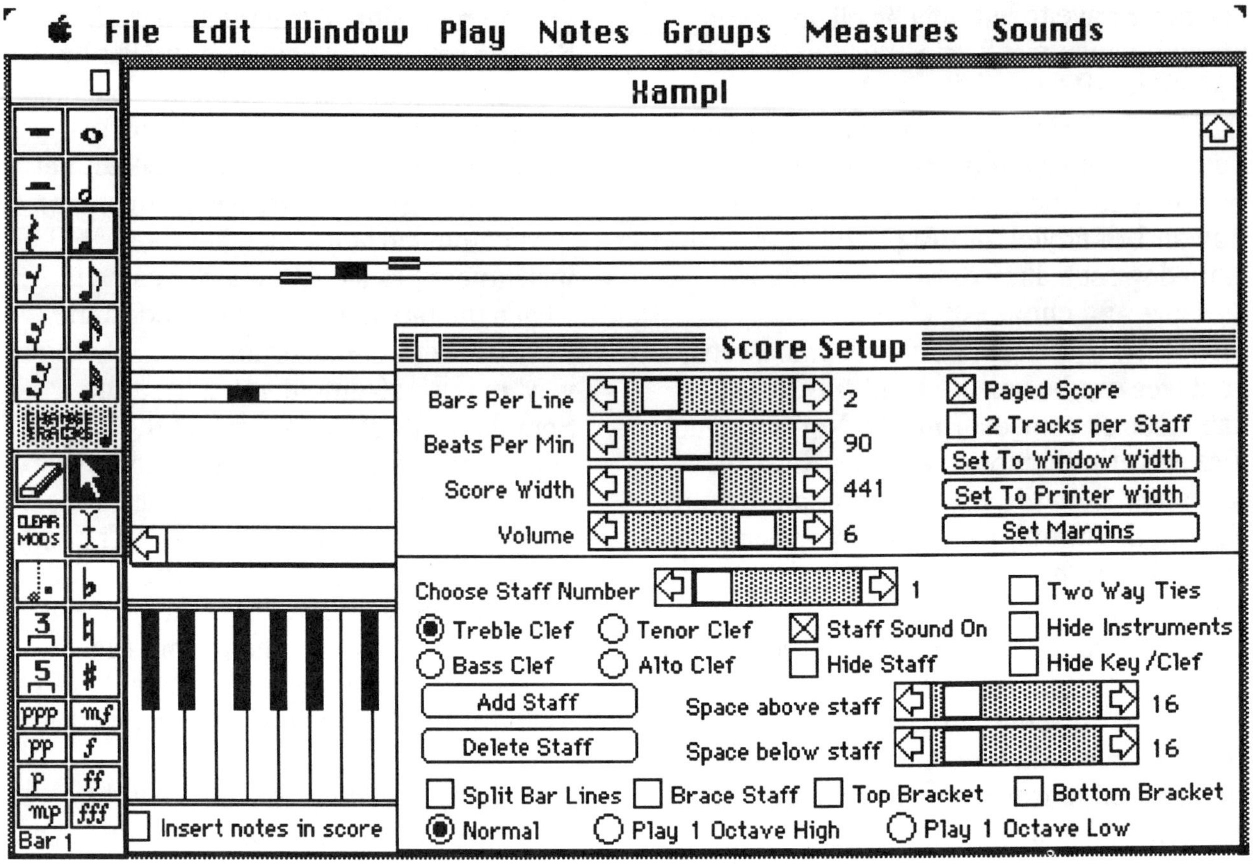

Score Setup

Bars Per Line ◄ [ ] ► 2
Beats Per Min ◄ [ ] ► 90
Score Width ◄ [ ] ► 441
Volume ◄ [ ] ► 6

☒ Paged Score
☐ 2 Tracks per Staff
[Set To Window Width]
[Set To Printer Width]
[Set Margins]

Choose Staff Number ◄ [ ] ► 1   ☐ Two Way Ties
◉ Treble Clef   ○ Tenor Clef   ☒ Staff Sound On   ☐ Hide Instruments
○ Bass Clef   ○ Alto Clef   ☐ Hide Staff   ☐ Hide Key /Clef
[Add Staff]   Space above staff ◄ [ ] ► 16
[Delete Staff]   Space below staff ◄ [ ] ► 16
☐ Split Bar Lines ☐ Brace Staff ☐ Top Bracket ☐ Bottom Bracket
☐ Insert notes in score   ◉ Normal   ○ Play 1 Octave High   ○ Play 1 Octave Low

staccato, dots appear above or below the note heads even when you Hide Play Styles. For maximum legibility and minimum clutter, be sure to hide them when you print the score.

In the place of Mac sounds, you can assign MIDI channels and patch changes to any measure. Typing command-M changes the Sounds menu to a MIDI menu. The current MIDI channel is shown with a check mark beside it. With the MIDI menu active, type command-M again to change MIDI channels at the insertion point. Command-A returns the menu to Sounds. MIDI channels and patch changes are entered just like instruments. When you give the Set Instruments… command, the channel and patch change checked in the MIDI menu are assigned to the current measure.

Playing and printing

To play a song file, just select Play Song from the Play menu or type command-P. If you're using a Mac to make music with no external instruments, it's assumed that you're using an external speaker for full fidelity. Since some bass sounds are too low to hear over the Mac's little built-in speaker, you can raise everything an octave by unchecking External Speaker (command-E), also from the Play menu. If Flash Notes is turned on, a real time piano roll notation displays each note as it plays, showing up to 12 voices of MIDI. You can also see the keys highlighted as they play on the Piano Keyboard, but if there's too much going on onscreen, it screws up the music.

You don't have to listen to the whole song every time you play something. You can select a section to play with the Play Section command (command-S). Put the insertion point in the first measure of the section and choose Begin Section << from Play, or better yet, type command-< (shift-comma). Then put it in the last measure and choose End Section >>, or command-> (shift-period).

The ultimate output of most Deluxe Music files is a printed manuscript. To make it look good, it has to be formatted correctly. Look in the Score Setup, and make sure that Paged Score is checked, so that staves are arranged in rows. Control the number of staves across the width of a page with the Bars Per Line scroll bar. For entering music, the page width was probably set to the Set To Window Width default. For printing, click Set To Printer Width, unless you want it wider or narrower. To indent the first system or other systems, click the Set Left Margin button.

Now you're ready to print. All you have to do is warm up your printer, choose Print Score from the File menu, and all your effort is put on paper.

Note Palette Keyboard Equivalents

whole note	w or 1
whole rest	shift-W or shift-1
half note	h or 2
half rest	shift-H or shift-2
quarter note	q or 3
quarter rest	shift-Q or shift-3
eighth note	e or 4
eighth rest	shift-E or shift-4
sixteenth note	s or 5
sixteenth rest	shift-S or shift-5
thirty-second note	t or 6
thirty-second rest	shift-T or shift-6
eraser	x
arrow tool	enter
clear modifiers	c
text tool	' (quote)
dotted tool	d
flat	b
natural	n
sharp	r
triplet	l
quintuplet	v
p, pp, ppp	hold p to scroll
mp	mp
mf	mf
f, ff, fff	hold f to scroll

ConcertWare+

Along with Macromind's **MusicWorks**, Great Wave's **ConcertWare** was one of the very first music programs for the Mac. Before those two programs, practically the only way to coax music out of the Mac was to run a program in BASIC or play a game that featured musical accompaniment. The original ConcertWare not only played four voices from the Mac, but it gave you the tools to create new sounds to play your compositions. A substantial number of song files were included on disk, and more selections were available. Then came the new and improved **ConcertWare+**, and later, **ConcertWare+ MIDI**, for playing music with MIDI instruments. Now ConcertWare+ is available in both MIDI and non-MIDI versions. Of course, the MIDI version can also play music from the Mac's sound circuit.

All versions of ConcertWare+ are actually three interrelated applications: **Music Player**, **Music Writer**, and **InstrumentMaker**. MIDI versions use the names **MIDI Player** and **MIDI Writer**. When you open a song file, it plays in Music Player. Music Player displays the instruments as they play, usually offering a text block describing the piece being played. Composing and arranging is accomplished in Music Writer. Music is entered, one voice on one staff at a time, from a music symbol palette, from the Mac keyboard, or from a MIDI instrument. InstrumentMaker lets you design instrumental voices to add to the instrument library. Define parameters like waveform, envelope, and vibrato, and even design an icon for each instrument.

Music Player/MIDI Player

Music Player (or MIDI Player) is the ConcertWare+ application that performs one or more selected songs, rather like a computer jukebox. To play a song, double-click its icon in the Finder or select it from a file dialog. When it opens, it plays immediately. To play a series of songs, select them in the Finder by shift-clicking or clicking and dragging around their icons. After they begin playing, you can cancel a series of selections with Forget Selections in the File menu.

The Music Player screen shows up to eight members of the orchestra on the left and right, and the current players surrounding a conductor icon in the middle of the screen. Scroll bars let you change tempo and volume, and active voices are checked. Only four simultaneous voices play from the Mac, or up to eight voices from MIDI instruments. Without MIDI, any four of the eight instruments shown can be playing at any given moment. As instruments change, the icons surrounding the conductor change.

To substitute members of the orchestra, choose **Set Instruments** from the Play menu. This calls up a dialog box with the instrument library shown as a scrolling list. Click the button for the voice number you want to change and select an instrument by double-clicking. For additional instruments, click their buttons and select new ones. To change a single instrument, save time by double-clicking its icon and select a new one from the instrument

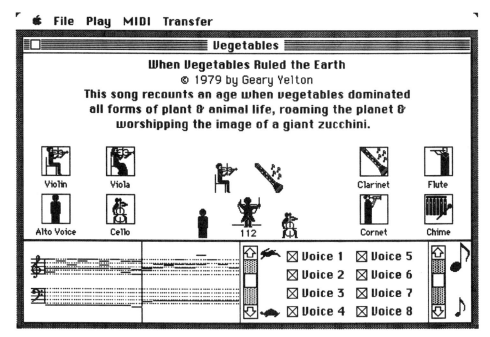

library. Though Music Player doesn't remember changes in tempo, volume, or which voices are playing, you can save instrumental changes as part of the song file. To changes these and other parameters, use the Transfer menu to open the same song in Music Writer.

As the music plays, a graphic representation of the score scrolls by in a window on the lower left. Unless you check Repeat Piece from the Play menu, ConcertWare+ keeps playing until the end of the song. To prematurely stop playback, choose Pause from the Play menu or type command-P. To continue, choose Continue or type command-G. Rewind to the beginning with the Start Over menu selection (command-S).

In MIDI Player, you can control whether voices play through MIDI or through the Mac by choosing Edit MIDI Parameters… in the MIDI menu. If MIDI is checked in the MIDI menu, no voices are heard from the Mac unless you turn it off. To

permanently change this, uncheck MIDI Default On and save your changes. The MIDI parameters dialog box also lets you specify the MIDI channel on which each voice plays, whether patch changes are sent, and MIDI interface clock speed. A set of MIDI parameters can be saved and opened with the Load MIDI Setup command.

Music Writer/MIDI Writer

Music Writer (or MIDI Writer) is the ConcertWare+ application for entering and editing musical performances. Each voice is transcribed onto its own staff, one voice at a time. Music can only be entered and edited in the currently active voice. To select one of eight voices, click a number button across the top of the window or hold the Command key and type the voice number. The arrow cursor keys also change the currently active voice. If Show Voice Above is checked, the current voice is shown at the top of the score window. Otherwise, it takes its position in the score with the first voice at the top.

The score's layout is formatted with the *ruler*. Click the ruler button to add braces or brackets, assign clefs, and hide selected voices. To change the distance between staves, use the *mover tool* at the top of the symbol palette to move staff bars in the ruler. The ruler also lets you assign multiple voices to the same staff. Rulers, key signatures, time signatures, tempo changes, repeats, endings, and double bars can be inserted in any measure with the *Insert* menu.

There's a *palette* of music symbols on the left side of the screen, and to its right, a range of pitches. You can place the palette at the top of the screen by choosing Edit Show/Hide from the MIDI menu. The note symbols select durations for notes and rests. To enter notes with the mouse, select a voice with one of the voice buttons (1-8). Click the desired duration, then the pitch. A note appears on the staff at the insertion point. If you want a sharp, flat, natural, or triplet to modify the note, click the *modifier* before you select the pitch. To enter a rest, click the desired duration and then the rest symbol. To enter chords, check the Chords box at the top of the screen. Select a duration and then a series of pitches. Click the Next Chord button or press Return to advance the cursor. Because each Mac voice is monophonic, the computer plays only one note in chords entered this way. All notes play over MIDI.

Like notes, rests, and chords, *dynamic markings* are also entered from the symbol palette. Dynamics affect playback volume from the Mac and velocity from MIDI instruments. MIDI velocities can be inserted from the MIDI menu. They show up as dynamics unless you use Edit Show/Hide… in the MIDI menu to show velocity values.

You can also enter music from the Mac keyboard. Choose *Step-Time Entry* from the Sound menu, then type numbers for durations and letters for pitch. The number keys specify duration, from a 32nd note to a whole note, and the bottom row of letters specify pitch. The middle row of letter keys enter notes with accidentals, but naturals, sharps, and flats can be added with the Q, W, and E keys. The R key enters a rest, and the T key, a triplet. The Shift and Caps Lock keys both transpose the pitch range up an octave, and the option key lowers it an octave. If you don't select Step-Time Entry before you begin typing, the keys still play the Mac like an instrument.

Use the same procedure to enter music via MIDI, but enter pitch from the MIDI instrument rather than the Mac keyboard. If you check the Chords box first, you can play chords into *Music Writer*. You can also record in real time and then insert what you record into a score. To do this, position the insertion point and choose Record from the Sound menu. A dialog box appears and a metronome begins clicking. The tempo can be set between 30 and 225 beats per minute. The voice boxes let you select which of the other voices play as you record. To begin recording, click the Start Recording button or just start playing. What you play is automatically quantized to the duration you specify. When you're finished recording, you can listen to what you've played, then choose to re-record or insert it into your score.

To select music for editing, click and drag across it. For long passages, click the beginning of the selection, then shift-click the end. Selected music can be cut, copied, cleared, and pasted with the Edit menu, and deleted with the Delete key. Music across staves can be cut or copied with *Multi-Cut...* and *Multi-Copy...* commands from the Edit menu, which summons a dialog box to check the voices you want to cut or copy. Using these commands changes Paste to *Multi-Paste...*, which summons a similar dialog box that lets you reassign voices as well. You can copy only a few of the notes in chords with the *Extract Copy* command. The *Merge-Paste* command lets you merge several voices into a single system. You can also copy and paste between song files, but if you close Music Writer, the contents of the Clipboard are lost.

Selected music can be altered in many ways. With the *Change* menu, notes can be transposed, groups of flagged notes beamed, durations modified, slurs added, and stem directions changed.

You can play songs in Music Writer as well as Music Player, so you can hear what you're composing. Command-G commences playing, command-P stops it, and command-S rewinds it to the beginning. Playback always begins at the insertion point. You can tell the program to move the insertion point to wherever you choose to stop. The ability is convenient when you're listening for something that needs to be changed.

There are eight instruments assigned to the eight voices. To change any member in the orchestra, choose *Set Instruments* from the Sound menu, then click the instrument you want to replace and select a new one. You can insert an instrument change at the insertion point by simply choosing an instrument in the Sounds menu. MIDI patch changes are inserted with the Insert MIDI Inst... command in the MIDI menu.

Choose Edit MIDI Parameters... from the MIDI menu to assign voices to MIDI channels and set up other details of MIDI performance. MIDI setups can be saved and recalled with the Load MIDI Setup command. Up to 128 MIDI messages, including continuous controller values and mode changes, can be inserted into any staff as *MIDI macros*. The Insert MIDI Macro... command opens a library of preset macros. New macros are entered as hexadecimal code in a dialog box summoned by choosing Edit MIDI Macro...

When you enter *lyrics* into your score, each word or syllable is linked to a note. When you delete or reposition a note, you delete or reposition its associated lyric. Click the symbol palette's text tool to begin entering lyrics. Three of the menus are replaced by Font, FontSize, and Style menus. Choose Gap from the Style menu to widen the space between notes so that lyrics aren't crammed together like general admission attendees at a Pink Floyd concert. Then click under the note to which the word or syllable is to be linked and type it in. Move the next note with the Tab key or select a new text insertion point. Another way to change the horizontal position of a note is to move its lyric with the symbol palette's mover tool.

InstrumentMaker

Yet another ConcertWare+ application is InstrumentMaker. Of the three interrelated programs in ConcertWare+, it's the only one that has nothing to do with MIDI. It synthesizes Macintosh sounds to be used as instruments in song files. InstrumentMaker instruments have always been among the warmest sounds synthesized by the Mac. Up to 256 instruments can be imported and saved into the *instrument library*. Additive synthesis and handdrawn waveforms are how sounds are designed. Envelopes and vibrato waveforms are also drawn with a pencil tool. You can even drawn or edit an instrument's individual icon, which visually represents the instrument in *Music Player*. Clicking a keyboard at the bottom of the screen lets you try out your new sound at different pitches as you develop it.

For *additive synthesis*, the amplitude of each of the first twenty harmonics can be

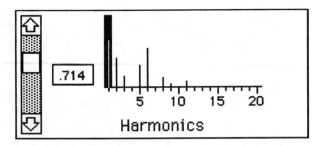

defined. Harmonics from the Mac's four-voice synthesizer are exact whole number multiples of the fundamental frequency. Each harmonic is represented by a notch on the harmonics ruler. To change a harmonic's loudness, click on its notch and use the scroll bar to enter a new value. Choose the Waveform menu command Compute from Harmonics Scaled To Fit to see your additive waveform shown in the waveform display. Place the cursor over the waveform display to edit and draw waveforms from scratch. The are 256 tiny dots spread across the horizontal axis, and you can redistribute them with a pencil tool to create a sound visually. It's also possible to import waveforms from other instruments with Get Wave & Harmonics from… in the WaveForm menu.

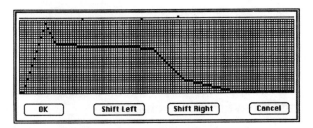

The *envelope* is divided by three lines into attack, sustain, and release stages. Reposition the lines in the envelope box by clicking and dragging them. Everything that happens before the first line is the attack. The sustain is the portion of the envelope between the first and second lines. When the sustain is reached, it's held

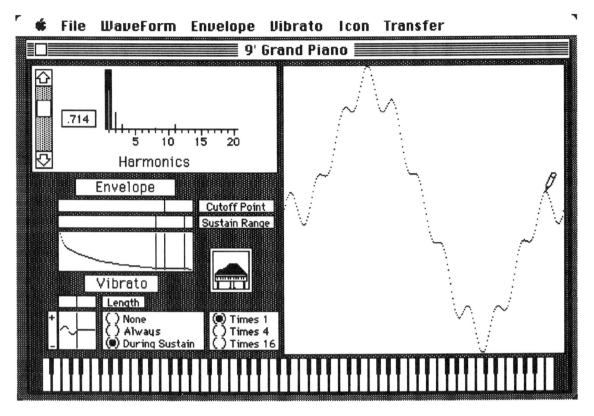

for the duration of the instrument. If the sustain isn't level, the loudness varies as it repeats. If you want a note to just die out without sustaining, drag the sustain points to the right. The release occurs after the sustain and ends at the cutoff point. The cutoff point doesn't have anything to do with filtering, as its name suggests, but indicates the end of an envelope. Rather than drawing a new envelope for every instrument, you can import envelopes from other instruments with Get Envelope from... in the Envelope menu. Envelopes can also be drawn in Fat Bits..., one pixel at a time, like a paint program at maximum magnification. Just click and drag the pencil tool to shape the envelope. Sometimes it's easier to draw a rough shape in the envelope box, then clean it up in fat bits.

Vibrato is a slight wavering in pitch employed by many performers to add expression to their playing. The vibrato waveform is shown in the vibrato box. Its positive and negative motion varies pitch around a base line, which is shown to the right of the vertical vibrato length line. You can govern whether vibrato occurs only during the sustain stage, always, or not at all. The vibrato's amplitude is multiplied by one, four, or sixteen. Like harmonic waveforms and envelopes, you can import vibrato waveforms from other instruments. They can also be drawn in Fat Bits.... Handdrawn vibrato can carry quite a bit of expressivity.

Length: ○ 30 (2 Hz)   ○ 20 (3 Hz)   ○ 15 (4 Hz)
⦿ 10 (6 Hz)   ○ 8 (7.5 Hz)   ○ 6 (10 Hz)
Height: ○ ±4   ○ ±8   ⦿ ±12   ○ ±16
Shape: ⦿ Sine   ○ Square   ○ Up   ○ Down
○ Random

[**Compute New Vibrato**]   [Cancel]

NoteWriter II

NoteWriter II, from Passport Designs, is a graphics-oriented scoring program with several methods of input, including typing command codes, pointing and clicking, numeric keypad, and an onscreen keyboard. NoteWriter II doesn't force you to conform to its idea about how printed music should appear. It has defaults for the placement of rests, clefs, beams, barlines, and ledger lines, but these defaults can be turned off. The program lets you make decisions about stem length and how far apart notes should be spaced, but it can also make these decisions for you. Once completed, entire scores or selected portions can be saved as MacPaint or Encapsulated PostScript (EPS) files for exporting to other graphics programs.

Some music notation software has rigid formatting capabilities, and often it's impossible to place a symbol exactly where you want it. With NoteWriter II, music symbols can be placed anywhere on a page, regardless of whether the result makes any musical sense. Using the PostScript font Sonata (available from Adobe), NoteWriter II can print a score that looks as good as any, or it can produce a complex score that nobody can read. A folder full of non-PostScript

symbol libraries is included, and you can import custom-drawn symbols from paint and draw programs.

When you begin a new score, you're presented with a series of windows. The first lets you designate the page size, margins, bracing, distance between staves, and the number of staves in each system. If you click one staff, you're asked if you want an initial barline. If you click two, choose between piano and instrumental bracing. If three, the choices are system, vocal-piano, and individual. If you click Other, you get a window in which you design a page by indicating staff positions, clefs, and braces. Once you select the number of staves, indicate the clef assignments and the key signature. You can place as many staves as you can cram onto a page, with up to a hundred pages in a file.

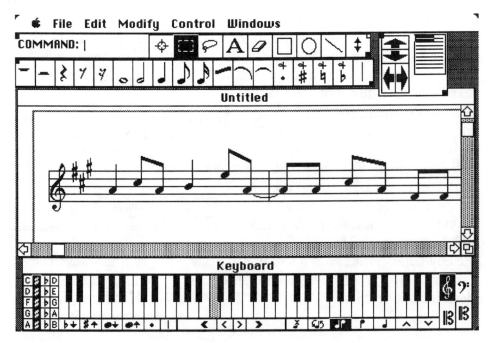

Entering music and words

Once you learn to use NoteWriter II, it's fast. All four methods of input can be used at all times. The standard entry method uses the *command window*. It has a *command line* for typing in command codes (abbreviations for music symbols), along with an insertion tool, selection tools, a text tool, an eraser, tools for drawing straight lines, rectangles, and circles, and tools to place guide lines. Typing a symbol's command code selects it for insertion. There's also an onscreen *image palette* for selecting nineteen common symbols and modifiers by clicking on them.

To enter notes and other symbols with the insertion tool, type the symbol's code or click on the palette, then click its location on the score. Rests and dynamic markings require only a single click to place them. Notes, staves, and beams require two clicks to indicate their height or width. For notes, click first where you want the note head to appear and again where you want the stem to end. Three clicks are needed for ties, slurs, and curves to indicate both ends and a center point.

The most recently placed note can be transposed up and down by half steps using the Mac's up and down cursor keys. Its horizontal position can also be changed with the left and right cursor keys.

It doesn't take long to learn the codes for symbols used most often. A whole note is w, an eighth note is e, a whole rest is rw, a sharp is sh, and a coda is coda. When you simply type a symbol's one- to four-letter equivalent, that symbol is selected. A command remains active until another command is given.

To add an accidental or make a note dotted, type the note's command followed by its modifiers, with no spaces. For example, a sharp dotted eighth note is abbreviated "e.sh". To select notes with modifiers from the image palette, click the note, then the sharp, flat, natural, or dot, before you place the note on the staff.

Choosing *Command List* (or typing its command key equivalent, command-`) from the Windows menu displays the command list, a screenful of 146 symbols and their command codes. When you click on a symbol, its code appears on the command line and the command list window disappears.

dw	g(	dsh	tc	b	fff	st	sl	tr	(
w	sm	sh	ac	a	ff	!st	$	ped	{
h	hh	n	tnc	b.	f	3/4	coda	*		
q	qq	fl	bc	a.	mf	c	oct	arp	-
e	sflag	dfl	!tc	b,	mp	c/	oct	/	\
s	dflag	sh1	!ac	a,	p	ks2	[3	//	|3
ts	tflag	sh3	!tnc	b2	pp	kf2	]3	///	-3
sft	qflag	fl1	!bc	a2	ppp	>	,	gtr	\3
dia	rw	gds	bl	b13	fp	_	lv	123	--
sdia	rh	gsh	dbl	sb	sfz	_	mord	=3	||
+	rq	gn	|.	sa	sf	_	turn	r23	x
G	re	gfl	.|	gb	<	^	o	RB	y
g	rs	gdf	'abc	ga	<	^^	db	R3	xy
gfs	rts	.	tie	gb2	12	ferm	ub	**Done**	
q1	rsf	..	slur	ga2	1d2	feru	%		

Most symbols are placed on an invisible grid. This grid can be turned off from the Control menu. Except for fine adjustments, it's best to keep the grid turned on.

Music can be more accurately positioned by turning on Alignment (command-L) in the Control menu, which displays the *Vertical Alignment Bar* on the staff. This evenly spaces symbols across the staff. Use the tab and space keys to advance the alignment bar, and move backwards by adding the shift key. Alternately, you can advance automatically by selecting Auto-Increment from the Control menu. Move to other staves with the alignment bar's scroll arrows. Some input methods require that Alignment is turned on.

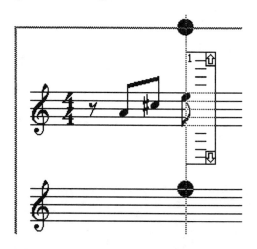

Another input technique called *QuickScrawl* lets you use the mouse to draw vague shapes which are magically transformed into music symbols. For example, a jagged vertical line becomes a quarter note rest. A straight angled line becomes an eighth note. Drawing the number 4 yields a treble clef symbol. Most music symbols are drawn with the pencil tool, which is accessed by holding down the shift key or pressing caps lock. Dynamic markings, articulations,

ornamentations, and accidentals are drawn with the crayon tool, which is summoned by holding down the command key. Still more notes and beams are available with the quill tool, activated by holding down the option key. If you use QuickScrawl a lot, save time by leaving the Caps Lock key down.

You can also enter and edit music from an *onscreen musical keyboard*, activated from the Windows menu. Alignment must be turned on to use keyboard note entry. To enter a note, first select its value, then click a key to select its pitch. The keyboard also has buttons to change pitches, add and change accidentals, indicate the accidentals of notes played from black keys, dot notes and rests, indicate stem direction, remove stems, insert barlines, and move the Vertical Alignment Bar.

The Mac's *numeric keypad* is yet another means to enter symbols. Once again, Alignment must be turned on to enter notes, though notes can be modified with it turned off. Keys 1 through 9 are used to enter notes by indicating the diatonic interval above the previous note. Pressing the Enter key along with a number key inserts a pitch below the previous one. If the last note inserted was a C, insert the E above it by typing 3, indicating an interval of a third. The zero key inserts a rest, and the period key adds a dot. Holding down the plus key scrolls through a list of accidentals to add. The asterisk changes stem direction, and the equals key erases stems in chords. The slash key adds a barline. The minus key steps back to the previous note, and the Clear key moves the alignment bar to the left edge of the next staff.

To enter titles, lyrics, and other *text*, click on the letter A, then click and drag where you want to place the text. How far you drag to the right determines the size of the text box. The Text Format command (command-W) in the Control menu lets you choose the font, style, and justification within the text box. Because NoteWriter II prints music at 75% of the size it's displayed, text printed as 12 point is shown onscreen as 16 point.

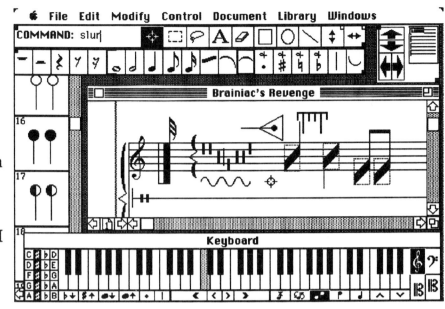

Maneuvering around the page is accomplished with normal Macintosh scroll bars or with NoteWriter II's *Scroll window*. Arrows in the Scroll window move your view of the score in four directions. There's a tiny representation of the page in the Score window in which you can move a selection box to the desired location. Command keys and menu choices also move your view to the next or previous staves.

Editing and printing your score

The Return key toggles between the insertion tool and the *selection tool*. The selection tool works just like the marquee tool in paint programs: dragging it diagonally draws a selection box, and everything within the box is highlighted. You can also select symbols on a staff by encircling them with the *lasso tool* or by clicking directly on their *control points*. Control points, small handles on every symbol, can be shown with the Control

menu. Once selected, music can be edited extensively, using commands from the Edit and Modify menus. Most menu commands have command key equivalents.

When a symbol is selected, you can pick it up and move it anywhere. You can also beam and tie notes, add and remove accidentals and ledger lines, and flip beams, stems, and ties. A stem's height can be changed by clicking on its control point and dragging it to its proper height.

Print quality depends on the type of printer you have and whether you have the Sonata printer font in your System folder. Draft-quality printing uses QuickDraw to print scores. Use this for printing on a dot-matrix printer. To print the same size as PostScript printing, choose Draft Print @ 75%. Show Overview (command-F) displays the current page, with the portion to be printed highlighted in black. Click and drag the black block to change the print area before printing.

Professional Composer

Professional Composer, from Mark of the Unicorn, makers of the sequencer Performer, was the first professional music program for the Macintosh. Composer notates music with a good variety of music symbols using the Adobe Sonata font. Even if you don't have the PostScript version, the display version of Sonata is included, along with a bit-mapped MusicFont and ChordFont. Composer lays out staff systems of a single staff, a grand staff, vocal and piano staves (a grand staff bracketed to a single staff), or any number of multiple staves up to its maximum 40 staves on a page. Compositions can be played back at three fixed tempi from the Mac's sound generator.

Most actions are carried out with menus and an icon palette. The Extras menu is where you tell the insertion point to go to a particular measure or rehearsal mark, when and where to insert and move text, change text styles, and add measures, and when to redraw the display. Hide the instrument names, clefs, and time signatures with the Hide Margins command. Extras also sets up headers, footers, and a title page with a fixed format.

Entering music

The current version of Professional Composer isn't a MIDI program. If you want to enter or play compositions using

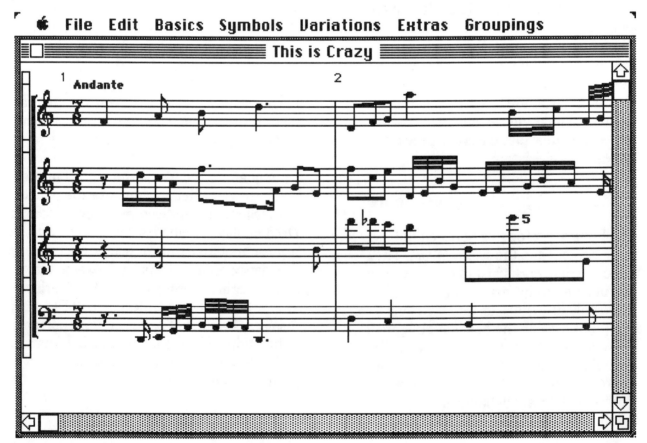

MIDI, you have to import or export them from or to Performer or some other sequencer that reads and writes Composer files. Performer can save sequences as Composer files, and it can open Composer files from its File menu. You can also use Performer to convert MIDI Files from other programs so you can transcribe them with Composer. If you have Opcode's sequencer Vision, you can convert files directly to Composer's format, and convert Deluxe Music files to Vision files, and then to Composer files, or back the other way.

When converting a MIDI sequence to Composer, be sure to first *quantize* everything to the duration of the shortest note. Selectively quantize portions to larger values anywhere it's possible. Without quantization, your sequence is interpreted too literally, and you're likely to end up with a bunch of tied 128th notes and rests, which are very difficult to read and edit. (Frankly, it's easier to edit note values within a sequencer environment.) For best results, quantize both the beginning and duration. Even with quantization, your playing should be pretty accurate with notes held legato to transcribe them to their full value. If, for example, you play a staccato eighth note, it may be transcribed as a sixteenth or thirty-second followed by a rest. If you don't quantize, and sometimes even if you do, notes that should fall directly on the beat may land somewhere else. As with any scoring program, transcribed sequences almost always need editing before they're acceptable.

Besides importing sequence files, Composer has two other means of input. Notes and rests can be entered directly into Professional Composer using the Macintosh keyboard to specify both pitch and rhythm. Notes, rests, single barlines, sharps, flats, and naturals can be simply typed in. It doesn't matter which key you hold down first, pitch or rhythm. Letter keys on the right side of the keyboard indicate pitch, with keys on the left side indicating duration, accidentals, and bar lines. When necessary, the Enter key serves as an insert command. If you make a mistake, delete it with the Delete key.

Chords are entered by entering a note, then placing the insertion point over that note to enter other notes in the chord. The ChordFont is available for typing chord names, abbreviations, and special symbols. Chords can be automatically inverted with Invert Chord (command-N) in the Variations menu.

Keys can also be used to move the insertion point to the left or right, up and down by lines and spaces, and up and down by staves. The cursor keys change the view without moving the cursor. They scroll left and right by screenfuls and up and down by staves. You can also scroll with shift-U, shift-P, shift-I, and shift-O.

You can also summon a series of *music symbol palettes* from a menu. To place symbols on a staff , click the intended location, then the desired symbol. Symbols include notes, rests, bar lines, clefs, and an assortment of ornaments, articulations, and dynamic markings. Music can be entered by any combination of mouse and computer keyboard, using the mouse only, keyboard only, mouse for pitch and keys for rhythm, or keys for pitch and mouse for rhythm. Since only basic music symbols can be typed from the keyboard, all others must be entered in point-and-click fashion.

When you're entering music, Composer doesn't automatically move the insertion point to the next measure just because the total rhythm in a measure equals its full duration. It will, however, check the rhythm on command and highlight any measures that don't add up. You can also select the menu command Rebar to add or move bar lines to conform to the meter.

Use the Basics menu to specify the key signature and meter anywhere in the composition, even in the middle of a measure. Tempo can be indicated by a list of traditional Italian terms or whatever you choose to type. Tempo can also be indicated in beats per minute by a metronome marking, but only at the beginning of the piece. Also from the Basics menu, you can globally control the space between notes and the vertical width of crescendos, as well as the distance between staves and crescendos,

decrescendos, octave markings, endings, tuplet numbers, and other symbols.

Entering and editing words

Even if it has no lyrics, printed music almost always needs text in the form of a title, copyright notice, and performance notes. Title Page in the Extras menu doesn't really create a title page; it creates a large header on the first page of music. If you type them into the title page text block, the title and copyright notice appear there.

To enter text, click any insertion point and choose Insert Text (command-;) from the Extras menu. A horizontal text block appears with a blinking insertion point, and the cursor becomes an I-beam when it's placed over this block. Just click and type. If you're typing lyrics, they can be aligned to the notes above them. The insertion point first appears flush left to the barline. Move it under the first note by pressing the Tab key, then tab to the next note to separate words and syllables. Shift-tab to move to the next measure. If placement isn't accurate, use the Space Bar when typing lyrics to increase the distance between notes. Press the Return key to type a second line of text below the first.

Words can be selected for editing by clicking a dragging over them; shift-clicking doesn't work. The only way to move a block of text is to select it, cut it, and paste it into a new text block.

Editing music

At any point during composition, symbols, measures, and staves can be selected and manipulated in many ways. Symbols and measures are selected by clicking and dragging or by shift-clicking, reversing black and white within the selection. If you select something and want it to stay highlighted after you've made a change, choose Retain Selection from the Basics menu. Measures are selected by double-clicking them. An entire staff can be selected by clicking in its staff box, a vertical rectangle to its left. Staff selection is retained when you select another staff. To de-select, click anywhere else. The tiny boxes above and below the staff boxes select the space between staves for inserting new staves. All the music on every staff can be selected by the Select All command in the Edit menu.

When one or more notes are selected, they're subject to grouping, variations, and all kinds of editing. Of course, music can be cut, copied, pasted, and erased in word processor fashion — no complicated choices here, just straightforward editing, true to the Mac interface. Undo Delete appears in the place of an Undo command — it doesn't necessarily undo the most recent action. Instead, it inserts whatever is on the clipboard, usually from the last cut or delete. One neat thing is that you can take a look at

what's on the edit Clipboard. Granted, it's not a very big Clipboard window, and it can't be resized, but you can identify what you'll get if you select Undo.

From the Variations menu, notes can be *transposed* diatonically, by interval name, or by key change. Multiple staves can be merged, putting all of their symbols on one staff, and later unmerged into their original form. This is how you notate two parts on one staff with Professional Composer, collapsing them together. Note that merged staves can't be edited. Other menu choices invert or flip groupings and sharps and flats, and place ornaments and dynamic markings on the other side of the staff. They also strip dots and ornaments from a selected range of music.

If two or more notes are selected, they can be connected in various ways from the Groupings menu. Notes are *beamed* by selecting them and choosing Beam or

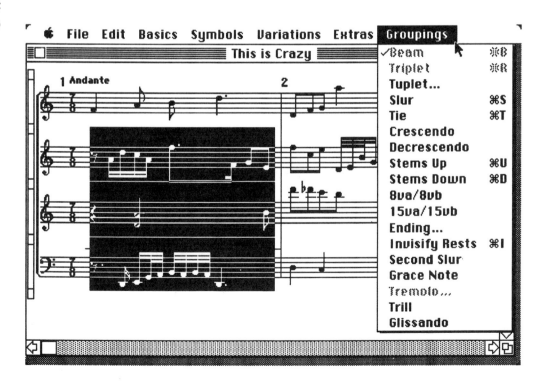

holding down the command key and typing a B. Any odd division of a beat, like three notes of equal duration written and played within the duration of two notes (a triplet),

Instruments

Alto Sax
Alto (voice)
Baritone Sax
Bass Clarinet
Bass Drum
Bass Guitar
Bass (voice)

up
down

○ Range High: G
○ Transpose: B♭
○ Range Low: E♭

☐ Hide Key Signature

Name: Bass Clarinet

Abbreviation: B.Clar.

Ledger Above: 4

Ledger Below: 3

Playback Waveforms:
○ Loud Brass
○ Soft Brass
● Single Reed
○ Double Reed
○ Loud Organ
○ Soft Organ

OK   Cancel

or five in the time of four (a quintuplet), or any other *tuplet* can be indicated in a dialog box summoned by another command in the Groupings menu. This is also where you indicate ties, slurs, and second slurs. To place a tie or slur above a note grouping, click and drag above the selected notes; to place it below, click and drag below. Notes can be grouped to indicate the beginning and end of a crescendo or decrescendo (gradually growing louder or softer). Any note can be turned into a smaller grace note by selecting it and choosing Grace Note.

Playback

Professional Composer's playback abilities don't threaten to turn the Mac into a musical instrument. Each staff can be assigned an instrument name, and each

instrument can be given characteristics like pitch range, transposition, and playback voice. A scrollable list of preset instruments takes care of range and transposition parameters. There's currently no MIDI playback, and only six rather similar Mac sounds and three tempi (56, 75, and 112 quarter notes per minute) from which to choose. Typing command-P begins playing the score from the insertion point. No more than one voice per staff is heard, and no more than a total of four voices. The only way to hear a chord is if each note is on a separate staff. Clicking anywhere during playback stops it at the end of the measure that's playing at that moment.

Page layout, previewing, and printing

At present, Composer's *page formatting* capabilities are rather limited. You don't have much control over the placement of staves on a page. Change the distance between staves by selecting a staff, choosing Instruments… from the Basics menu, and changing the number of ledger lines above or below. More ledger lines increase the space, and fewer ledger lines decrease it. You can globally affect the width of measures with the Set Spacing command in the Basics menu.

Though you can't change the distance between the title and the top of the page, you can change the distance between the title block and the first staff by changing the number of ledger lines above the staff.

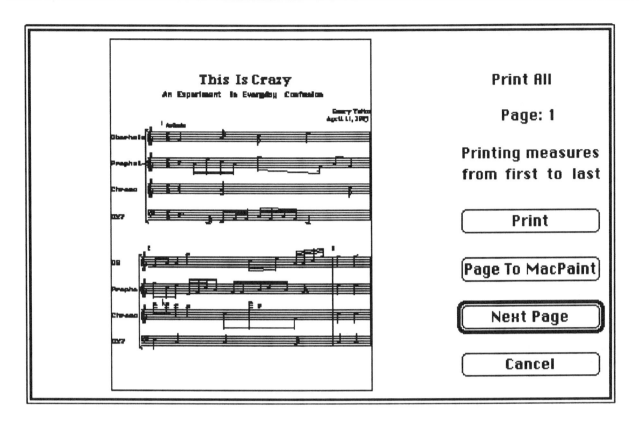

It's possible to print complete scores or part extractions with Professional Composer. When you select Print All…, Print Partial…, or Print Parts…, you're first presented with a scaled-down, full-page preview of approximately what your score will look like. If you have a PostScript printer, you can print very attractive scores. Only the PostScript Sonata symbols are high resolution, though. The bit-mapped MusicFont and ChordFont symbols have a resolution of only 72 dots per inch, exactly the same as the Macintosh display screen. Even at 72 dpi, with a printer like the Apple ImageWriter, music printed with Composer is pretty legible.

To print an entire score, choose Print All… from the File menu. After you preview the first page, you can view other pages, give the print command, or save the file into a bit-mapped format which can be opened by

graphics programs like MacPaint. Parts can be extracted by selecting the staves to be printed and choosing Print Partial… or Print Parts…. Print Partial… prints only the selected staves, and Print Parts… also prints tempo markings, measure numbers, and other marks at the top of the whole score. The Measure Range command in the File menu lets you specify first and last measures to be printed.

Composer only lets you view the score at full size. If you really insist on seeing a smaller or larger version of your score, here's a round-about way to change the view: In the File menu, choose Page Setup. Increase the Reduce or Enlarge parameter to, say, 150%, then click OK. Choose Print All…, click Okay, and you see a reduced preview of the beginning of the score. Click on Next Page until you see what you need to see reduced or enlarged. Using this technique, 250% gives you an actual size view; anything smaller than 250% is reduced and anything larger is enlarged.

The *instrument name* appears in the left margin of the first measure, and on all the systems below, its abbreviation. If you don't want the instrument names to print, just leave the Name and Abbreviation fields blank in the Instruments dialog box that's summoned from the Basics menu.

If you do a good job, and you have the PostScript version of Sonata and a PostScript printer, Professional Composer scores can look polished and professional. Just be sure that the appropriate printer driver is chosen in the Chooser desk accessory, and okay your choices in the Print Setup dialog box. If you try to print a manuscript on a laser printer when you're set up for an ImageWriter, it won't look like what you expect.

Music Publisher

Music Publisher, a professional music scoring program from Australia, includes its own PostScript music font, *Repertoire*, for high-quality music printing. It also comes with a special keypad for musical input and two short cables: one for connecting the keypad to the Mac Plus and another for connecting to all later Macs via ADB. The *Presto* keypad is a short, typewriter-like keyboard, arranged in four rows of seven keys, representing four octaves of C, D, E, F, G, A, and B. At the top of the keypad are eight function keys. Music is entered by typing pitches on the Presto pad with one hand, while typing note values, rests, accidentals, and a vast array of additional music symbols on the

Mac keyboard with the other hand. Pitch can also be entered in step time from a MIDI instrument. To enter music via MIDI, simply press the rhythm key on the Mac keyboard and play the note. Accidentals are entered automatically, depending on the key signature.

Music Publisher gives you plenty of control over the appearance of music on paper. It's very page-oriented, like a desktop publishing program for music. A movable *Toolbox palette* contains tools to enter and select music, position staves, select pages and systems, insert barlines, draw straight lines and boxes, enter and edit text, and add slurs, dynamic markings, crescendos

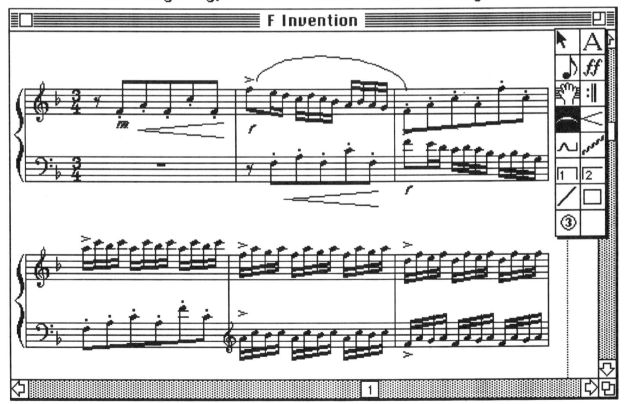

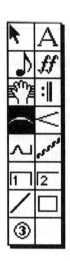

and decrescendos, pedal markings, fingering numbers, glissandos, and repeat endings. With menus, you can set up and alter the page, add and customize systems, change key and time signatures, transpose, beam and tie notes, change stem direction, indicate note spacing, number measures, extract parts, select and play voices, specify fonts and typestyles, align lyrics with notes, and more.

Scoring

Begin a new score by indicating the size of the page and the width of the margins in the Publication Format dialog box. Once a score is formatted, you can show this box again, but you can't change it. Place the first system of staves on the page. A handful of pre-formatted systems are included, ranging from a single staff to a bracketed system for four voices and piano. You can also design and save your own customized staff configurations and call them up for use in other scores. Insert bar lines to determine the number of measures across the page.

Four sizes of music can be combined in a Music Publisher score: small, standard, large, and big note. Notes, rests, and other symbols can be proportionally spaced within measures by rhythm, then manually adjusted. Choose Note Spacing from the Music menu to change the distance between notes in

proportion to measure width. Select a preset spacing or type in a new ratio.

The music symbols used most often are available straight from the Mac keyboard, with pitch provided by the Presto pad or MIDI input. Keyboard symbols include note rhythms from a double breve to a 128th, sharps, flats, naturals, clefs, repeat marks, accents, fermatas, codas, segnos, pedal signs, and numbers for multiple measure rests. Pressing the Shift key accesses rests, double flats and sharps, small accidentals, small clefs, grace notes, note heads, bow markings, and more accents. Choosing Percussion Keys from the Music menu has the same effect as holding the Option key. This keyboard level includes all kinds of percussion notes, accents, mordents, turns, tremolos, and accidentals within parentheses. Additional markings are found in the Toolbox. Most Toolbox symbols may be placed anywhere on a page.

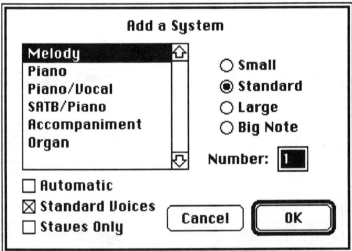

When you enter a note or a rest, the cursor advances automatically according to rhythm. To enter chords, press the Chord function key on the Presto pad, then enter pitch and rhythm for each note. Advance to the next chord by pressing the space bar. Press the space bar a second time to repeat the chord, or press a rhythm key first to repeat it with a different rhythm. Pressing the Chord key a second time returns to single-note mode.

If you're scoring charts for studio work, you may need chord slashes. When Guitar Slashes is checked in the Music menu, entering notes results in slashes rather than notes. To enter a grace note, type its rhythm, press the M2 function key, enter its pitch, then enter the next normal note. Double and triple dotted notes can be entered by pressing a dotted rhythm key more than once.

Music Publisher has a unique way of dealing with triplets and other tuplets, which the Music Publisher manual calls *grouplets*. Before entering the tuplet, enter the total rhythm of the tuplet, press the equals (=) key, type a number to indicate how many notes are in the tuplet, enter the rhythm of each note, then enter the pitches. Pressing the equals key again returns you to normal input. It sounds tedious, but once you get used to it, it's very logical and fast. A tuplet can be indicated by a slur and a number, a bracket and a number, or a number alone, aligned to either note heads or stem ends.

Selecting Time Signature from the Music menu calls up a dialog box to define meters and determine how flagged notes are beamed. Time signatures can be placed at the beginning of any measure. The default meter is 4/4, but you can set up almost any time signature you can think of, within reasonable limits. You can't have more than 99 beats per measure, and a beat must be a fraction of a whole note divisible by 2,

up to 128. You can decide how notes are beamed by indicating where the beat falls in complex meters. A measure of 5/4 time could be played 4+1 or 1+4 or 2+3 or 2+1+2, etc. If you check the Show Complex Pattern box, these numbers appear in the place of the beats per measure in the time signature.

Slurs are drawn manually with the Slur tool in the Toolbox. You can draw slurs between any two notes, even on different systems. Click on the first note and drag to the final note in the slur. The way you drag determines the the shape of the slur and whether it's above and below the notes. It's all in the wrist. A slur in Music Publisher is a Bézier curve with a handle in the middle and one at each end. Change the width of a slur by dragging one of the end handles. Change its curvature by dragging its middle handle. To move a slur, click it anywhere but on a handle and drag.

Editing

Music symbols must be selected to change them. Most selecting is done with the Music tool, by pointing and clicking, double-clicking, option-clicking, clicking-and-dragging, option-clicking-and-dragging, and my personal favorite, triple-clicking. When notes and other symbols are selected, they show as outlines

rather than in reverse black and white.

To select any note, even a single note in a chord, just click it (click it good!). Accidentals or other modifiers are selected automatically. To select a whole chord, option-click it. Double-clicking a note selects its measure.

Triple-clicking selects a whole voice, just like the Select Voice command in the Voice menu. To select a group of notes in one voice, click the first and drag to the last. Shift-clicking doesn't do it. Select a whole system by option-clicking it with the Layout tool. Also use the Layout tool to select a whole page by option-clicking in its margin. Select dynamics, bar lines, slurs, crescendos, pedal markings, glissandos, repeat brackets, straight lines, boxes, and fingering numbers with the appropriate tool in the Toolbox.

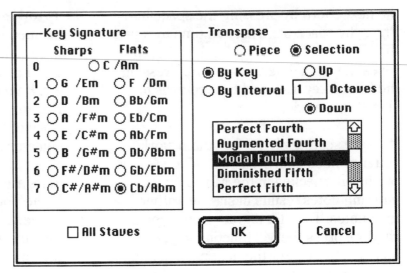

Selected music can be cut, copied, and pasted as you expect. Change a note's pitch by selecting and entering a new pitch. Change accidentals the same way. To change the rhythm of a note or a rest, select it, delete it, and enter a new value. You may have to delete several notes to make it fit in the measure. Stems can be made longer or shorter by option-clicking them, holding the option key, and using the arrow cursor keys. Several markings can be lengthened by clicking and dragging their handles. Move a marking by selecting and dragging it to a new position.

Sometimes symbols clash, running into each other in cramped measures. You can move a note, chord, or rest horizontally by option-clicking it and using the left and right arrow keys. Option-arrow moves it one point at a time, and shift-option-arrow moves it four points at a time. Change the position of an accidental by selecting its associated note and using option-arrow and shift-option-arrow.

Selected music or entire scores can be *transposed* in a number of ways. Choose Transpose (command-K) from the Music menu to summon a dialog box. Either pick an interval from a scrolling list of 32 or pick one of 15 new keys. If transposing further than an octave, type in the number of octaves. Click the Up or Down button to control whether you're transposing your selection up or down in pitch. If changing key, any new measures are in the new key.

Playback

A selected voice can be played back by the Mac's internal four-voice synthesizer. Only one voice at a time may be played, with chords up to four notes. Select the portion to be played, or triple-click any note to select the whole voice. Begin playback with Play Selection in the Voices menu. To change the tempo, use the Metronome... command in the MIDI menu.

If you have MIDI instruments, you can play all the voices simultaneously. Call up the Voices Setup... dialog with in the MIDI menu to give each voice a name, a MIDI channel, and a patch number. Since you

Name	Solo	Mute	Channel	Patch
Piano	●		13	120
Guitar		●	12	3
Bass		●	11	18
Drums		●	10	0

Voices Setup

can't play only selected parts over MIDI, you can solo and mute voices in the Voices Setup... box. Playback always begins at the measure in which the insertion point is placed. Begin MIDI playback by choosing Play or holding the Command key and typing a 1. Stop it with command-2.

Putting words to music

With the Text tool, Music Publisher has the means to place words almost anywhere and to align lyrics with their associated notes. Create an insertion point for text just by clicking and typing. Unlike a lot of programs, you can mix fonts, sizes, and styles in the same text block, which is whatever length you type. Words are edited word processor-style. You can't click and drag to move text blocks; you have to cut them and paste them to their new locations.

The Type menu accesses sub-menus that list fonts, styles, sizes, leadings, and alignments for selected text, very much like a desktop publishing program. Alternately, the type specifications can be entered in the Specifications... dialog box (command-D). The Type menu also offers a choice of four music symbol sizes and tells the program to line up lyrics with notes.

When you choose Lyric/Note Alignment from the Type menu and click to create an insertion point, it highlights the closest note of the most recently selected voice. Lyrics are automatically centered under notes. Type the first word or syllable, and the cursor advances when you press the SpaceBar, Tab, or the hyphen (-) key. Type hyphens instead of spaces between syllables, and the hyphens are centered. To extend lyrics over ties and slurs, type the word or syllable, then press shift-hyphen to advance to the next note. Do this as many times as necessary.

Type Specifications

Type Style
- ☐ Bold
- ☐ Italic
- ☐ Outline
- ☐ Shadow
- ☐ Underline

Leading
- ○ Auto
- ◉ Manual
- By: 11.5

Font Name:
- Times
- ToulouseLautr...
- Uncials
- Univers 55
- University Ro...

Font Size: 10.0

[Cancel] [OK]

Finale

Coda Finale is best known as the first Mac program with the ability to put musical performances into print by transcribing what's played directly into it via MIDI, in real time. A *floating quantization* feature graphically displays music with quantized durations without changing the recorded performance. For writing musical scores, Finale offers an almost overwhelming choice of options and unprecedented control over the placement of symbols on a page.

its greatest asset and its greatest hardship. Really mastering Finale requires such discipline, such patience, such devotion, that it becomes something more than a computer program — it becomes a way of life. Those willing to undertake the path are rewarded by more than a glimpse of tomorrow's music tools today. Remember when the clergy were the only ones who knew how to read and write? Experienced Finale users can create and edit printed music that other musicians can't. Finale's

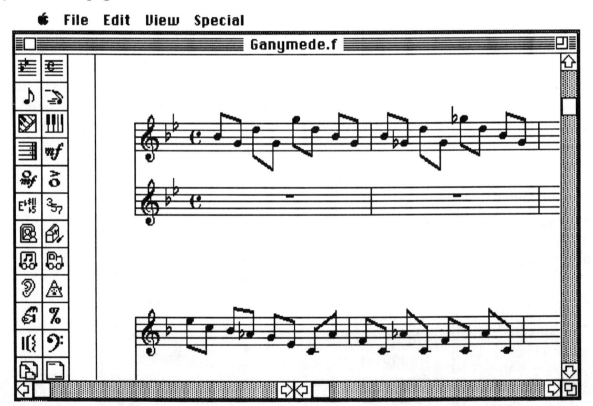

Few programs are as versatile as Finale, and few have such a steep learning curve. To really plumb its depths, it may require most of your attention for a few weeks or maybe months, depending on how deep you want to go. Its sheer versatility is both

challenging maze of decisions at every turn leads to a musical pot of gold at the end of the rainbow, in the form of a pretty powerful tool for composing and arranging the architecture of music.

After you've set up a staff and all the options, Finale can capture what you play, turn it into standard notation, and play it back pretty much just as it was performed. The next step is editing, where you correct your errors and any errors made in transcription. Along the way, you can extensively alter the way the music looks and sounds. Then, if you know what you're doing and you have a good PostScript printer, Finale produces a printed score that looks like it came from an honest-to-goodness music engraver.

A music scoring program that gives new dimension to the word flexibility, Finale comes luxuriously packaged on several disks with several manuals. The program itself is too big for an 800K floppy, and requires a bare minimum of a megabyte of RAM in your computer (as should be expected from any power program). Finale comes with the PostScript music font *Petrucci*, which includes dynamic markings, ornaments, and notes and rests as short as a 4096th. If you need symbols that aren't in Petrucci, other PostScript fonts are available from Coda, including symbols for musicology, guitar chords, jazz, percussion, and a unique (and nonstandard) notation for MIDI events.

In the documentation that accompanies Finale, instructions are given in a sort of shorthand called a *map*. A map is nothing more than a list of step-by-step directions to accomplish something, expressed in a very limited vocabulary and syntax called a *Finale Abbreviated Description*, or FAD for short. Though FAD may look like some sort of high-level programming language at first glance, it's actually a simplified form of English. For instance, FAD says "dblClick InstAttrTool" instead of "double-click the

Instrument Attribute Tool". Like traditional maps, Finale maps are a means to navigate unfamiliar territory without getting hopelessly lost. Once you quickly comprehend how maps work, they're supposed to make directions foolproof. Until you understand maps, though, a lot of material in Finale's manuals is undecipherable.

Ideally, Finale is most useful as a big sketchpad for developing musical ideas by displaying music you play in standard notation. It lets you deal with recorded music in transcribed form. Everything from short thematic phrases to complete symphonies is fair game for this hybrid MIDI recorder and music copyist's toolbox. Don't mistake Finale for a sequencer, though. It lacks the ability to deal with music as anything other than some sort of music notation. It also lacks sequencer functions like speed, punch recording, loop recording, track sliding, precise event editing, location shuttling, and other conveniences. Start and stop commands aren't carried out immediately. For serious MIDI playback and editing, **Finale PowerPlus** can export scores into any sequencing program that supports MIDI Files. For importing files from sequencers, Finale PowerPlus captures more than just quantized note information, but the conversion process is rather slow.

Tools and techniques

Finale has a huge collection of tools and techniques for notating music. Some of its functions are accessed by pull-down menus, but most tasks are accomplished by clicking on a tool palette on the left side of the computer screen, sometimes followed by clicking the score. Selecting a

tool or a menu item may open a dialog box, and clicking a button on the dialog box may lead to another dialog box, which may lead to another dialog box, ad infinitum. With its barrage of dialog boxes, Coda extends the Mac's menu metaphor further by offering its user so many choices.

There are two ways of viewing a Finale score: page view and Igor's view. *Igor's view* shows the score scrolling to the right like most music programs, and *page view* gives you a preview of your score as it will appear on paper, with one system below another. There are several *templates* included with systems in place for beginning a new Finale document. These templates include a lead sheet, a grand staff, a small orchestra, and a choral score with a piano staff. The *instrument attributes tool* lets you define each staff's instrument name, clef, transposition, and MIDI channel, as well as hide and show symbols like time signatures, repeats, and expression marks. The *key signature tool* can create key signatures with any number of sharps and flats, and the *time signature tool* can create simple and unusually complex meters.

There are no fewer than seven ways to enter music into Finale, using combinations of the Mac keyboard and numeric keypad, the mouse, and/or a MIDI instrument. Each method has its advantages and shortcomings, but they're all useful at one moment or another. Four

tools from the tool palette select the method of input: the HyperScribe tool, the transcription tool, the simple note entry tool, and the speedy note entry tool. Using Finale PowerPlus to import a MIDI File is an eighth way to get music into Finale.

The most obvious technique is *simple note entry*. Simple note entry puts a single voice on a single staff. When you click the simple note entry tool, a palette of music symbols replaces the tool palette. To enter notes, simply click the desired symbol, then click where you want it to go. Things progress more quickly when you use the numeric keypad to choose rhythmic values — the 3 key is a sixteenth note, 4 is an eighth, 5 is a quarter, etc. To enter a rest, position a note with the proper duration, then click it once with the eraser tool. To actually erase it, click it twice with the eraser. You can also add and delete ties, dots, sharps, flats, and grace notes with the simple note entry tool.

Speedy note entry lets you enter one or two voices on a staff, one measure at a time. Notes and rests are entered with MIDI input for pitch and the numeric keypad for rhythm, the Mac's letter keys for pitch and the keypad for rhythm, or the mouse for pitch and the keypad for rhythm. Notes can be clicked and dragged vertically to transpose them. Use speedy note entry also to add and delete accidentals, tuplets, ties, and grace notes. The apostrophe key lets you toggle between two voices.

```
┌─────────────────────────────────────────────────┐
│  HyperScribe™                    ⊠ Refresh Screen │
│                                                   │
│  State  Duration   Division   MIDI                │
│   I     [0     ]   [0     ]   [$00][$00][$00] ☐ Listen │
│   II    [0     ]   [0     ]   [$00][$00][$00] ☐ Listen │
│   III   [0     ]   [0     ]   [$00][$00][$00] ☐ Listen │
│                                                   │
│   Tap   [1024  ]   [2     ]   [$B0][$40][$7F] ☐ Listen │
│                                                   │
│      ( H/4 ) ( H/8 ) ( (3)H/4 ) ( (3)H/8 )        │
│                                                   │
│  Key Split  ⦿ None  ○ Passive   ☐ No Voice Two    │
│  Receive MIDI Channel [0   ]    ⊠ Ties Over Barline│
│                                 ☐ Float Quantizing │
│        ( OK )  ( Cancel )        ☐ HyperClick™     │
│                                 ☐ MIDI Thru       │
└─────────────────────────────────────────────────┘
```

The *HyperScribe tool* is one of the most intriguing means of musical input. HyperScribe is the technique used to record MIDI performances and turn them into notation as you play. Begin by clicking the HyperScribe tool. This summons the HyperScribe dialog box, which presents a possibly bewildering set of choices, but things are simpler than they seem. If you want to see your performance transcribed as you play, "refresh screen" should be turned on. That way, when you're recording and you finish a measure, it appears as real music notation, just like that. If it's turned off, the music isn't transcribed until you stop playing and you leave HyperScribe by clicking its icon again.

The three *states* make it possible to record music that changes meter. To record in HyperScribe without stopping, State I, State II, and State III are user-defined meters that you can step between. Finale lets you assign certain functions to MIDI notes, so that when you play the note you've set up to trigger State II, it steps

from its current time signature to the time signature you set up in State II. States I and III also change the meter when they receive an appropriate signal. If your music doesn't change meter, you don't have to deal with states. The four buttons below look even more cryptic, but they're used to set the time signature, defining the kind of beats in a measure. The first two are for duple time (4/4, 3/4, 3/8, etc.) and the other two are for triple time (9/4, 6/4, 6/8, etc.).

The *transcription tool* is Finale's multitrack sequencer. It transcribes real time MIDI performances, including continuous controller information and tempo changes. Unlike HyperScribe, the transcription tool lets you record many tracks simultaneously, punch in and out, and overdub while listening to previously-recorded tracks. It records up to 16 MIDI channels at once, so you can record directly from a sequencer as it plays into Finale. The *Transcribe* menu lets you specify splits, view and quantize resolution, transcription and input filtering, and so on.

To begin recording, click the transcription tool and the starting measure, then click Record at End and Start. If you click Wait Till instead of Start, recording begins when you start playing. Click anywhere to stop recording. As you record, musical information graphically appears in piano-roll notation. Note data appears in most of the window with the top portion reserved for rhythm data. Beats and measures are entered as time tags after recording notes.

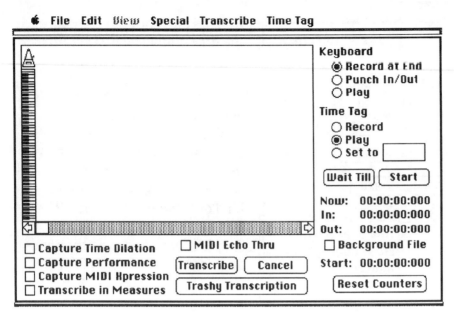

There are three *intelligent notation tools* used to design and position symbols that affect playback. These are the note expression tool, staff expression tool, and score expression tool. Symbols placed with these tools can change tempo or send MIDI messages like controller values, pitch bends, patch changes, and the like. You can create whole libraries of such symbols with these tools and the *shape designer*.

Record at End begins recording at the current measure. You can also punch in and out to replace part of a track without affecting what comes before or after. When you click and drag in the data window, the beginning and ending of your selection are shown as In and Out points. Click the Punch In/Out button to record between these points. To punch in on the fly, designate a punch preroll in the Transcribe menu. To transcribe your recording into music notation, click and drag or choose Select All to select the music data, set the options, and click the Transcribe button.

Other tools are used to create and enter lyrics and other text, tuplets, and chord names, and to edit the music you transcribe. When you click on the *playback tool*, then click a measure of music, MIDI playback begins at that measure after you okay a number of options and the playback file is loaded into RAM. You can also audition music with the playback tool by dragging the cursor over a group of notes while holding the Option key.

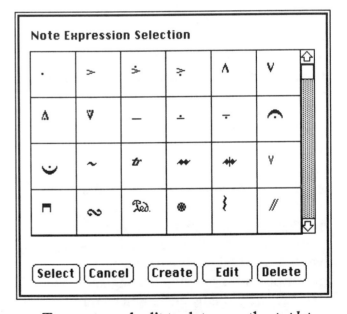

To create and edit tuplets, use the *tuplet tool*. Clicking the first note in a group of notes with the tuplet tool causes handles to appear on the notes. Double-click on one of the handles to open the *tuplet temporal definition* dialog box, where you define the parameters of the tuplet. A *chord tool* analyzes chords you play or transcribe and assigns names to them from a library of chord suffixes. You can also enter chord names and Finale correctly plays back the chords over MIDI. When you transpose notes, the chord suffixes are automatically transposed as well.

Words are entered with the *lyrics tool* or the *text block tool*. Each tool has its own built-in text editor. When you use the lyrics tool, each word or syllable is automatically linked to a note. You can even export text to or import text from a word processing program. To export, enter the text editor of either tool, then select and copy the text to the Scrapbook. Open your word processor, copy the text from the Scrapbook, and paste it in. Follow the same steps in reverse to import from a word processor, pasting the text into the *mass create* dialog box. For importing to work, dummy lyrics must first be inserted into the score. For large text files, use Finale PowerPlus to extract text from a word processor document.

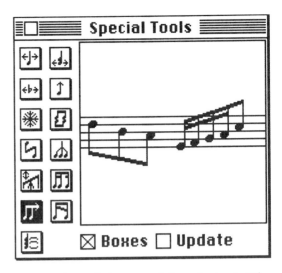

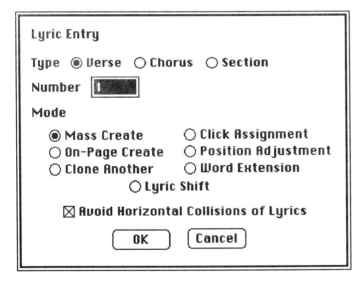

mover tool, and the special tools tool. The *mass mover tool* selects whole measures for edit operations. With the mass mover tool, click a measure to select it, or select multiple measures by shift-clicking or clicking and dragging. Clicking in the left margin selects an entire staff. To selectively cut, copy, paste, and mirror measures, double-click the staff to open the mass edit dialog box. The *note mover tool* copies, cuts, pastes, deletes, and transposes notes only. When you select the note mover tool and click on a measure, handles appear on every note in that measure. Rests and other symbols are unaffected. Select the notes you want to edit, and a dialog box lets you choose the type of editing. The *special tools tool* adjusts the horizontal position of notes and accidentals, stem attributes like length and direction, beaming attributes like height and angle, and so on. Many edit functions are performed with the same tools used to create symbols, assigning identification numbers to select clefs, brackets, shapes, and other symbols.

Scoring editing, layout, and printing

Many tools and menu selections are used to edit the details of Finale scores, including the mass mover tool, the note

Finale has lots of other interesting and useful features for composing and arranging music. You can merge several staves into a piano reduction with the *implode* function, or *explode* a grand staff into a full orchestration with correct transpositions for each instrument. Define your own custom clefs with the *clef tool*. (By the way, you can't enter a clef into a measure unless it already has notes or rests in it) With the *hocket tool*, you can copy and paste a measure, so that the copies are linked to the original. Whenever you edit the source measure, the changes you make are reflected in its copies, called *mirrors*. The *arbitrary music tool* creates measures of music that exist only as graphic symbols. They're linked to existing measures and can't be played back. Finale includes preset *libraries* of staff layouts, key signatures, meters, clefs, chord suffixes, microtonal scales, dynamic markings, tempo markings, transpositions, spacing allotments, tool set combinations, macros called *meta tools*, and sets of command keystrokes.

Finale gives you complete control over the layout and design of pages, staves, measures, and notes. Everything on a page can be relocated. You can globally or individually change the spacing between notes. There are numerous page layout and printing options, including the ability to compile the score into a pure PostScript file. When you download a PostScript file to a laser printer, you get better print resolution and smoother curves than using the Print Score command.

Music Education

If you had the finest music tutor in the world, what

qualities would that teacher possess? He or she would be thoroughly knowledgeable about all aspects of music, absolutely expert in performance, completely open minded, diplomatically nonjudgmental, infinitely patient, always on call, and of course, relatively inexpensive. Until you find such a teacher, music education software fulfills quite a few of these requirements. Patience is its best virtue. You can go over an exercise over and over without the computer showing the slightest hint of boredom. You can concentrate on your weakest areas without fear of embarrassment. You can work at any time of the day or night, at your own pace, without bothering anybody or paying for overtime. If you have a Macintosh, you have the most expensive part of educating yourself already. With one or two rather modest investments in software, you can teach yourself a lot of useful things about music.

What kinds of things? The first one that comes to mind is ear training. Ear training is a course of study in which you learn to recognize pitches, rhythms, scales, melodic patterns, intervals, chords, and timbres. Traditionally, the ultimate goals of ear training are 1) to learn to transcribe music directly from your mind, through your hands, and onto paper; 2) to immediately sing or play music you hear in your head; and 3) to instantly recognize exactly what someone else is playing, often so you can play along. In an ear training class, the teacher plays successive examples, often on a piano, as the students try to write down in musical notation what they hear.

Like the words "ear training" suggest, it improves your ability to hear musically. You'll learn songs more quickly, read music more easily, and improvise more smoothly, alone or with other players. The advantage of computer software is immediate feedback. It asks questions and your answers are judged as soon as you give them.

Closely intertwined with ear training is another course of study called music theory. Music theory teaches you to understand how musical elements (notes, chords, rhythms, etc.) work together, what they're called, and how to put them on paper in a form that anyone who reads music can understand. Music theory tries to analytically explain what makes music sound like music. Perhaps the most useful skill that comes from a good knowledge of music theory is the ability to gracefully communicate musical ideas with other musicians. Traditionally, it also teaches you how to get around on a musical keyboard.

A number of software packages are available for learning music theory and ear training. These include Listen, Practica Musica, Perceive, 7th Heaven, and similar programs from academic institutions. Each has its strengths and weaknesses. Some software, like Guitar Wizard and Harmony Grid, teach you something about putting music theory into practice. In this chapter, we'll take a close look at some of the products that are on the shelves in computer and music stores.

Practica Musica

Practica Musica, from Ars Nova, does a fine job of teaching both theory and ear training. Originally developed for use in a classroom, it automatically keeps a record of your progress, making it useful with or without a human music teacher. Its strengths are teaching you to recognize intervals and scales by their sound, teaching you to name the notes in intervals, scales, and chords, and teaching you to write music you hear. Practica Musica comes with a very useful workbook/theory text entitled *Windows On Music*.

When you first open Practica Musica, you're presented with an onscreen keyboard and a grand staff. An Activities menu offers a series of eleven musical exercises. If no activity is selected, the program is in practice mode, labeled *practice with harmony*. When you use the mouse to click on any two, three, or four keys, or place the notes on the grand staff, or play them on a MIDI instrument, the program analyzes the interval or chord and displays its name. By the way, Practica Musica only recognizes traditional 19th century harmony, the type taught in classical music studies, and not modern harmony, as taught in jazz studies. As a result, when you play a chord which doesn't conform to a classical triad, like a suspended fourth, the program calls it "unidentifiable".

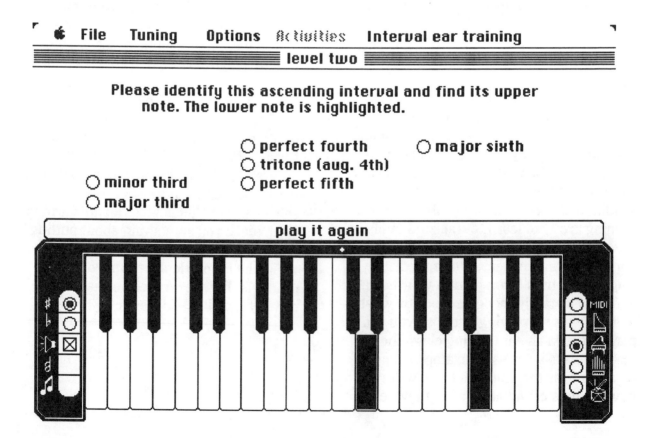

By clicking a button in the lower left corner, you can also *practice with melody*. This shows the relationship between notes on the keyboard and on the staff. If you're learning to recognize tunings other than the standard 12-note equal temperament, eight alternate tunings are available from the Mac's sound circuits.

Tuning

✓12-note equal
12-note Meantone
12-note Pythagorean
Extended Meantone
Extended Pythagorean
Kirnberger 1/2 comma
Silbermann 1/6 comma
Tempérament ordinaire
'just' scale (in C major)

Each activity has four levels of difficulty. Some activities require that you complete a level to graduate to the next, by accumulating a certain number of points. Points are added to your score for each correct answer (for certain activities, within a limited time frame) and subtracted when you make too many errors. When you give a complete response, an encouraging comment like, "Excellent! That was both fast and accurate," or "Not bad! You lost a few points for errors, though," may appear with the score. Help screens detailing the music theory behind the exercise can be summoned for a few activities. When a level is completed, a check mark appears in the menu beside the level's choice, and the computer bursts into an unconvincingly spontaneous show of respect and appreciation (digitized cheers and applause).

Activities

Pitch reading displays a series of ten notes on the grand staff. You're supposed to play the same notes, either onscreen with a mouse or on a MIDI instrument. The level determines whether the notes are all naturals or include accidentals, and whether key signatures appear. Basically, this exercise teaches you to recognize notes quickly, a skill that's necessary for sight reading.

The *Scales* activity gives you the name of a scale and asks you to correctly transcribe or play it. The right answer earns you 80 points, and if you give the key signature, that's an extra 20 points. Wrong notes in your response subtracts from these scores. You can listen to either the scale or your response without losing points. The first level is all major scales, and the second is all natural minors. The third level presents harmonic and melodic minor scales. The fourth level includes every natural mode, plus whole tone scales. You can also concentrate on a particular scale without saving your score to disk.

In *Interval playing*, you're given the name of an interval and its starting note, told whether it's ascending or descending, and you have to either click on the two notes or play them via MIDI. Depending on the level, the intervals could be diatonic or chromatic, and the first note natural or with accidentals. *Interval spelling* has the same four levels, but you have to click on notes with precisely the right accidentals (double-flats and double-sharps included) or place them on the staff. Unlike Interval playing, enharmonic equivalents don't count. *Interval ear training* plays an interval, then asks you to identify (by

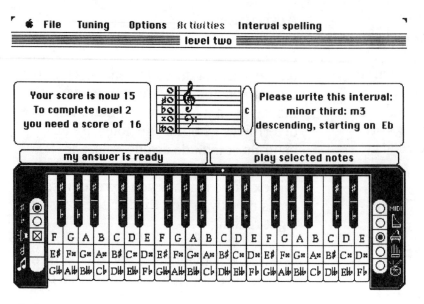

clicking or playing) the right notes on the keyboard and select the interval name from a number of choices. Each level contains a particular range of intervals.

The *Chord playing* activity tells you the name of a chord (Ab minor triad in first inversion, for example), and you respond by playing that chord or clicking on the notes that comprise it. The first level is all major and minor triads in root position, and the second level includes inversions. Third level includes seventh chords plus augmented and diminished triads in root position, with inversions and augmented sixth chords in the fourth level. *Chord spelling* is like interval spelling, with the same levels as chord playing.

All the exercises discussed so far are good preparation for learning to take melodic dictation. Dictation itself is addressed by melody ear training. The computer plays a melody, and you either write it in musical notation or play the same notes. Melody ear training is divided into three activities: pitch, rhythm, or both pitch and rhythm.

The melodies played by Practica Musica come from three sources: a library of forty selections from the classical repertoire (ranging from "My Country 'Tis of Thee" to Bartók and Stravinsky), up to forty user-programmable melodies written by you or your teacher, and tunes generated by the computer within parameters specified by the user. A metronome, in the form of a digitized human clap, can be turned on to keep the beat in any meter. You can change the tempo at any time.

When you choose *Melody ear training: pitch* and a level, you're given a choice of ten melodies. You can click on buttons to hear either the complete melody or just the first part, up to three times without losing points. A menu choice determines the number of notes past your current position that are played by the "Play first part" command. The first note is shown, and the cursor assumes the rhythmic shape of the next note. Just click on the appropriate staff line or space, and the cursor changes to the next note. Rests appear automatically. When you've completed the melody, the computer evaluates your response, highlighting any errors and displaying your score.

Melody ear training: rhythm works much the same way, but the pitches are supplied while you select rhythms, rests, ties, and barlines from a palette of music symbols.

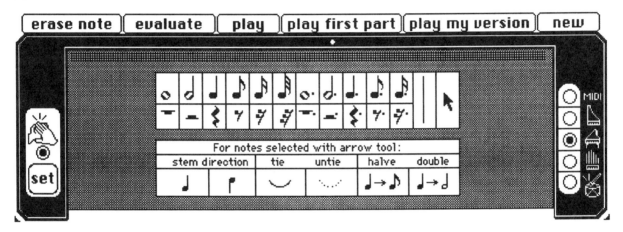

Full-fledged melodic dictation is found in *Melody ear training: pitch and rhythm*. The computer plays a melody and you have to write all the correct pitches and rhythms. When you click on Evaluate, it checks the rhythm and gives you a chance to correct any mistakes before it evaluates the pitches and issues a score. The clapping metronome is very handy for melodic dictation, especially if there are pick-up notes in the first measure.

Melodic material can be generated by the computer for all melody ear training exercises. You can choose the scale type (major,

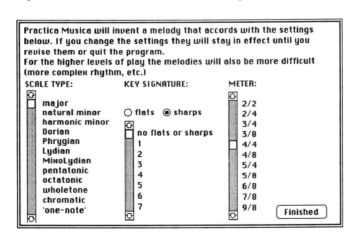

variety of minor or modal, or chromatic), the key signature, and the meter for generated melodies.

You can also write your own melodies for melodic dictation by selecting *Melody writing*. Up to ten custom compositions can be saved to disk if they're short enough to fit on the staff across the Mac screen. The same palette used for melody ear training is used to enter music symbols, by clicking on the needed symbol, then clicking where you want it to appear on the staff.

Listen

Imaja's **Listen** teaches you to recognize pitches and harmonies. Designed as an ear training tool only, it's also one of the few programs that let you play up to four simultaneous Mac voices from a MIDI instrument. Listen is strictly an ear-training tool, with exercises for recognition of pitches, intervals, and an impressive variety of chords, including triads, 7ths, 9ths, 11ths, 13ths, and random, non-triad-based chords. It also performs melodic dictation, though all the notes have the same duration and all the melodies are computer-generated. It doesn't save your scores like Practica Musica. Instead, it keeps track of the number of right and wrong answers and displays two corresponding horizontal bars that lengthen with each response, only for the length of each exercise.

There's an optional "time-out" penalty for taking too long to answer an exercise. This can be any duration from one second to four minutes, with the passage of time indicated by a running hourglass window. You can also show how much time has passed since beginning each exercise.

There are three main windows in Listen: a piano keyboard, a guitar fretboard, and a "progress and explanation window", where scores are displayed and you can click buttons to repeat or respond to an example. The instrument windows are handy if you're trying to match notes on a piano and a guitar. When you click on any key or string, the same note is highlighted in the other window. When no exercise is selected, you can play single notes from the Mac sound generator in either instrument window or

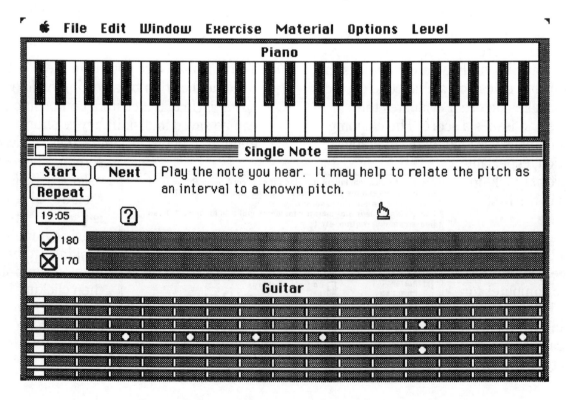

via MIDI. A variety of computerized sounds on the Listen disk can be opened to use in exercises. A Control window lets you change the volume, length, and vibrato of the tones. The program remembers your control window settings the next time you start.

Each Listen exercise has five levels of difficulty for tailoring to your personal skills. The first level may be confined to all white keys within one octave, or all major and minor triads in a single key, while the fifth level includes every pitch in every imaginable harmonic permutation. There's also a User Level for selecting a lot of variable parameters: which pitches or scales are included, how high or low they get, the starting pitch, which chords and inversions are used, and so on. Some of these are automatically requested if you

```
┌─────────────────────────────────┐
│ Exercise                         │
├─────────────────────────────────┤
│ No Exercise              ⌘N      │
│ Single Note                      │
│ Two-Note Melody                  │
│ Growing Melody                   │
│ Melody                           │
│ Interval                         │
│ Triads                           │
│ 7th Chords                       │
│ 9th Chords                       │
│ 11th Chords                      │
│ 13th Chords                      │
│ Random Atonal Chords             │
│ Tuning                           │
│ Interval Naming                  │
│ Triad Chord Quality              │
│ 7th Chord Quality                │
│ Triad Inversion Naming           │
│ 7th Chord Inversion Naming       │
└─────────────────────────────────┘
```

check Auto-Select Materials in the Options menu. Then, when you begin an exercise, a series of dialog boxes appear to set up these options. You can also set the pace of the examples — the time between notes in melodic exercises and the time before Listen automatically plays the next example. Pitch Sets and User Options are remembered for next time.

Three keys on the computer keyboard can substitute for equivalent buttons: S for Start, N for Next, and R for Repeat. You can also assign any three notes on your MIDI instrument to substitute for the same three buttons, so you can respond without taking your hands off your instrument.

Exercises

All the exercises in Listen are either matching drills or multiple choice. Matching responses are given by clicking the appropriate key or string on the computer screen or by playing the note on a MIDI instrument. Other examples require that you click on an answer button.

The object of the *Single Note* exercise is simply to match the note played by the computer. This drill is good for learning to recognize pitch relative to the previous example. In *Two-Note Melody*, two tones are played in succession. The first note is highlighted, and you have to match the second one. *Growing Melody* plays a note, and if you match it, plays it again followed by another note. If you match them both, three notes are played, then four, then five, adding another note to the computer-generated melody each time you play it back without errors. If you answer wrong, it repeats the series of notes. The *Melody* exercise plays a series of notes that you have to match. The length of the melody, from one to ten notes, depends on the difficulty level or user settings.

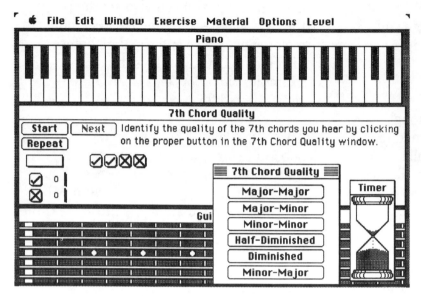

The *Interval* exercise plays two notes and the first is highlighted. The goal is to match the second note. If Arpeggiate Chords is checked in the Options menu or if you're at levels one or two, the two tones are played one after another. Otherwise, in the upper two levels, they're played at the same time. The same is true of *Triads*. When the computer plays a chord, you must match the notes in the correct order, from the lowest to the highest. The same method applies to *7th Chords, 9th Chords, 11th Chords,* and *13th Chords. Random Atonal Chords* plays groups of two, three, or four notes without regard to their harmonic logic. If the tones are played in succession rather than simultaneously (that is, if Arpeggiate Notes is checked), this exercise is essentially two- to four-note melodic dictation.

Tuning is quite different from the other exercises. The Mac plays two out-of-tune tones together, and you're supposed to

move a scroll bar until they're in absolute unison. Close doesn't count. Keep clicking the Repeat button until you think you have it right, then click Check. This exercise is just about impossible for most people unless you lengthen the tone's duration in the Control window so you can scroll the box as you listen. Click on the gray part of the scroll bar for coarse tuning and the arrow itself for fine tuning. With practice, you'll quickly learn to recognize perfect unison, but tuning a good guitar is probably easier.

Interval Naming is a multiple choice exercise. Two tones are played, either in succession or simultaneously, and you respond by clicking the button with the name of the interval. Another multiple choice, *Triad Chord Quality*, prompts you to indicate whether a chord is major, minor, augmented, or diminished. The *7th Chord Quality* exercise plays a chord, then you click a button to indicate whether you think it's major major 7th, major minor 7th, minor minor 7th, minor major 7th, diminished 7th, or half-diminished 7th.

Triad Inversion Naming is just what it sounds like — you guess whether the chord played is in root position or in first or second inversion. (If the 3rd's in the lowest note, it's in first inversion; if the 5th's at the bottom, it's in second inversion.) *7th Chord Inversion Naming* is identical, but with four note chords and third inversions to boot.

Perceive

Coda's **Perceive** is yet another ear trainer for the Macintosh. It's divided into five related applications called Tutor, Drills, Tunings, MiniDrawWave, MiniDesign Wave, and Sound Machine. Tutor and Drills use either MIDI or one of four basic Mac sounds for output and keep score for each exercise. Scores can be saved to disk so you can take up where you left off. The four other applications demonstrate principles of musical sound by generating sound from the computer, rather than quiz you on recognition skills. The program is accompanied by a textbook which teaches the basics of music theory and a workbook to reinforce what the textbook teaches. Perceive illustrates some of the concepts presented by the text.

Tutor gives melodic dictation from a selected scale in one selected key or all keys. Major, natural minor, harmonic minor, melodic minor, dorian, phrygian, lydian, mixolydian, locrian, pentatonic, whole tone, diminished, and full chromatic scales are included. Computer-generated melodies can be any length, from one to a hundred notes of equal duration. The tonic for each example is played and displayed on an onscreen musical keyboard, then the melody is played. You respond to each example by clicking on the matching keys. Click on the Compare button to see how well you've done, then click Hear New Example to progress to the next.

Drills plays scales, intervals, and chords which you identify by name. Scales plays an ascending or descending example, and you decide whether it's one of the seven natural modes or harmonic or melodic minor. You can limit the number of choices to any combination of scales before you begin.

Intervals are played ascending, descending, or simultaneously. Again, you choose which intervals are include in the exercise, from unison to major 9th. Triads and Seventh Chords arpeggiate three or four notes up or down or plays them simultaneously, and you identify the chord value. The screen always displays the number of questions, responses, and correct responses so far. When you're finished with an exercise, you can view an Analysis window with a final score.

Tunings offers five historical temperaments and an avant garde tuning from which to choose, then plays a C major scale, a C, F, or G major triad, or a cadence (a short chord progression) with the selected tuning.

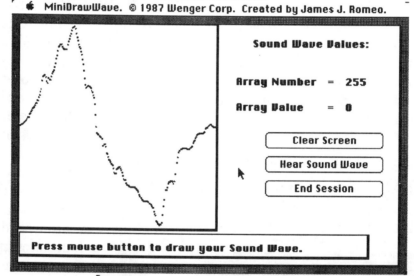

MiniDrawWave. © 1987 Wenger Corp. Created by James J. Romeo.

Sound Wave Array:

```
 0    0    0    0    1    1    2    3    4    5    6    8   10   10   14
15   17   19   21   22   23   25   27   28   31   31   35   38   42   45
56   61   62   63   63   60   55   53   59   59   57   57   61   65   67
69   73   78   84   88   94   99  100  102  102  102   99   97   96   96
96   96   96  102  106  109  113  116  120  123  124  124  125  122  116
111  107  102   99   97   93   89   83   77   69   59   51   47   48   49
50   50   49   48   47   44   42   38   35   27   14   -1   -9  -10  -11
-11  -13  -14  -14  -16  -25  -25  -23  -23  -26  -34  -35  -39  -42  -43
-45  -47  -48  -49  -53  -58  -59  -59  -54  -53  -52  -51  -51  -53  -55
-58  -62  -66  -67  -67  -71  -73  -73  -74  -75  -75  -76  -76  -76  -76
-76  -76  -77  -78  -79  -80  -82  -85  -87  -87  -89  -91  -92  -93  -93
-93  -93  -93  -93  -94  -94  -96  -96  -97  -99 -101 -101 -106 -109 -111
-118 -119 -121 -122 -123 -122 -122 -120 -110  -99  -91  -91  -79  -79  -76
-71  -69  -69  -68  -68  -69  -71  -68  -59  -59  -45  -38  -32  -30
-30  -28  -28  -27  -27  -27  -27  -27  -27  -28  -28  -28  -27  -26
-25  -24  -20  -18  -17  -14  -12  -10   -9   -9   -8   -8   -8   -8   -8
-8   -7   -6   -2   -1   -1   -1    1    2    3    3    2    1    1    1
 1
```

Click Mouse to continue.

click the appropriate box, the computer plays the pitch A-440.

A number of basic waveforms are available in *The Sound Machine,* including sine, square, triangle, sawtooth, pitched noise, and a sine wave mixed with noise. When you select a sound, the Mac plays a chromatic run, a major scale, and a quasi-random pattern using that sound.

The three remaining exercises teach you something about harmonic structure and how different waveforms sound. *MiniDrawWave* lets you draw a single wave with the mouse, then it calculates and displays a "sound wave array" as the computer plays a chromatic scale, a major scale, and a cadence with the sound you've drawn.

MiniDesignWave is similar, but you design a sound by specifying the number of partials (from one to fifteen) and their relative amplitudes (from one to a hundred). The screen shows you what the sound looks like, and if you

MiniDrawWave. © 1987 Wenger Corp. Created by James J. Romeo.

Sound Wave Values:

Array Number = 255

Array Value = 0

[Clear Screen]
[Hear Sound Wave]
[End Session]

Press mouse button to draw your Sound Wave.

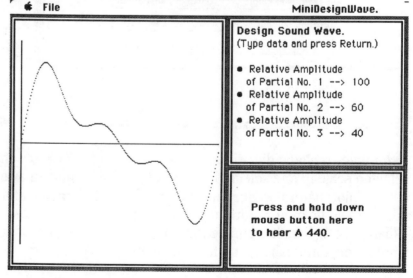

File   MiniDesignWave.

Design Sound Wave.
(Type data and press Return.)

• Relative Amplitude of Partial No. 1 --> 100
• Relative Amplitude of Partial No. 2 --> 60
• Relative Amplitude of Partial No. 3 --> 40

Press and hold down mouse button here to hear A 440.

Guitar Wizard

If you play the guitar, you should definitely check out Baudville's **Guitar Wizard**. Basically, Guitar Wizard is a chord and scale computer for the guitar. All four facets, Chord Wizard, Scale Wizard, Fretboard Wizard, and Improvisation Wizard, may be open at the same time. In three of its windows, Guitar Wizard graphically displays roots, chords, and scales on an onscreen guitar fretboard. In the fourth, you can choose a scale for interactive display in the other three.

Scale Wizard displays the very same guitar fretboard, but with the fret dots indicating single-position fingering for any of 19 different scales in any key, including major and minor pentatonic, two blues scales, and all the natural modes. The root, scale, and note names are displayed, along with fingering numbers, intervals, or notes. Again, you can scroll to different positions on the fretboard.

Fretboard Wizard shows either chords or scales in all positions and inversions over the entire fretboard. You can see which frets are pressed when you add notes by clicking on the row at the bottom of the window. You can also use the small scroll arrows immediately to the left of each string to see the fret positions when you change the way the strings are tuned. Alternative tunings can even be saved and opened.

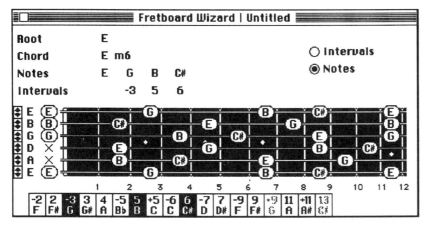

Chord Wizard opens a window that displays 32 different chords (one at a time, of course), ranging from major and minor to 7+9-5 and 13-9, in all inversions (also one at a time). The chord name, its root, and the notes within it are named. White dots show which frets are pressed, and radio buttons let you determine whether these dots show fingering numbers, interval numbers, or note names. The scroll bar changes the chord's inversion.

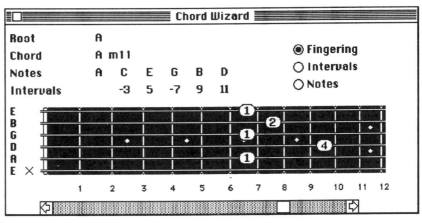

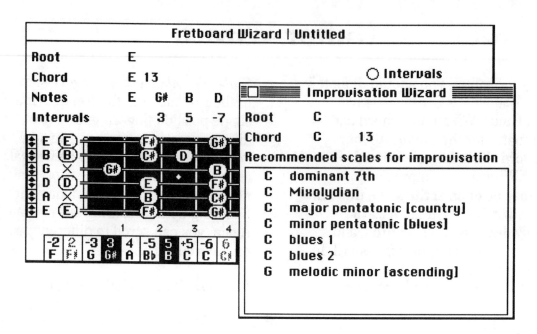

Improvisation Wizard lists up to nine appropriate scales for improvisation over any selected chord. Specify a root and a chord value, and a list of scales appears. Any scale listed works over the given chord, depending on its context within a song. Select a scale by clicking on its name, and it's automatically shown in the Scale Wizard and Fretboard Wizard windows.

Root	Chords	More Chords	Scales
C	major	7	major
C#	minor	9	melodic minor [ascending]
Db	aug	7+5	natural minor
D	dim7	7-5	harmonic minor
D#	6	7+9	major pentatonic [country]
Eb	maj7	7-9	minor pentatonic [blues]
E	maj9	9+5	blues 1
F	6add9	9-5	blues 2
F#	add9	7+9+5	dominant 7th
Gb	m6	7-9+5	diminished
G	m7	7+9-5	half-diminished
G#	m9	7-9-5	whole tone
Ab	m11	7sus4	Ionian
A	m maj7	11	Dorian
A#	m7-5	11+	Phrygian
Bb		13	Lydian
B		13-9	Mixolydian
			Aeolian
			Locrian

Desktop Orchestras: MIDI Instruments

Because the Macintosh's sound-producing capabilities

are so limited, you need MIDI instruments to make serious music. Under the computer's control, MIDI instruments are electronic sources of musical sounds. Some MIDI instruments can be picked up and played like other musical instruments. You can use them to enter musical information into a computer. Other MIDI instruments depend on external MIDI signals for musical input. MIDI instruments include synthesizers, samplers, playback modules, and drum machines. They're available for a wide range of prices, from a couple hundred dollars to a couple hundred thousand. If you want to put together a desktop orchestra, this chapter may help you decide where to start.

Unless you're especially proficient on MIDI guitar, sax, drums, or marimba, and lousy on piano, your first MIDI instrument will probably have a built-in musical keyboard. Like a traditional keyboard instrument, a MIDI keyboard instrument can be thought of as two parts: the part that the performer plays, the keyboard itself, and the part that makes sound. Keyboards and other controllers with no sound-producing electronics are available as separate components for a MIDI system.

A lot of MIDI instruments are free-standing, self-contained boxes that can only be played from external MIDI controllers. Often, these boxes are "rack-mountable" for stacking in a professional, 19" audio rack. Some modular instruments are exactly the same as their keyboard-sporting counterparts, only minus the keyboard. The Roland D-550, for example, is basically a D-50 without the keyboard, and the Korg M1R is the modular version of the M1.

All instruments are limited in the number of notes (voices) they can play at the same time. Old synths like the Minimoog and ARP 2600 are *monophonic*, meaning that they only produce one voice at a time. Traditional monophonic instruments include all woodwinds and brass instruments. Modern synthesizers are *polyphonic*, meaning that they have multiple voices. Some can only play six voices at a time, others sixteen, and some as many as thirty-two. In many instruments, all voices are identical, because the sound of every voice is created by the same patch. (A patch is a collection of parameters defining an electronic sound.) If it's a violin patch, all voices sound like a violin.

In a MIDI system, it's very important to know if an instrument is *multitimbral*. Multitimbral instruments can produce several different sounds simultaneously. They're usually capable of receiving messages on more than one MIDI channel. Owning a multitimbral synthesizer is like owning several synthesizers, each capable of producing sounds from a different patch. A single multitimbral instrument may play the piano part, the bass part, and the drums all at the same time. The number of voices played by each timbre may be fixed, or it may be dynamically allocated, with timbres stealing voices from other timbres as necessary. If you're looking for MIDI instruments to use with your computer, you could do worse than to start out with something multitimbral.

If two sounds are played by the same note, they are said to be *layered*. With layering, you can combine timbres to form richer composite sounds. By playing two instruments on the same MIDI channel, one is layered with the other. If a keyboard plays one sound with half its keyboard and another sound with the other half, it's said to be *split*. Some multitimbral instruments have keyboards that can be split up into multiple zones, with each zone playing a different timbre.

Synthesizers

When someone says, "MIDI instrument", what's the first thing that comes to mind? "Synthesizer"? That's it, isn't it? Synthesizers are the primary instruments of electronic music. If you're dabbling in MIDI, you probably have at least one synthesizer. Most synthesizers have keyboards, but thanks to MIDI, there's also a wide variety of self-contained synth modules without keyboards. After more than two decades of technological evolution driven by the demands of the marketplace, synthesizers are the most flexible and easiest-to-expressively-use instruments available to the modern computer musician.

A synthesizer generates sound from electronic sources called *oscillators*. Some synthesizers have voltage-controlled oscillator (VCO) circuits where sounds originate. These are called *analog* synthesizers, and they create sound by filtering harmonically complex waveforms. This process is called *subtractive synthesis*. Most analog synthesizer oscillators produce only sawtooth waves, pulse waves, and unpitched noise. Analog filters cut and boost certain harmonics in these waveforms. Ten years ago, all synthesizers were completely analog.

In modern analog synths, signals from a microprocessor are converted into voltages that control analog circuits like oscillators and filters. A microprocessor is also necessary to communicate with other MIDI machines. Even though they're really digital, some subtractive synths with digitally-controlled oscillators (DCOs) are referred to as analog synths. In fact, most so-called analog synths have DCOs.

Digital synthesizers use their microprocessors to fabricate oscillators by juggling numbers and turning them into audio signals. Analog synthesizers have hardware oscillators, and digital synthesizers have software oscillators. There are dozens of methods used by different synth manufacturers to generate sounds digitally. Each method has its own distinctive sound. Yamaha synthesizers generate sounds by frequency modulation, or FM synthesis. Roland synths use linear arithmetic, or LA synthesis. Some Casios rely on interactive phase distortion, or iPD synthesis. Then there's additive synthesis, wavetable synthesis, digital re-synthesis, and a host of other techniques for creating timbres algorithmically.

Even though their means of sound generation may differ completely, many analog and digital instruments feature similar controls, giving us some common ground in the human interface with synthesizers. The majority of circuits (analog) or functions (digital) in a synthesizer are for controlling or altering the characteristics of the sounds made by oscillators.

Envelope generators, usually with digitally-generated envelopes, are found in almost all synths. The most important function is an envelope generator paired with an amplifier, which literally shapes a sound's loudness. Most synthesizers also have an envelope generator to shape harmonic content. On a subtractive synth, this is paired with a lowpass or multipass filter. Other standard synth features include low-frequency oscillators (LFOs) to create vibrato and other articulations, and manual controllers to change the behavior of other functions, like oscillator frequency (pitch bend) or the rate and depth of vibrato.

When you modulate the frequency of a simple waveform with another simple waveform, the result is a more complex waveform. The techniques of generating sound by frequency modulation is called *FM synthesis*. Yamaha makes a very popular line of digital FM synthesizers,

including the classic DX7. Each voice of an FM synthesizer has either four or six *operators*. An operator is a digitally-generated waveform paired with an envelope generator. Operators are combined to form complex waveforms. An operators is either a carrier, which produces the sound, or a modulator, which controls its tone color. Pitch is determined by the carrier, with the waveform and frequency content determined by the modulator. You can dynamically control the harmonic content of an FM sound by changing the depth of the modulator's output with envelopes.

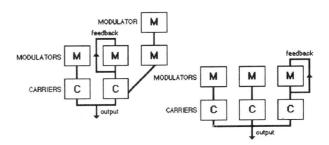

Operators are arranged in various preset combinations called *algorithms*. Programming an FM sound from scratch usually begins with choosing an algorithm. Instruments with 6-operator synthesis have 32 algorithms, and 4-operator instruments have eight. To harmonically enrich the modulating waveforms, some algorithms have modulators that modulate one another, and some have modulators that modulate themselves. In one algorithm, all operators are carriers.

Many instruments employ *wavetable synthesis*, in which a selection of digitally-recorded or digitally-generated sounds are stored in ROM (read-only memory) chips. These sounds may be acoustical instruments, including drums, and samples of other synthesizers.

Typically, as little as a single wave of an instrumental sound is sampled and looped. Instruments that use *PCM synthesis* fall into this category. PCM stands for pulse code modulation, which is just a type of digital recording. Casio makes a series of inexpensive PCM synths with MIDI. Some Kawai synthesizers, including the popular K1, also use recorded wavetables for sound sources. Korg's M series, including the M1 and M3, contain a large number of high-quality sampled wavetables. Some instruments have wavetables synthesized by additive synthesis rather than samples.

Many Roland synthesizers use a synthesis technique called *linear arithmetic*, or *LA synthesis*. These include the Roland D series (D-50, D-10, etc.) and CM series (CM-32L and CM-64) of synthesizers. LA synthesizers combine wavetable synthesis with subtractive synthesis. A number of short samples are provided, usually instrumental attacks. These are mixed with basic waveforms from digitally-controlled oscillators. The resulting sound is filtered, shaped with envelopes, and modulated in various ways. LA synthesizers have onboard signal processors for reverb and delay effects. Effects settings are saved as an integral part of each patch.

Only a few synthesizers employ *additive synthesis*, including the Kawai K5 and the Bohm DE 4X9. A few samplers also have limited additive synthesis capabilities. With Digidesign's Softsynth program for the Mac, it's possible to synthesize waveforms additively and transfer them to a sampler. In additive synthesis, many sine waves are combined to form complex waveforms. Each sine wave has a different frequency and amplitude, both of which can be controlled by an envelope. This is great,

because you can create sounds whose harmonic complexity changes over time like most acoustical instruments. Additive synthesis, though tedious, is capable of emulating instrumental sounds with great realism.

Samplers

A sampler is an instrument that digitally records and plays back sounds under MIDI or keyboard control. With a sampler, you can capture any sound and play it as you would play a piano. Samplers are most often used to record and play back the sounds of acoustic instruments, voices, and sound effects. Almost all samplers are by nature multitimbral, capable of producing as many different sounds at one time as there are voices.

What kind of sounds can you sample and what can you do with them? Record real orchestral instruments and play a symphony. Record a duck and play a symphony of ducks. Sample a vintage analog synthesizer and make it polyphonic, velocity-sensitive, and MIDI-controllable. Digitize your vocalist singing a lyric absolutely perfectly, and whenever the lyric appears in a song, trigger the sample. Stack background vocals on tape, sample them, and play them at live gigs to give your band a big vocal sound. Record Foley and sound effects for a radio spot and synchronize them to picture with MIDI software.

Digital sampling instruments have been around since the introduction of the Fairlight CMI in 1979. A couple of years later, E-mu introduced the first Emulator for a fraction of what the Fairlight cost. The Emulator put sampling into the hands of working musicians and serious hobbyists.

Through the 1980s, the high cost of digital sampling fell steadily, and today's musician can choose from a large number of popular samplers, both with and without keyboards. As prices continue to fall, sampling technology continues to improve.

The process of sampling involves measuring the dynamic amplitude of sound at periodic intervals, rather like the way a movie camera snaps a picture thirty times a second. Each "snapshot" is a single sample, and the frequency at which samples are taken is called the *sampling rate* or *sampling frequency*. Most samplers let you choose from a number of fixed sampling rates, and the highest sampling rate varies from one instrument to another.

According to a formula called the *Nyquist theorem*, the sampling rate must be twice as high as the highest audio frequency being sampled. If you're sampling a sound with harmonics that go up to 18 kHz, the sampling rate should be 36 kHz or higher. In reality, the sampling rate should be even higher than twice the highest frequency, due to the limitations of sampling hardware. Trying to sample frequencies higher than half the sampling rate results in *aliasing*, which creates overtones not present in the original sound. To avoid aliasing, samplers have anti-aliasing filters to block frequencies they can't reproduce.

Changing the sampling rate changes the frequency bandwidth. A high sampling rate results in crisp, clear samples with a wide range of frequencies. A low sampling rate yields a narrow bandwidth and poor audio quality. So why not always use the highest sampling rate? The higher the rate, the more memory it eats up. As a result,

sampling rate has a direct effect on how long your sample can be. If you half the rate, you double the time, and vice versa. For example, if your sampler has enough memory to record for five seconds at 36 kHz, then changing the sampling rate to 18 kHz lets it record for ten seconds. To gain time, you have to give up quality. To gain quality, you have to give up sampling time. Different samplers offer different sampling rates, but most give you a limited choice of rates.

Another major difference between samplers is *bit resolution*, which determines the accuracy of the data describing a sample. Most popular models are 12-bit, some are only 8-bit, and others are 16-bit. In general, the higher the bit resolution, the better the audio quality, and the more expensive the sampler is to build. Low bit resolution, like low sampling rates, results in samples that sound gritty. Resolution is the number of bits used to describe each sample. When a sound is digitized, its dynamic changes in amplitude are quantized. The number of divisions of amplitude is determined by the bit resolution. If a sample is 8-bit, its dynamic range is divided into 256 levels, but a 16-bit sample is divided into 65,536 levels. Some samplers change resolution as they record, but in general, a sampler's bit resolution can't be changed the way you change sampling rate.

When you record with a sampler, carefully set its input level like you adjust the input on a tape recorder. If the recording level is too high, the sound is clipped. If it's too low, there's too much noise. The ideal sampling level lies somewhere in between — as loud as possible without clipping.

Most samplers can be triggered manually or automatically. With triggering manually, recording begins as soon as you push the button. With automatic triggering, recording doesn't begin until the input senses an audio signal. You can usually adjust the triggering threshold, so a sound must reach a certain level before sampling is triggered. This prevents noise from starting the recording, but since it takes time for the sampler to react to an incoming signal, it can miss important transients during the sound's attack. It's a trade-off: if you auto trigger, you may lose part of the attack, but at least you don't have to truncate the beginning. If you trigger manually, you need enough sampling time for the moment between pressing the record button and the beginning of the sound.

When a sample plays back at the rate it was recorded, it plays at its original pitch. When the sample playback rate is changed, the pitch is transposed. If you sample a singer singing a single note, you can then play that singer's voice with a MIDI instrument, transposing its pitch as you play up and down the keyboard. Of course, you wouldn't have to transpose it very far for it to stop sounding like a real voice and more like a cartoon voice. That's why sounds are *multisampled*. Several pitches are recorded, and each is assigned to play from a particular part of the keyboard.

Record low notes for the lower range and high notes for the upper range. With multisampling, a sound isn't stretched so far that it loses its realism. The challenge of multisampling is that the division between adjacent zones has to be as seamless as possible. If it's difficult to tell on which note one sample ends and another begins, then it's the result of good multisampling.

Each sample's original pitch is assigned to a key, then the highest and lowest keys that play the sample are defined. This is how samples are split into zones across the keyboard. If two or more samples are assigned to the same key, those sounds are layered. Each sample can also be velocity scaled to affect its sensitivity to how hard it's played. Because samples may be recorded at slightly different levels, you can also change its overall volume to achieve a balance between zones.

Some samplers are capable of digital synthesis, offering raw waveforms as a sound source in addition to recorded samples. These waveforms may be triangle waves, square waves, and sawtooth waves for subtractive synthesis, or they may be sines waves that can be combined for additive synthesis. Some samplers offer a palette of complex wavetables that must be processed to make them useful. A sampler with digital synthesis capabilities is a multitimbral synthesizer in its own right.

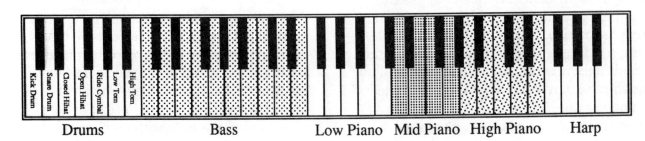

Which sampler is the right one for you? That depends on what you want to do with it and one what you can afford. Samplers go from relatively cheap to very expensive. As you can see, there are many factors that make one sampler different from another: the amount of memory, bit resolution, sampling rates, number of voices, number of samples, ease of editing, processing features, and so on. You really have to use your ears when choosing a sampler. Does it reproduce sound realistically? Does it sound good when you play chords? Is it clean or gritty? Is there a large library of samples already available for it, or do you plan to create your own? What about its user interface? Is it complicated to record and edit samples? Do you plan on using a Mac-based sample editor? If so, does the sampler connect to a computer via SCSI or RS-422 port, or via MIDI only? Should you buy last year's model, this year's big seller, or the latest thing? If you're buying a sampler, ask a lot of questions before you decide which one is right for your needs.

Drum machines

In most MIDI systems, drum machines provide the sounds of percussion. Some drum machines are built into synthesizers, but the majority are free-standing modules. Most of the time, drums, cymbals, and other percussion instruments are digitally recorded and permanently stored in a drum machine's memory circuits. A few drum machines are really specialized digital samplers. Some machines feature velocity-sensitive pads on their surfaces for

playing individual sounds, but each sound can also be triggered by playing a note on any MIDI controller. Often, there are separate audio outputs for each voice, as well as stereo outputs with sounds panned appropriately. Like any electronic instrument, drum machines can only play a limited number of voices simultaneously.

Like samplers, drum machines are multitimbral — they produce a wide range of sounds at the same time. It's not unusual to have a choice of snare drums, kick drums, and tom-toms, as well as open and closed hihat cymbal, ride cymbal, crash cymbal, snare rimshot and sidestick, handclaps, cowbell, tamborine, and maybe a few Latin or African instruments like congas, bongos, timbales, and so on. Because they're digital samples, the length and number of sounds is limited by the amount of available memory. Some drum machines have ports for changing the sounds in memory via ROM cartridges or even built-in floppy disk drives.

Drum machines contain specialized sequencers for arranging rhythmic patterns. Composing a pattern is a matter of arranging several instruments for a measure or two. Typically, a pattern loops over and over as you add instruments. Record the kick drum in the first pass, then the snare, then the hihat, and so on. Patterns are then strung together to form complete songs. Songs can be stored in the drum machine's memory, played into an external sequencer, and sometimes dumped to a MIDI librarian program. If you have a sequencer for your Macintosh, though, it makes more sense to forget the drum machine's sequencer and record directly into the computer, using the drum machine only as a sound source.

Most MIDI drum machines can be played from an external MIDI controller. Even drum machines without velocity-sensitive pads respond to velocity when played from a keyboard or a sequencer. Each note plays a different percussion sound. You can usually remap which key plays which drum. Some drum machines even change songs or patterns when they receive a patch change.

MIDI controllers

Like a traditional piano, most MIDI instruments have musical keyboards. As the interface between a performer and his or her instrument, the keyboard is the primary means of musical performance and MIDI input. MIDI keyboards differ in a number of ways. Most MIDI keyboards have 61 keys instead of the piano's 88 keys, though a few have 76 or 88. A few have wooden keys and weighted actions, which make them feel more piano-like (and heavy), while most have plastic keys with a light action typical of synthesizers and electronic organs.

Many keyboards are *velocity*-sensitive, meaning that each key responds to how hard it's struck. Playing a note produces a velocity value between 0 and 127, which is applied to change the loudness, brightness, or some other parameter of the sound. Some instruments respond to MIDI velocity from external sources, but their keyboards aren't velocity-sensitive. Only a few inexpensive MIDI instruments don't respond to velocity at all.

Some keyboards also feature *aftertouch* or pressure-sensitivity. They respond to how hard you press a key after it's struck. Most pressure-sensitive keyboards have channel aftertouch, meaning that pressure applied to the keyboard affects all notes being played. Some have polyphonic key aftertouch, with each voice responding to the pressure applied to keys individually.

Details of the Musical Instrument Digital Interface

Until just a few years ago, electronic musicians lived in a sort of pre-digital Dark Ages, waiting for something to sweep them into the mainstream of the recording industry. And that's just what MIDI's done: it has given us sophisticated, reasonably affordable music production tools that have become almost essential to modern recording. The development of MIDI has made it possible to write software for desktop computers that every component in an integrated music production system can understand on its own level.

Music is usually best when a number of musicians play together. One may play bass, another plays piano, and another plays something else, and when they play together, they create a whole greater than the sum of its parts. Man has always dreamed of the day when one musician could play several instruments at the same time. MIDI makes it possible. Never before could a single person express his or her richly orchestrated musical vision in finished form without a big, expensive multitrack recording setup. With the benefits of MIDI, a more-or-less live solo concert can be played by dozens of invisible, replicated hands. In the studio, complex, finely-tuned musical arrangements can be recorded onto tape in just one take. Even a non-musician can noodle with professional-quality musical gear on his or her day off.

Because the components of a MIDI system are modular, you can assemble exactly the right system for your needs, whether it's a system for computer-aided composition or a full-blown tapeless studio. Because all MIDI instruments are inherently compatible, it's possible to begin with a modest system and build onto it without running into very much equipment obsolescence. Using your favorite MIDI keyboard, guitar, drum pads, or any other master controller, you can play any number of external instruments.

With MIDI, a keyboard-controlled instrument no longer needs its own keyboard. It may be a six-voice synthesizer that plays up to six voices of the same sound. If it's multitimbral, it may play six different sounds with one voice each, or four voices of one sound and two of another, or myriad other possible combinations. These voices could sound like bass guitar, flute, French horn, glockenspiel, machine-gun fire, resonant growl, or whatever you need at the moment. Instead of a synthesizer, an instrument could be a playback module that sounds like a grand piano or a string section, a digital sampler that sounds like anything you can record, or a drum machine that sounds like dozens of different drums.

MIDI grew up pretty quickly. Someone told a bunch of music scientists to drum up some ideas for a simple connection between any two synthesizers, and they gave us an interface so well-conceived that it allows the complete control of musical events by computer. Alas, a synthesizer without a computer to latch onto is lacking something. It's a good thing we have machines as marvelous as the Macintosh in our homes, offices, and studios.

Why has a four-letter word changed so much about music? Think of all the fields that have been radically changed by the use of computers: banking, printing, design, architecture, manufacture, medicine, education — institutions that affect our lives all the time. Like these areas, music is a natural for computers. All that's required is a bridge to link computers and music. MIDI is that bridge.

So what is music, anyway? It's a constant flow of information about pitch and rhythm, sound and silences. This information can be expressed in numbers, and therefore, as digital data. MIDI is the pathway through which musical data flows.

In addition to being the physical link between instruments and computers, it's the actual form that musical information takes. MIDI is both the medium and the message. The language of MIDI makes it possible for various parts of an electronic music system to share musical ideas. They exchange messages like, "Play a soft, high A# here for half a beat," or "Now bend the pitch this far," or even, "Here's a list of parameters that makes a DX7 sound like a xylophone." Some messages are meant for any instrument tuned to a particular channel. Some are meant for one synth and one synth only. Others are meant for every device that's tied into the network.

Physical connections

When you connect instruments to a computer, you're networking their microprocessors, creating what's called a *MIDI system* or *MIDI network*. This is true any time you link two or more instruments together so one controls the other. There are a lot of advantages to networking musical instruments and other musical equipment with desktop computers, as you no doubt realize.

The most basic MIDI connection occurs when you plug one end of a MIDI cable into an instrument's MIDI Out port, and the other end into another instrument's MIDI In port. If the second instrument is listening on the same channel that the first one's talking, you can play the second one with the first. Every time you strike a key, both instruments play.

A more complex network might include a computer and a master keyboard controlling dozens of synthesizers, samplers, a couple drum machines, some audio effects processors, an automated mixing console, and a stage lighting system. Musical data streaming from the computer could be synchronized to time code information recorded on a videotape's audio track, so what the instruments play is synched to what's happening on the television screen. With enough instruments and a computer, complete record albums can be extensively produced before anything gets recorded on tape.

With a Macintosh, a MIDI interface, some software, and a MIDI-equipped musical instrument or two, you can accomplish quite an assortment of musical chores, from recording your own arrangement of a classical concerto, to jamming off what the computer improvises when the cursor is dragged across the screen.

Communications hardware

Inside every MIDI instrument, there's at least one computer chip, called a microprocessor or CPU (central processing unit). With the proper connections, this microprocessor can receive MIDI data in an 8-bit serial stream at a rate of 31,250 bits per second, or 31.25 kBaud (kiloBaud). That means it can accept a series of digital words (units of information called bytes), each exactly eight bits (or letters, if you will) long, one bit at a time, one after another, in single file. That's why MIDI is called a *serial interface* — bits are sent and received in series.

A *parallel interface*, by contrast, transfers an entire word or more simultaneously, like a crowd of well-organized commuters passing through a turnstile into the open doors of a subway train. Serial is like a line of cars coming out of a parking lot, each containing a lone driver, and parallel is the same row of cars, each with eight passengers. In this analogy, passengers are bits. It takes longer to clear the lot if everyone drives his or her own car; more people get home in time for dinner if they carpool. Yeah, that's it: Carpooling is a parallel protocol. Lunch line in the school cafeteria is serial. (Amusement park lines may be one or the other.)

The only real advantage of using a serial interface is that it's inexpensive. Economy was a critical consideration when MIDI was formulated. The hardware had to be as cheap as possible, so it wouldn't appreciably add to the cost of instruments incorporating MIDI. If it cost too much, it had less chance for widespread acceptance. To add MIDI to an instrument, all that's required from the electronics shop is two or three low-cost DIN jacks, a few strands of wire, a switch called an opto-isolator, and an integrated circuit called a UART.

To get information from one machine to another, you need a *MIDI cable* for communication in one direction, or two

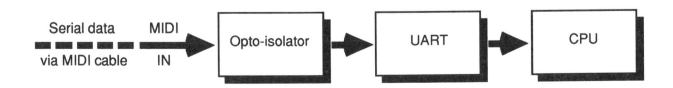

Serial data via MIDI cable → MIDI IN → Opto-isolator → UART → CPU

cables for two-way communication. MIDI data moves in only one direction through a single MIDI cable. That's why there are at least two MIDI ports on any device that sends and receives MIDI — one for sending (MIDI Out) and another for receiving (MIDI In). A *MIDI port* is a female 5-pin DIN jack. At each end of a MIDI cable, there's a male 5-pin DIN plug which plugs into this jack. Only three pins are actually used for MIDI. The conducting wires are attached to pins 4 and 5, with the shield connected to pin 2.

MIDI cables, except by special permission of Her Majesty the Queen of England, are by definition no longer than 50 feet (but don't tell her I said so). Without special assistance, you risk losing vital data if you stretch things too far. Exact mileage may vary, depending on factors like the gauge of the cable's wire. There are devices available for extending the range of MIDI, of course, and even for wireless MIDI transmission. The *MediaLink* protocol uses fiber optics for high-speed, long-distance MIDI transmission.

The *MIDI In* port accepts messages that pass through the MIDI cable. If the information is addressed to a particular instrument, or that instrument's channel, or all devices in the system, the circuitry at the receiving end of its MIDI In port may respond to messages by playing a note, changing a filter setting, turning a stage light or an echo effect on or off, or whatever it's told to do. A keyboard controller or any other device with no reason to receive MIDI messages doesn't need a MIDI In port.

The *MIDI Out* port sends information from any source capable of transmitting MIDI.

This source may be a computer interface sending a multitracked studio performance, a slave module sending patch data, a MIDI controller sending note and velocity data — the possibilities are almost endless. A *MIDI controller* is anything that transmits MIDI information under a performer's control, especially note information. Messages from a controller determine what sounds emanate from your instruments. When you play one, it sends out messages about what notes you play, how hard you hit them, what knobs you turn, and all the usual performance stuff. A MIDI controller may be a free-standing keyboard, synthesizer workstation, drum pads, guitar, marimba, horn, saxophone, leather boot, or what-have-you — if it has a MIDI Out port.

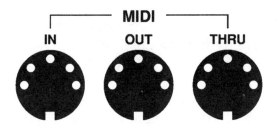

A third port, called *MIDI Thru* (note the spelling), appears on a lot of MIDI machines. It's considered optional, but essential for connecting more than two instruments. When data enters a device's MIDI In port, it gets passed directly to the MIDI Thru, as well as to the device's microprocessor. Whatever comes in through MIDI In, goes out through MIDI Thru, unchanged and practically instantaneously. There are MIDI devices called *thru boxes* that take a MIDI In signal and pass it to a number of MIDI Thru outputs. Thru boxes let you distribute a signal from a master controller or a computer to a lot of MIDI instruments and devices.

Mac interfaces

Unlike the Atari ST series of computers, the Macintosh doesn't have built-in MIDI ports. It needs an external device to convert the MIDI signals into a form the Mac can handle. This device is a MIDI adapter, commonly called a MIDI interface, although it's obviously redundant to call something a musical instrument digital interface interface. The interface plugs into the Mac's modem port, printer port, or both. It has one to four MIDI In ports and one to eight MIDI Outs.

Most MIDI programs for the Macintosh offer a command to summon a dialog box to set the MIDI options. This is where you tell the software about the interface you're using. You can indicate which port is connected, and you're usually given a choice of interface clock speeds, the rate at which the computer and the interface exchange serial data. The usual selections are 500 kHz , 1 MHz (megaHertz, or million cycles per second), and 2 MHz. There's also an optional Fast clock speed supported by certain interfaces. Virtually all commercial Mac interfaces run at 1 MHz. A few years ago, there were a few 500 kHz units made, but I don't think I've ever seen a 2 MHz interface. The first Opcode interface had a switch for selecting clock speeds, but now it's done in software.

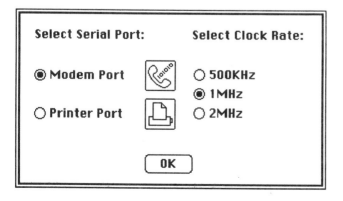

The Mac's RS-422 interface is faster than MIDI's rate of 31,250 bits per second. Some interfaces, including the Southworth JamBox 4+ and Opcode's Studio 3, are capable of accelerated transfer of MIDI data to and from software which specifically supports it. Why would you want to increase the rate of communication? By increasing MIDI's transfer rate, more information can be packed between each MIDI clock pulse, increasing the amount of musical data that can be communicated without getting MIDI logjams.

MIDI channels

One of MIDI's basic concepts is that most messages are sent on *channels* to instruments or voices assigned to receive on those channels. According to the MIDI Spec, there are 16 channels for transmitting and receiving data. Information transmitted on any single channel is acted upon by any instrument set to receive on that channel. An instrument can be told to receive data sent on just one channel and ignore other data it receives. If a synthesizer is receiving on MIDI channel 5, it makes sounds in response to signals sent on channel 5. The signals sent on any channel determine the sounds made by all instruments that are set to receive on that channel.

Cable television is an obvious metaphor for the idea of MIDI channels. Let's say you subscribe to a cable television service with a selection of 16 channels. All 16 channels are simultaneously passing through one cable, hooked up to your TV. You can select a single channel for viewing, just as a MIDI instrument listens to messages on a single channel. Like an instrument, your television ignores all the other channels until you switch the channel number it's receiving. It doesn't matter how many televisions are connected; you can tune as many televisions to as many channels as necessary without affecting the quality of the cable signal. With the right hardware, any number of instruments or voices can be connected to each MIDI channel.

only 16 separate channels, you may have to send duplicate information to two or more receivers. Some Macintosh software makes it possible to double the number of MIDI channels by transmitting 16 channels from the modem port and another 16 out from printer port. For this, you must have two MIDI interfaces or an interface that connects to both ports. This capability is essential if you have more than 16 MIDI machines that you want to control independently.

Multitimbral instruments can receive on several different channels at the same time. One of these channels is the *basic channel*, which is the channel on which it receives patch changes, mode messages, and so on. Some eight-voice synths, like the Kawai K-1 or Yamaha TX81Z, can receive on up to eight channels, with each channel controlling a different musical sound. With an eight-voice sound source, no more than eight sounds can be heard at any one moment, but an eight-track sequence may include parts for piano, bass, drums, and string quartet, with the sounds of as many as eight instruments coming from one instrument. (Let's see you do <u>that</u> with any traditional member of the brass or woodwind family!)

What if you're lucky enough to have more than 16 MIDI receivers? Because there are

What kinds of messages?

There are two basic kinds of MIDI information: channel messages and system messages, which are further divided into channel voice, channel mode, system common, system real time, and system exclusive messages. Voice messages are directed to devices on a single channel, and usually tell an instrument to do something, like play a note or turn on vibrato. Mode messages are sent on the basic channel to which an instrument is tuned. They tell devices whether to react to information on all channels or particular channels only, and whether to play only one voice per channel or more.

System real time messages synchronize devices in a MIDI network played by a sequencer. System common messages provide information like which sequence to play or how many beats have passed since the first beat. System exclusive (*sys ex*) messages are addressed to specific MIDI devices, allowing the digital exchange of patch information between a computer and an instrument, or between one instrument and another. Sys ex messages may also control non-standard parameters such as LFO and envelope settings. A synthesizer could have one LFO, or three, or none, and almost any number of envelope generators with almost any number of stages. If parameter changes couldn't be addressed to one specific instrument, some of them could be interpreted strangely by different instruments on the same channel. Another tremendous benefit of system exclusive is that it makes it possible to write librarian and editor software for specific instruments.

Channel voice messages

There are two kinds of channel voice messages: *commands* and *values*. A *command* might tell a synth to play a note or change patches, while the *value* tells it which note or patch to play. There are 128 possible commands (called *status bytes*) and 128 possible values (called *data bytes*) in MIDI. Only some of these messages are defined by the MIDI Specification, leaving lots of room for future expansion.

Probably the most important voice message is *note on*. Its status byte tells an instrument to play a note, and its data bytes tell it which note to play and at what *velocity*. For keyboard instruments, velocity tells an instrument how hard a key is

struck, which may affect its loudness or any other parameter programmed into a patch. Remember, synthesizers are flexible. Most, but not all, recent MIDI instruments respond to velocity information. If a controller doesn't provide velocity data, it's sent at a default value of 64. If a receiver can't respond to velocity data, it's ignored.

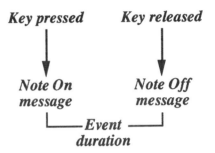

A *note off* message tells an instrument to stop playing a note and includes its *release velocity*. A few instruments respond to release velocity, or how quickly a key is released, but most controllers send a default value of 64. Some MIDI controllers don't send a note off message, but substitute a note on message with a velocity of zero.

Pressure data, also called *aftertouch*, tells an instrument how hard a key is pressed after it's down, changing a note's loudness, brightness, vibrato, envelope times, or whatever parameter is programmed to respond. If a controller is pressure-sensitive, it may send channel pressure or polyphonic key pressure messages. If pressure is applied to a MIDI keyboard, *channel pressure* sends that information to all notes that are playing on all instruments assigned to the same channel. Only a few controllers support *polyphonic key pressure*, which sends individual pressure information for every note.

Control change messages send information from a continuous controller, like a modulation wheel, footswitch, or breath controller. These messages control parameters such as vibrato depth, portamento time, volume, and sustain. The sustain on and off commands (MIDI controller #64) control a note's release time, just like a piano's damper pedal. Volume commands (MIDI controller #7) let you dynamically change the balance between instruments in a sequence. *Pitch bend* tells a note to momentarily raise or lower its pitch by a certain amount. *Program change*, also called a *patch change*, tells a MIDI device to switch to another patch or program number. This may cause a synthesizer to go from sounding like a violin to sounding like a trumpet, or cause an echo unit to switch from one preset effect to another.

MIDI á la modes

Channel mode messages set up an instrument so it knows how to respond to incoming channel voice messages or on what channels to send these messages. It may respond to or transmit on all channels or specific channels (Omni mode on or off), and it may play only one voice at a time or several simultaneous voices (Poly or Mono mode), resulting in four MIDI modes.

Mode number one is *Omni On/Poly*. Omni On means that a device isn't tuned to any particular channel, and it accepts or sends information on any and all channels. Poly mode lets a polyphonic instrument play more than one voice at a time. MIDI mode two is *Omni On/Mono*, which means that it receives or transmits on any channel, but it can only play one voice at a time. *Omni Off/Poly*, mode number three, instructs an

instrument to send or respond to messages on one channel only and to play multiple voices. If an instrument is multitimbral, this mode lets it play polyphonically on its basic channel and any other voice channels to which it's assigned. Omni Off/Poly is the most useful mode for controlling several instruments in a network. The fourth mode, *Omni Off/Mono*, makes each voice respond to a single MIDI channel. Each channel controls only one voice, which is useful for playing monophonic voices from a multitimbral instrument, or assigning a different channel to each string in a MIDI guitar controller, so that each controls a single voice in a six-voice synthesizer, for example.

Local control is a mode message that determines whether an instrument responds to controller data from its own keyboard (or if it's not a keyboard instrument, whatever part the performer actually plays). If local control is on, it plays normally. If local control is off, it only acts on messages sent over its assigned MIDI channel(s). An instrument can control itself with local off by routing its MIDI Out back to its MIDI in. (See the chapter on Sequencers for more information on local on and off.)

All notes off does just what it says; it sends the equivalent of a note off message to all 128 MIDI notes. *Reset all controllers* is similar in that it returns all continuous controller values to their default values. Pitch bend is reset to zero, volume is reset to its full value, and so on.

System messages

System messages aren't encoded with a channel number, so they're sent to every device in a MIDI system. However, *system exclusive* messages are addressed to a particular make and model instrument, like a Casio VZ-1 or an E-mu Proteus, and are encoded with its manufacturer's MIDI identification number. Since all MIDI devices are different, sys ex messages contain information only useful to one type of machine. This information may contain all the parameters for one program or for a full bank of programs, or it may change a single parameter not addressed by channel voice messages, like selecting an oscillator waveform or a filter resonance setting.

System common messages are mostly used for playing a MIDI system with a sequencer. *Song position pointer* counts the number of beats since the beginning of a sequence, so that the current location in a sequence is defined. Without it, you might have to start at a sequence's beginning whenever you stopped and restarted its playback. Song position pointer is essential for synchronizing a sequence to recorded time code, so that the computer plays in sync with a tape recorder no matter where in the sequence you begin playback. Closely related is *MIDI Time Code Quarter Frame*, which indicates location in real time rather than in the number of beats since a sequence's beginning. It also provides a sequencer with the capability of relocating itself to any point within the sequence, like a very precise fast forward and rewind on a tape recorder. If a song file includes multiple sequences, *song select* picks out one sequence by assigning a number to each. Then there's the system common message which has nothing to do with

sequencing, but it's useful if you have synthesizers with analog oscillators. This is *tune request*, which initiates the autotune function of analog synthesizers, so you can tune a bunch of them from a master controller.

System real time messages are also necessary for sequencing and synchronization. A sequencer may be computer software, or it may be hardware, like a free-standing sequencer or the sequencer circuit in a drum machine. The most important Real Time message is the *timing clock*, a digital pulse which "keeps the beat" in a sequence to determine the tempo. Each beat is divided into 24 pulses, so that a sequencer sends out 24 clock signals for every beat. A beat is usually defined as a quarter note or an eighth note, depending on the song's meter. In 4/4 time, one measure equals 96 timing clocks. If the tempo increases, the clock signals are sent more frequently. If the sequence slows down, the clocks decrease in frequency. MIDI clocks are sent even if a sequencer isn't running, so that everything plays in sync from the very first beat.

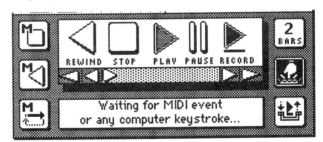

So how does a sequencer know when to start and stop? Start, stop, and continue messages are responsible for functions that, if they controlled a tape recorder, would include play/record, stop, and rewind. The *start* signal begins playing or recording a sequence from its beginning. I surely don't need to tell you what *stop* does.

Because start rewinds to first beat of a sequence, it serves as both the play and rewind controls, so there's *continue* command to restart a sequence from wherever it stops. If a sequencer supports song position pointer, the continue command lets you commence playback from any location, even before the first beat.

MIDI Time Code (MTC) is a format which indicates location in real time rather than referring to a start point like song position pointer does. A *MIDI Time Code quarter frame* message is sent 120 times a second, allowing ten times the precision of MIDI timing clocks for accurately triggering events. What kinds of events? Well, if you're scoring a film and you want to precisely synchronize a sound effect or a musical hit point to something happening onscreen, you need all the accuracy you can get. SMPTE-to-MIDI converters can read an audible time code signal off tape or film and convert it to MTC quarter frame messages.

If a MIDI cable is accidently unplugged while a performer or a sequencer is playing, the serial flow of MIDI messages is interrupted. This may cause notes on messages to be sent without their respective note offs, resulting in a dreaded phenomenon called stuck notes. Some instruments send an *active sensing* message every 3/10ths of a second. If the MIDI path is interrupted, an instrument that supports active sensing automatically turns all notes off when these messages cease.

There's one more system real time message, called *system reset*. The reset command returns all instruments in a system to their power-up states. This resets an instrument as if it had just been turned on, which turns all notes off and returns all controllers to their zero values. Older MIDI instruments may default to Omni On/Poly mode, as originally suggested in the MIDI Specification, but many newer ones remember their MIDI mode and channel settings from before the reset command.

Continuous controllers continued...

Continuous controllers are wheels, sliders, levers, knobs, buttons, switches, pedals, and other devices that are part of a master controller like a MIDI keyboard. They send messages that affect pitch, timbre, envelope, portamento, panning, and other parameters that can be varied in real time. Most of them are used to add expression to your playing. With sequencing software that supports continuous controllers, if you change these parameters as you record, those changes will be duplicated when the sequence plays back.

According to the MIDI Spec, there are theoretically 128 possible continuous controllers, but most of them are presently undefined. A few are standardized by assigning each its own number, so that if controller number 92 controls one instrument's tremolo depth, sending the same message to another MIDI instrument on the same channel also controls its tremolo depth. The advantage is that you can use a master controller to send continuous controller messages to a variety of MIDI machines. Without standard controller numbers, you would have to translate each message's effect on each instrument's performance parameters.

MIDI instrument manufacturers have agreed on numerical assignments for continuous controllers to assure that their instruments are as compatible as possible. The most common or potentially useful controllers are defined in the MIDI Spec. These include the modulation controller (#1), a wheel or lever which controls vibrato depth on most instruments, but may be assigned to control other parameters such as loudness or filter frequency. The effect of the modulation controller depends on how the instrument applies the modulation signal. Controller #2, the breath controller, usually controls modulation as well. It's found on most

Yamaha MIDI instruments, and thanks to standardization, it can control modulation on non-Yamaha instruments.

Continuous controller #7 controls volume. It lets you dynamically change an instrument's loudness level. With a number of sequencer tracks, you can actually do an automated mixdown of a MIDI performance by changing the value of controller #7 for each track. The foot controller (#4), data entry controllers (#6 and #38), and data increment (#96) and decrement (#97) controllers can usually be assigned to perform a variety of functions, depending on the instrument and the

MIDI Controller Numbers

#	Function	#	Function	#	Function
0	Undefined	40	LSB for value 8	84	Undefined
1	Modulation wheel or lever	41	LSB for value 9	85	Undefined
2	Breath controller	42	LSB for value 10	86	Undefined
3	Undefined	43	LSB for value 11	87	Undefined
4	Foot controller	44	LSB for value 12	88	Undefined
5	Portamento time	45	LSB for value 13	89	Undefined
6	Data entry MSB	46	LSB for value 14	90	Undefined
7	Main volume	47	LSB for value 15	91	Undefined
8	Balance	48	LSB for value 16	92	Tremelo Depth
9	Undefined	49	LSB for value 17	93	Chorus Depth
10	Pan	50	LSB for value 18	94	Celeste (Detune) Depth
11	Expression Controller	51	LSB for value 19	95	Phaser Depth
12	Undefined	52	LSB for value 20	96	Data increment
13	Undefined	53	LSB for value 21	97	Data decrement
14	Undefined	54	LSB for value 22	98	Non-Registered Par. #LSB
15	Undefined	55	LSB for value 23	99	Non-Registered Par. #MSB
16	General Purpose #1	56	LSB for value 24	100	Registered Par. #LSB
17	General Purpose #2	57	LSB for value 25	101	Registered Par. #MSB
18	General Purpose #3	58	LSB for value 26	102	Undefined
19	General Purpose #4	59	LSB for value 27	103	Undefined
20	Undefined	60	LSB for value 28	104	Undefined
21	Undefined	61	LSB for value 29	105	Undefined
22	Undefined	62	LSB for value 30	106	Undefined
23	Undefined	63	LSB for value 31	107	Undefined
24	Undefined	64	Sustain (Damper pedal)	108	Undefined
25	Undefined	65	Portamento	109	Undefined
26	Undefined	66	Sostenuto	110	Undefined
27	Undefined	67	Soft pedal	111	Undefined
28	Undefined	68	Undefined	112	Undefined
29	Undefined	69	Hold 2	113	Undefined
30	Undefined	70	Undefined	114	Undefined
31	Undefined	71	Undefined	115	Undefined
32	LSB for value 0	72	Undefined	116	Undefined
33	LSB for value 1	73	Undefined	117	Undefined
34	LSB for value 2	74	Undefined	118	Undefined
35	LSB for value 3	75	Undefined	119	Undefined
36	LSB for value 4	76	Undefined	120	Undefined
37	LSB for value 5	77	Undefined	121	Undefined
38	LSB for value 6	78	Undefined	122	Local control
39	LSB for value 7	79	Undefined	123	All notes off
		80	General Purpose #5	124	Omni mode off
		81	General Purpose #6	125	Omni mode on
		82	General Purpose #7	126	Mono mode on
		83	General Purpose #8	127	Poly mode on

patch. Other standard controllers govern portamento time, portamento on and off, stereo panning and balance, expression pedal, soft pedal, sostenuto, hold, and the depth of various effects.

As with all MIDI messages, if an instrument is incapable of responding to a continuous controller message, it ignores it. For example, if a MIDI synth receives a message that says, "Turn on your portamento," and it doesn't have a portamento function, the message has no effect.

In sync with the real world

In multitrack recording, the usual procedure is to record one or more tracks in the first pass and then overdub subsequent tracks while listening to tracks already recorded. In this manner, it's possible to not only get the sound of more instruments playing more parts, but to make creative discoveries along the way.

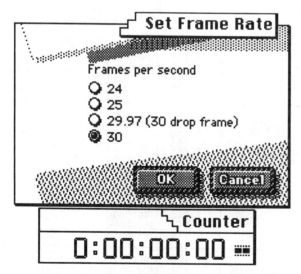

This process occurs in both tape recording and sequence recording. Sometimes it's desirable to synchronize a multitrack tape and a MIDI sequencer, so that when

recorded tracks are played, the computer plays along. This is possible by recording something called *time code* on one track. For synchronizing MIDI messages to audio tape, videotape, and film, *SMPTE Time Code*, first adopted by the Society of Motion Picture and Television Engineers in 1969, is the standard interface protocol.

SMPTE code is a complex audio signal containing information in the form of hours, minutes, seconds, and fractions of seconds called frames, sub-frames, and bits. Because it's an audible signal, it can be recorded on tape or film. When code is *striped* on a tape by pre-recording it on one track, every recorded moment on the entire tape is individually time-stamped. This code can be used to locate any point on the tape by its relation to where the SMPTE signal begins. If you want to begin recording a new song exactly five minutes and ten seconds after the time code's start point, you can tell your equipment to begin playing at that exact point.

There are two kinds of SMPTE code. *Vertical Interval Time Code*, or VITC, is recorded between frames on video tape. It can be read no matter what speed a tape is running, even in "freeze-frame", but it can't be recorded on audio tracks. *Longitudinal Time Code*, or LTC, can be recorded to an audio track on tape or film. LTC is necessary to sync computer software to tape. Its disadvantage is that a tape must play at the speed and level it was recorded or the code will be "dropped".

Time code comes from a circuit or device called a *SMPTE generator*. A tape is striped by recording the generator's signal, and the computer plays in response to signals from a *SMPTE reader*. For use with computers, SMPTE Time Code is converted into MIDI clocks, or for greater accuracy, into MIDI Time Code. This conversion is accomplished by an interface with a built-in reader, or by a peripheral SMPTE-to-MIDI converter. These devices are combination time code generators, readers, and converters.

Like MIDI, SMPTE is indispensable for getting diverse equipment to work together. It makes it possible to build auto-locators, which can repeatedly rewind a tape not just to the first measure of the song, but to the beginning of the bridge before the second chorus. Because of SMPTE, a synchronizer can slave one 32-track recorder to another for 60-track recording. Most important to the Macintosh musician is that SMPTE makes it possible to slave a sequenced performance to a recorded performance.

Why do you want to synchronize a tape machine and a computer? You have a limited number of MIDI instruments at your disposal. It's easy to sequence more tracks than you have voices to play them. If you record all the tracks your instruments can handle in the first take, and you want to record additional tracks, can't you just rewind the tape and then start it and the sequencer at the same time? This method isn't very precise, so a sync signal like SMPTE is called for. Once you've recorded the first pass, mute, or turn off, the sequencer tracks you've just recorded on tape. When you rewind and start the tape, the sequencer rewinds and starts too. As the computer plays the remaining sequencer tracks, the instruments they play are recorded on additional tracks of tape. This process is repeated until recording is complete.

Even if your MIDI arsenal is absolutely huge, recording MIDI instruments this way lets you use your best instruments over and over for different tracks. By recording one 16-voice instrument 24 times, you can play as many as 384 voices, even without bouncing tracks down. Another reason to sync tape and sequence: If a human voice or an acoustic instrument like a guitar or piano is recorded on tape that's striped with SMPTE, that tape can control a sequencer as it plays back. Live instruments, under MIDI control, play in sync with the recorded tracks on tape. This makes it possible to work on sequenced tracks while listening to recorded tracks.

SMPTE-driven software makes it possible for samplers to play sound effects in perfect sync with action in a video or film. Using edit decision list software such as Digidesign's Q-Sheet, you can precisely align sampled sounds to exact moments in time, like playing a sampled crash at the exact instant a vase hits the floor. "Hit points" can also be recorded on sequencer tracks, and you can even individually name recorded events in a sequencer's markers window, but edit decision list software makes the task a lot easier.

Hooking up a MIDI system

There are many possible MIDI system configurations, depending on your equipment and your applications. You may have a single keyboard synthesizer and a computer, or you may have dozens of instruments, processors, and synchronization devices. Your setup may be a complete pre-production studio, or it could be a setup for performing live on a concert stage. Let's take a look at a few of the possibilities.

The simplest network involves a Macintosh and one synthesizer. Musical information from the synth is sent to the computer, where it's stored, perhaps edited, and later returned to the synth. Anytime you get a Macintosh involved with MIDI, a MIDI interface is required. This plugs into one of the Mac's serial ports and provides a means to get MIDI signals into and out of your Macintosh. Plug one end of a MIDI cable into the interface's MIDI Out port and the other end into the synthesizer's MIDI In. This lets the computer control the synthesizer, telling it what to play, sending patch information, and so on, and the synth becomes the Mac's audio output hardware. To use the synth as an input device for getting music into the computer, connect the synthesizer's MIDI Out to the Mac interface's MIDI In. (Don't forget to plug your synth's audio output into an appropriate amplification source, or at least plug some headphones into its headphone jack, or you won't be able to hear what gets played.)

A typical system for a more serious user might include a Macintosh, a master keyboard controller, and a number of MIDI instruments or slaves, perhaps including a multitimbral synth module, a sampler, and a drum machine. If an effects processor is part of the system, its preset effects can be recalled by changing patch numbers. For such a complex system, the MIDI Out from the master controller should be routed to the computer's MIDI In. With most software, its signals can be echoed to the computer's MIDI Out, then sent to the various instruments.

If your interface has only one MIDI Out, how do you plug one MIDI cable into more than one slave? Well, obviously you don't. Instead, you make use of MIDI Thru. Create a *daisy chain* by plugging the computer's MIDI Out into one instrument's MIDI In, then direct a cable from that instrument's MIDI Thru port to another instrument's MIDI In, then out its MIDI Thru to the next one's MIDI In, until you come to the last machine in the series.

If you have more than four or five instruments in a daisy chain, the delay between the transmitter and the final receiver may be undesirably noticeable. The alternative is to use a thru box to form what's called a *star network*. Run the computer's Out to the thru box's In, then run MIDI cables from the thru box's outputs to each receiver's MIDI In. The advantage of a star network is that the MIDI signals reach each receiver simultaneously, rather than passing through each one's circuitry before getting passed on to the next receiver in a daisy chain. Some Mac interfaces feature multiple MIDI Outs, diminishing the need for a MIDI thru box.

Data transfer

Sometimes a MIDI user needs to export information from one medium to another, like from one sequencer program to another, or from a sequencer to a scoring program. Every sequencer has advantages that other sequencers lack. Suppose that you're recording in your usual sequencer program, and you want to do something that it can't, but another sequencer can. What do you do? The solution is to get one sequencer to talk to another. How do you do it? One way is to connect one computer

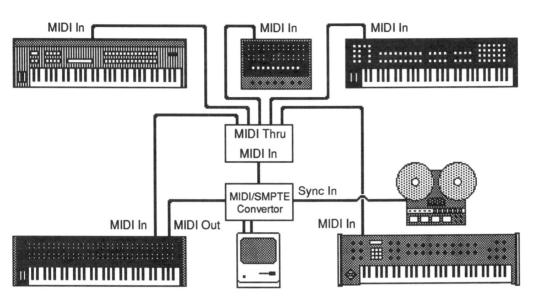

You can send up to 16 tracks on 16 different channels in real time. Some sequencers will record all channels at the same time on a single track, then unmerge this track into separate tracks, one for each channel. When carrying out this procedure, be sure to assign each track to a different MIDI channel beforehand. If you have more than 16 tracks, you can play up to 16 at a time in as many passes as necessary to record them all.

to another, with the transmitting computer's MIDI Out sending to the receiving computer's MIDI In. The transmitting computer must be synchronized to the receiving computer, with the sending computer providing the beat. When you click the record button on the receiving computer, it waits until you hit play on the other one before recording begins. If both sequencers support tempo changes, these will be recorded along with other data.

An easier way to export sequences from one program to another is via *MIDI Files*. MIDI Files is a standard data format for exchanging information between MIDI applications and even between different types of desktop computers. If a program lets you save sequences in MIDI File format, you can open them in any sequencer that reads MIDI Files. Not all information stored by one sequencer can be read into another, however, and incompatibilities do arise.

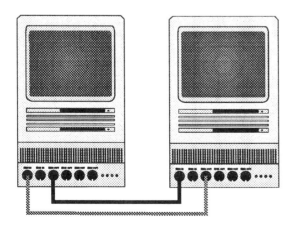

Another file exchange format that has been written into the MIDI Spec is the MIDI Manufacturers Association's *Sample Dump Standard*, or SDS for short. This allows the exchange of sample data between different kinds of samplers, or between samplers and computers. Without a standard sample data format, for sample editing software to communicate with your sampler, it must have a software driver that's specific to the sampler's make and model. Unfortunately, very few samplers support the Sample Dump Standard, so fortunately, sample editing software usually includes drivers for many popular samplers.

There are several other standard formats for storing sample data in software. The most popular is the Sound Designer format, the native format for Digidesign's sample editors. Some sample editing programs can read files written in various file formats, including Sound Designer, Audio IFF (the result of another standardization agreement among different companies, including Apple), Mac SND resource, and native formats from other programs.

Sequencers

To a musician with one or more MIDI instruments, the most useful music software is probably the sequencer. A sequencer memorizes anything you play, and plays it back on command. Sequencers are multitrack recorders, not for recording sound, but for recording musical information. Most sequencing programs for the Macintosh let you view and alter this data. There are other ways to enter music in addition to playing it. Musical information becomes a multitrack performance when the sequencer plays it back on MIDI instruments. Performances are stored on disk, then loaded into the computer's memory to be recalled at the press of a key or the click of a button.

For composers, a sequencer is indispensable for hearing combinations of rhythm, harmony, and tone color, without the need for other musicians. It makes a great sketchpad for recording musical ideas, as well as a platform for developing them in fine detail. In live performance situations, a sequencer is an invisible band playing real electronic instruments. In the recording studio, a sequencer lets you edit your music in thousands of ways you never could with tape, well before the tape starts rolling. A floppy disk is a whole lot cheaper than a reel of 24-track recording tape, and typically, sequencing time is cheaper than recording time in the studio. For totally electronic music, every part of all the songs on an entire album can be recorded, edited to perfection, and saved to disk. For music that's partially acoustic, a sequencer can be synchronized to a recorded performance on tape, so the computer plays MIDI instruments in tandem with the tape.

All you need is a single MIDI instrument to record dozens of tracks. Depending on the music's complexity, you may need additional instruments to hear every track played back at the same time. If the number of recorded instrumental voices exceeds the number of voices being played, some tracks may rob voices from other tracks, and some tracks may not play at all. At any rate, you hear only fragments of the whole recording. In most situations, sequences are recorded for instruments you have at hand, with each track assigned to play instruments set to the same MIDI channel.

Not all sequencers are software. Sequencers also exist as free-standing, external hardware devices, and sometimes they're built into an instrument's programming. Drum machines have built-in sequencers, and so do some synthesizers, samplers, and playback modules. A primary advantage of using a desktop computer instead of a dedicated sequencer is that its display monitor is so much larger, you can see a lot more sequence information all at once. Computers often have more memory than dedicated sequencers. Software upgrades are much easier for a computer. Instead of replacing an integrated circuit to change a sequencer's operating system, all you have to do is pop in a new disk. Some hardware sequencers with disk drives have caught onto this idea.

Sequences, tracks, and channels

A *sequence* is a musical performance recorded by a computer. It may be a complete piece of music, like a song or a symphony, or only part of a complete piece, like a riff, a verse, or a movement.

Sequences are saved to disk as song files. Some sequencers let save the parts of a song, like an intro, verses, a bridge, and a chorus, as separate sequences in the same song file, then link them to form a complete song. Sequencers all have the same purpose, but with different user interfaces, each takes a unique approach to recording music.

Each track plays back over a specified MIDI channel. Most Mac sequencers can send any track to any combination of MIDI channels through a MIDI interface connected to either of the Mac's serial ports. A track's channel determines which instruments it plays in a MIDI system. For example, the bass track could play instruments on channel 11, while the strings track plays instruments on channels 1, 2, 3, and 7.

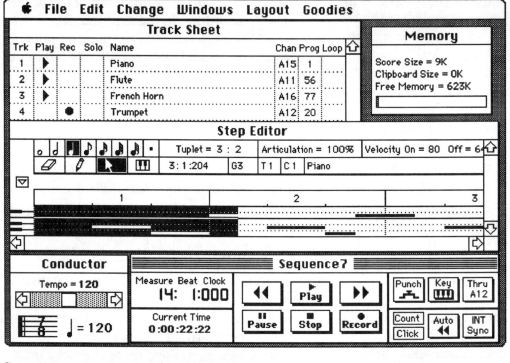

Getting around

Every Macintosh sequencer has a *control* window which serves the same purpose as the transport controls on a tape recorder. It has buttons for functions like play, record, stop, rewind, and fast forward. Most sequencers also let you shuttle directly to a given location in time by entering the number of the measure, beat, and fraction of a beat. That way, you can begin recording or listening from any point in the song without rewinding all the way to the top.

Sequences are arranged in *tracks*. A sequence is a number of tracks that play together, just as musicians play songs together. One track usually plays a single musical part, like a bass part or a solo or a piano accompaniment, on one or more MIDI instruments. The entire part may be recorded on a single track (a set of drums, for instance) or it may be spread out over several tracks (individual drums or right and left hand piano, recorded separately). A track may be a single live performance recorded all at once, or it may be pieced together one phrase at a time.

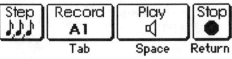

Most sequencers let you place *markers* to indicate a position in the sequence, like the beginning of the third verse, for example, or the exact moment in the film when the cowardly scarecrow explodes into a frightful ball of flame. Then, by clicking on the marker in a list of markers, you can shuttle directly to its location.

Another window is a *counter*, which displays how long it's been since the first beat of the sequence. The counter displays the measure number, the beat number, and the fraction of a beat. Some counters can optionally display the passage of real time or SMPTE location. Depending on the meter, a beat is usually a quarter note or an eighth note. Beats are divided into ticks, clocks, or units. Depending on the sequencer, there may be 192, 240, or 480 divisions per beat. The higher the number of divisions, the better the recording resolution. Better resolution means more accurate reproduction of what's played into the sequencer. If a beat was divided into, say, only 12 units, the playback would be somewhat robotic and unnatural. By offering higher resolution, a sequencer catches all the rhythmic subtleties of a performance, like tape does.

Recording musical events

An event is a MIDI message, like a note on or a patch change. Each track is a series of recorded musical events. The number of events you can record is limited by the amount of RAM in your computer. Some sequencers give you an exact readout of the number of events you can record

before memory runs short, and others display a gauge to make you aware of memory status.

There are two ways of entering music into a sequencer: real time and step time. *Real time* recording records what you play as you play it. Here's how real time, multitrack sequencing works: click the record button, then play your instrument, and when you're finished, click stop. Then click the rewind and play buttons to hear it played back. Sound familiar? The user interface of most sequencers is based on the tape recording metaphor. Add more tracks and record yourself playing additional parts as you listen to what you've recorded. If you have instruments assigned to different MIDI channels, you can send each track to one or more instruments, or several tracks to each instrument.

An audible metronome keeps the beat as you record, if you like. The metronome may be a steady tick from the computer or a note from an external instrument, like the tap of a hihat cymbal from a drum machine.

Sequencers turn mere mortal musicians into virtuosi. A sequence doesn't have to be recorded at the same tempo it's played back. You can slow down to record difficult passages, and speed up when they're

played back, which means you can record parts you could never play live. If you speed up a performance that's recorded on tape, it plays back at a higher pitch than it was recorded. In a sequencer, playback tempo has no effect on pitch. Even recording at a slow tempo is considered real time recording; it's still real time, it's just slowed down.

Step time recording lets you enter music one note or chord at a time. First specify each event's rhythm, either by clicking its value onscreen or by pressing a key on the computer keyboard. Enter pitch by

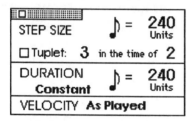

playing notes or chords on a MIDI instrument. Click an icon or press a Mac key to signify a rest. The disadvantage of step time recording is that, since all notes are precise rhythmic values, playback sounds stiff and mechanical. For some musical styles, sometimes this is desirable. Fortunately, a few sequencers let you "humanize" the feel by adding a bit of randomness to the track's rhythm.

Loop recording, also known as drum machine-style recording, is a variation on real time recording. In loop recording, you specify a number of beats or measures that repeat while recording. This technique lets you build up a track over several passes, recording a pass and then layering new material on top of it, again and again.

By turning on a track's *MIDI Thru* or *MIDI echo*, you can direct your controller's signal to its receiving instruments without rearranging any MIDI cables. The

controlling signal goes both to the Mac and to the instrument or instruments set on the same channel as the track that's selected to record. If channel 1 is brass and channel 2 is strings, when you enable record on a track assigned to channel 1 and play your controller, brass plays; when you enable record on channel 2, strings play.

If an instrument's MIDI setup has *local on*, it responds to its own controller. When using a sequencer's MIDI Thru, it's best to turn *local off* on the instrument you're playing, so it makes sound only when it receives information from the computer. Otherwise, every note you play sends two note on signals — one from the controller and another from the computer echoing the controller. You hear the controlling instrument as well as the instrument being controlled. If a controller has local on and it's controlling itself, its polyphony is cut in half if MIDI Thru is on. Since two identical notes sound for every note you play, a 16-voice instrument becomes eight-voice, and an eight-voice instrument becomes four-voice.

When you press the record button at the beginning of a sequence, what happens depends on how things are set up. Usually by default, recording begins immediately and the counter advances. If you tell the sequencer to *wait for an event*, however, recording doesn't begin until you send a MIDI message by playing something, pressing a switch, or something like that, or until you press a Mac key. If you tell it to play a *countoff* first, the metronome ticks for a measure or two before recording begins and the counter advances. If the computer is slaved to an *external clock*, like time code from a tape, nothing happens until the clock signal starts.

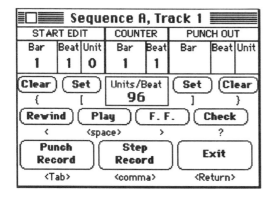

An essential feature for any sequencer is the ability to automatically *punch in* and *punch out* while recording, very much like recording on an automated tape machine. Punching lets you replace part of a track, but keep what's recorded before the punch in and after the punch out points. By specifying a precise point where recording begins, and another where recording stops, you can easily repair mistakes. Punching in "on the fly" involves listening to the sequence just before the punch in point, then playing the new part when recording punches in, and the sequence keeps playing after recording punches out. Anything you play before or after the punch points isn't recorded.

Sometimes you want to record on a track without erasing what's already on the track. That's when you need to select *overdub* or *sound-on-sound* to merge what you play with what you've already recorded on the same track. Recording this way may be useful if you're trying to limit the number of tracks listed onscreen, so things fit nicely.

Most Mac sequencers are capable of recording any MIDI messages you throw at them. A few sequencers have a limited or incomplete MIDI implementation, and may not record things such as polyphonic

aftertouch, release velocity, system exclusive, or undefined continuous controllers.

It's not always desirable to record every message. Sending aftertouch data for a patch that doesn't use aftertouch is a waste of memory and increases the chances of a MIDI logjam. Sometimes MIDI guitar controllers send useless messages like spurious pitch bend zeros. It's usually possible to filter MIDI data so that only meaningful messages are recorded. This is accomplished by opening a MIDI filter window and choosing the types of data you want to record, with all others filtered out. Sometimes you can also thin MIDI data, so that controller messages are recorded less often than they're sent, decreasing logjam problems.

Instead of actually recording MIDI events, they can often be inserted one at a time into a track you've already recorded. Such events are merged with the information that's there. Common events for insertion are notes, patch changes, continuous controller changes, pitch bend, and so on.

Editing sequences

Since data in a computer exists only as numbers, editing any kind of information is just a matter of changing those numbers. One of the main advantages of sequencing is the ability to extensively edit what's been recorded. In most Macintosh-based sequencers, every MIDI message recorded on any track can be displayed in an editing window. Some editing windows display MIDI as a list of events, and others display it graphically. Messages can be changed, deleted, and inserted anywhere in a track.

▽ 🖼 ⊠ 🖫 🔊 I ⚡	Hihat (Rap Up)

2|1|000 ↺ until 10|1|000 :infinite
2|2|000 ♪Eb1 ↓85 ↑64 1|240
2|4|000 ♪Eb1 ↓85 ↑64 0|410
3|1|001 ♪Db1 ↓75 ↑64 0|017
3|1|241 ♪Db1 ↓82 ↑64 0|017
3|2|238 ♪Db1 ↓83 ↑64 0|018
3|3|239 ♪Db1 ↓82 ↑64 0|017
3|4|235 ♪Db1 ↓82 ↑64 0|016
3|4|477 ♪Db1 ↓83 ↑64 0|017
4|1|238 ♪Db1 ↓83 ↑64 0|016
4|2|242 ♪Db1 ↓78 ↑64 0|021
4|3|243 ♪Db1 ↓83 ↑64 0|017

Typically, an *event list* window shows each event's measure, beat, sub-beat, event type, value, and duration. An icon may symbolize the event type, like a note event, a controller change, a patch change, or a tempo change. A graphical *piano roll-style* display shows music on a grid, with pitch as the vertical axis and time as the horizontal axis. Notes appear as bars on the grid; the longer the bar, the longer that note's duration. Pitch determines its height on the grid. Other information, like tempo, pitch bend, or controller data is graphically displayed as a continuous waveform deviating from a fixed value to signify changes.

There are all sorts of ways that music can be edited. To change event information, it must be selected. You can select an entire sequence, a single track, part of a sequence or a track, a few notes, or a single event. To select an event or a group of events, open an editing window and select like you would in a word processor or graphics program, by clicking, clicking and dragging, shift-clicking, etc. When something is selected, it's subject to whatever editing operation you want to perform.

Sequencers that don't feature an editing window for each track let you select events to be modified by specifying the beginning and end points for the modification. Sequencers with editing windows let you specify edit points this way, too, as an option. This method is usually best for simultaneously selecting parts of more than one track.

One of the most common types of note editing is *quantization*. When an event is quantized, it is aligned to the nearest fraction of a beat division. Think of a measure as a grid divided into fractions with 2 to 1 ratios. In 4/4 time, a measure equals one whole note. It can be divided into two half notes, four quarter notes, eight eighth notes, 16 sixteenth notes, and so on. The unit of division is called the quantization value or resolution. If you quantize to an eighth note, all eighth notes fall exactly on the eighth note pulse, and notes with greater rhythmic value are also aligned to the nearest eighth note pulse. If you quantize a part with four sixteenth notes in a row to eighth note resolution, they may end up playing as two 2-note eighth note chords. When you quantize music, you "round off" its note values so that everything falls into place and the rhythm is precise, because everything is lined up to a rhythmic grid.

Track A1: "Strings"		
1 · 3 · 0		
1 · 4 · 0		
44 · 1 · 0 581 Events		
1 · 1 · 0 Text: Strings	**Undo Edit**	Transpose Selection...
1 · 1 · 0 Bb4 0·240		Quantize Selection
1 · 1·224 G4 0·240	Cut Selection	Set Up Quantize...
1 · 1·476 D5 0·240	Copy Selection	Modify Notes...
1 · 2·231 G4 0·240	Paste Selection	Set Instrument...
1 · 3· 10 G5 0·240	Clear Selection	
1 · 3·244 D5 0·240		Reverse Time
1 · 3·473 Bb4 0·240	Merge Selection	Scale Time...
1 · 4·237 G4 0·240	Insert Clipboard	Change Tempo...
2 · 1· 10 Bb4 0·240	Repeat Paste...	
2 · 1·234 F#4 0·240	Get Times from Clipboard	Play from Selection
2 · 1·473 D5 0·240		Play Selection
2 · 2·227 F#4 0·240	Insert Blank Time	Jump to Selection
2 · 3· 1 F#5 0·240	Delete Selected Time	View...
2 · 3·231 D5 0·240	Move Events...	Select...
2 · 4· 3 Bb4 0·240		Select All
		Split Notes...

You can also *quantize duration*, so that note values are exact. If you quantize durations to an eighth note, any note whose duration is close to an eighth note becomes exactly an eighth note, and anything resembling a quarter note becomes exactly a quarter note. If a quarter note is divided into 480 units, and you quantize the duration of a note whose duration is 505 units, or 457 units, that note's duration is changed to 480 units. When you quantize so that each note begins on an exact multiple of a beat, and the duration of each is an exact division of a beat, that's called *hard quantization*. This sort of quantization is usually necessary if you intend to export a sequence to a transcription program for scoring.

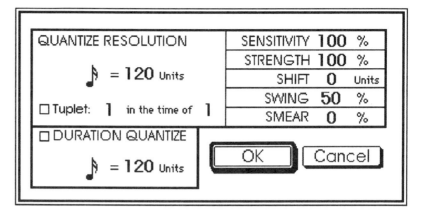

Quantization doesn't have to be quite so precise. Most Macintosh sequencers let you specify *quantization strength*. This determines how closely notes are aligned to the quantization value. For instance, if a note is recorded on a measure's 260th tick, and you quantize it hard, it will be moved to tick 240. If the quantization strength is 50%, it gets moved only halfway, to tick 250.

Another variable is *quantization sensitivity*, which selectively quantizes events that are a certain distance from the quantization value division. Depending on the sensitivity value (expressed as a percentage), only notes that are close enough to the grid are quantized if sensitivity is positive. Events that aren't close enough are unaffected. With negative sensitivity, only notes that are far enough from the grid are quantized, and the close ones are unaffected.

Another possible variation on quantization is *humanization* or quantize *smear*. This type of modification moves events away from the quantization grid. This is extremely useful if you have a sequence that's too stiff because it's quantized too hard. By humanizing it, you ease its computerized feel. When you import a song file from a scoring program and you want it to sound like it was played in rather than typed in, smear is what you need to loosen it up.

Selected notes can be *transposed* by any interval. Transpose a single note by selecting its pitch, then typing or playing a new pitch, or by a scrolling numerical field with an up-down arrow cursor. When you select events and give the transpose

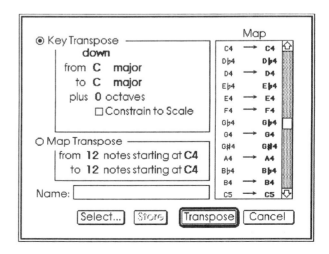

command, you're presented with a dialog box to indicate the interval that you want to transpose the selection.

You can also *change velocity*, or how hard the notes were played, in many ways. When you select a track or a group of notes, you can set all velocities to a particular value between 0 and 127. If a track has several notes that stick out because they were played too hard, limit the velocity so it never goes over a certain value. If the whole selection has too much velocity, or not enough, but the velocities are balanced in relation to one another, just change all velocities by a percentage, like changing to 80% or to 120% of the current velocity.

Different instrumental sounds have different attack times. Sometimes it's necessary, when you're playing an instrument with a slow attack, to anticipate the beat a little so the note "hits" on the beat. Other times, you may want to put something on top of the beat, or behind the beat, or somewhere not exactly on the quantization grid. In both situations, it's useful to *slide* the track, to push it a little ahead or behind in time, maybe just a few ticks, maybe more. At least one sequencer lets you slide tracks in real time so you can find the best offset by ear.

Tracks, or selected portions of tracks, can be *looped* or repeated a specified number of times or until the sequence is stopped. Indicate where the loop begins and ends, and the number of repetitions.

A sequencer is one type of music processor. As such, it's possible to *cut, copy, and paste* music from one part of a track to another, from one track to another, and so on, temporarily placing it in the Mac's memory buffer, the clipboard. A few sequencer clipboards let you see what's on the clipboard in the form of information about its data.

Some sequencers let you *insert* events from the clipboard at a given point in the track, causing the events already there to slide to a later point in the sequence. This is sometimes called *splicing*. Let's say you want an extra verse before the chorus. Just insert it where the chorus begins, and the chorus and everything after it moves out of the way to make room. If, on the other hand, you want to cut out part of a track and the rest moves to fill in the gap, that's *snipping*. Then there's taking data from the clipboard and pasting it into a track without removing what's already on the track. That's called *merging*.

Playback

A sequencer wouldn't be much use if you couldn't listen to your sequences. If you have enough MIDI instrument voices, you can hear all the tracks playing the whole song, or play it from one location to another. It's usually possible to go to a predetermined measure when you click rewind, and to loop a section of the sequence so that it plays over and over until you stop it, very much like the autolocate functions on a multitrack tape recorder. You can also turn off a track with the *mute* button, or turn off all the other tracks with the *solo* button, as you can with a mixdown console in a tape studio.

Most modern sequencers record tempo changes. A list of tempo changes called a *tempo map* is often recorded on its own *conductor track*. You can open an editing

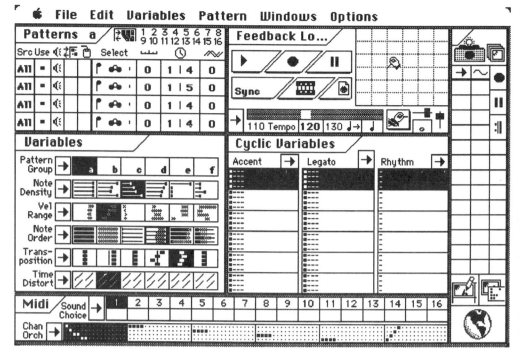

Importing and exporting music files

Most Macintosh sequencers can exchange sequences saved in a standard data format called *MIDI Files*. If you're recording in Pro 4, and you want to perform an operation that only Vision can do, it helps if you can open your sequence in

window for that track and modify it as you would any other track, deleting, inserting, and modifying tempo changes at will. Often you can edit the tempo so that it changes gradually from one speed to another at a rate calculated by the computer.

Sometimes it's possible to *chain* sequences so that one plays immediately after another without missing a beat. Recording a chain of sequences may not require that you duplicate all the information in those sequences if you can record *subsequences*. A sequence made up of subsequences is simply a list of markers that point to the original source sequences, so that all the parts play back in the right order without pausing.

different sequencers. Such an exchange makes it possible to record and edit music using the strengths of more than one MIDI program. MIDI Files contains all the sequence information in a form that other MIDI programs on other computers can read. Since different sequencers have the ability to record different information, though, some of this information may be lost when exchanged. The MIDI File standard is rather recent, so an older program that reads MIDI Files may not read files written by a newer program.

A more direct means of exchanging MIDI
data between programs is with Apple's
MIDI Management Tools. In MultiFinder,
via the Patchbay, it's possible to direct a
MIDI sequencer's output as it plays into
another program's input as it records.

Performer

Mark of the Unicorn's **Performer** is a full-function sequencer with loads of bells and whistles that give it extremely flexible recording and editing capabilities. Thanks to its "fast" user interface and sheer depth, Performer is popular with recording studios and professional musicians, and thanks to its logical layout and ease of use, it's equally popular with beginners and hobbyists. It can record any MIDI event, and events can be visually displayed and edited in windows. The number of tracks in a sequence, and of sequences in a file, is theoretically limited only by the amount of RAM available. With numeric keypad equivalents for most transport functions, you can record, play, pause, rewind, punch

in and out, and shuttle from one position to another, all without touching the mouse or even changing the position of your hand.

In Performer, positions within the sequence are expressed in measures, beats, and ticks. There are 480 *ticks* per beat, with the number of beats per measure defined by the time signature. If a beat is defined as a quarter note, that means an eighth note is 240 ticks, an eighth note triplet is 180 ticks, and a 128th note is 15 ticks. This high degree of resolution combined with Performer's full MIDI implementation allows for very accurate reproduction of recorded performances.

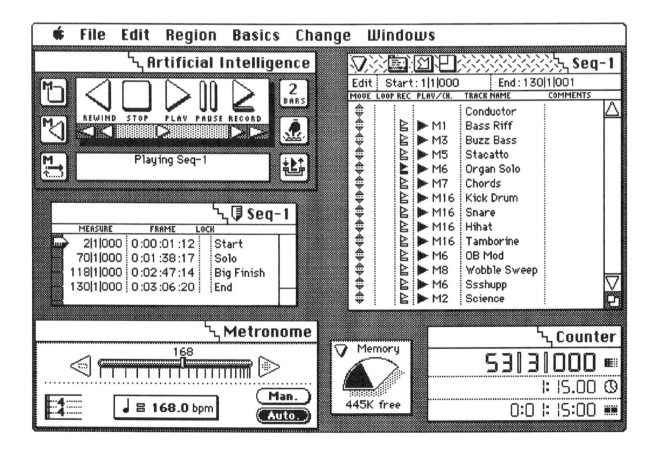

Many functions in Performer are split up into windows, which can be made active, hidden, and moved around as needed. Most windows offer mini-menus, tiny pop-up menus seen by clicking the menu icon on a window's selection bar. Mini-menus are used to select specific actions or to set up the window's display.

The current location in time is shown in the *counter window*, expressed in measures, beats, and ticks. Mini-menu selections change the display to show the passage of real time or SMPTE Time Code instead of or in addition to measures.

The *tracks window* shows all the tracks in a sequence, including track names, MIDI channel numbers, and other relevant information for the active sequence. Its mini-menu commands add, delete, and solo tracks, open editing windows for selected

tracks, and make it possible to record several tracks on several channels at the same time. Use the MultiRecord command to play an external sequencer directly into Performer. A list of sequences is shown in the *sequences window*, opened from the Windows menu. The tracks windows for several sequences can be onscreen simultaneously, but only one is active at a time — only one plays, and only one is capable of recording, until you select another sequence.

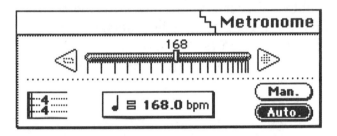

Performer's *metronome window* shows the current tempo and meter. Change tempo by typing in a new value, by dragging the tempo indicator, or by clicking on the plus or minus triangles. When set for manual, the tempo remains constant. When set for auto, tempo changes can be recorded into a conductor track. If the tempo or meter change, so does the metronome's display. A metronomic click can be turned on and off from the Basics menu.

A *markers window* can be called up from the Windows menu. This lets you indicate significant points in your sequence so they're easy to find quickly. Markers are especially useful for creating a cue list to synchronize music or sound effects to picture. When an event occurs onscreen, its location can be marked, and by locking the marker, its location remains constant even if you change tempo or other aspects of the music.

MOVE	LOOP	REC	PLAY/CH.	TRACK NAME	COMMENTS
				Conductor	
		►	M1	Cellos	JX-8P
		►	M3	Violins	Matrix-12
		►	M4	Violas	Matrix-12
		►	M6	Harp	Akai S612
		►	M7	Piano	Prophet
		►	M12	Xylophone	TF#1
		►	M13	Fr. Horn	TF#2
		►	M14	Trumpets	TF#3
		►	M16	Trombones	D-50
		►	M10	Snare/Kick	LinnDrum
		►	M11	Hihat/Crash	Alesis
		►	M11	Toms	Alesis
		►	M15	Farm Animals	FZ-1
		►	M2	Shimmer	Matrix-6
		►	M8	SFX-1	D-10
		►	M9	SFX-2	D-10

Edit   Start: 1|1|000   End: 37|1|001

	MEASURE	FRAME	LOCK	
	1|1|000	0 :00 :00 :00		Intro
	9|1|000	0 :00 :14 :23		Verse
	17|1|000	0 :00 :29 :16		Chorus
	20|2|311	0 :00 :35 :25	🔒	Hit
	25|1|000	0 :00 :44 :09		Vamp Out
	33|1|000	0 :00 :59 :02	🔒	Ending

Recording and playback

The *controls window* serves as a tape transport control panel in Performer's tape recording metaphor. Buttons in this window control record, play, pause, fast forward and rewind, cue forward and back, punch in and out, overdub, countoff, and wait for event functions. A scroll bar in the controls window follows the sequence's progress, and its thumb can be dragged to any point in the sequence.

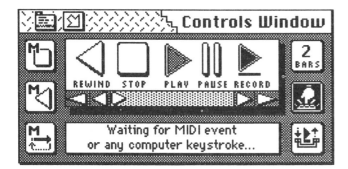

All but one control button can be accessed from the Macintosh's numeric keypad, to the right of the keyboard on all but the oldest Macs. Using this keypad is the secret to using Performer with efficiency and speed. The Enter key is the play button. The keypad equivalents for stop, rewind, pause, and record are 0, 1, 2, and 3. Like the record button, the 3 key lets you manually punch in and out on the fly. The slash (/) and asterisk (*) keys enable Wait for Event and overdub mode. The 4, 5, 6,

and minus (-) keys rewind the sequence quickly or slowly, and play it in slow motion or fast forward. The equals (=) key turns on the countoff. Its length can be changed by double-clicking its button. Memory functions are controlled with 7, 8, 9, and plus (+), or by control buttons. These functions include setting automatic punch in and punch out points, automatic stop when a point is reached, automatic rewind to a specified point, and automatic replay of a given section. Only the button to enable punch-in recording cannot be accessed from the keypad.

Two keys on the numeric keypad make selections in the Basics menu and the counter window. The Clear key turns the metronome's click on and off, just like typing command-5. Typing a period (.) on the keypad highlights the measure number in the counter window and shuttles to the beginning of the current measure. With the measure number selected, the position displayed in the counter moves to whatever measure number you type. Typing another period selects the beat number, and another period selects the tick number. Typing Return or Enter de-selects the highlighted number and moves to the position entered into the counter. Using the period key as a "go to…" command works only if the counter window is open and Measures is selected for display in the counter. This technique can be used even during playback.

Event list editing

Select a track by clicking its name in the tracks window, and open its *event list window* either by double-clicking it or by selecting it and choosing Edit from the tracks window's mini-menu. When an event list window is open, each event is shown as a horizontal strip containing mostly numbers. Its location is followed by the event type, its value, and if it applies, its duration in beats and ticks. Events are represented by icons. Any event type can be hidden by changing the settings in the View Filter, summoned from the window's mini-menu.

↳ Legend				
Location	Pitch	On	Off	Duration
1|1|000	♪C3	↓64	↑61	1|000
♪		Note		
⌁		Pitch Bend		
■		Patch Change		
▲		Controller		
⌄		Mono Key Pressure		
⌄⌄		Poly Key Pressure		
□		System Exclusive		
⟳		Loops		
⚑		Markers		
4/4		Meter Change		
Eb Major		Key Change		
♩ = 120.0		Tempo Change		

In the example shown below, there's a note event at measure 71, beat 3, and tick 000. The note is a D5, and it's played with a velocity of 97 and released with a default velocity of 64, probably indicating that the instrument which played it doesn't support release velocity. Its duration is exactly one beat and 221 ticks, just short of a dotted quarter note. Other events displayed in the window include meter, a patch change,

▽▤⊠□◀I⟍	Event List (A)			
1|1|000	4/4	click ♩		
	■ #33			
2|1|000	⚑	Start		
69|4|440	▲#64	Off		
70|1|000	⚑	Solo		
	♪Db5	↓106 ↑64	0|086	
	▲#1	0		
70|1|027	♪D5	↓106 ↑64	2|020	
70|2|473	♪C5	↓100 ↑64	0|217	
70|3|231	♪A4	↓100 ↑64	0|306	
70|4|009	♪C5	↓90 ↑64	0|289	
70|4|254	♪D5	↓82 ↑64	0|282	
71|1|042	♪F5	↓106 ↑64	1|017	
71|2|018	♪E5	↓90 ↑64	1|023	
71|3|000	♪D5	↓97 ↑64	1|221	
71|4|445	♪Eb5	↓90 ↑64	0|133	
71|4|462	♪E5	↓100 ↑64	0|303	
72|1|258	♪D5	↓90 ↑64	0|176	
72|1|479	♪C5	↓100 ↑64	0|227	
	▲#1	1		
72|2|039	▲#1	2		
72|2|050	▲#1	5		
72|2|080	▲#1	11		
72|2|089	▲#1	25		

markers, sustain footswitch (controller #64) off, and left-hand modulation (controller #1).

To select an event, just click on it. If you highlight the *speaker icon* before you select a note event, it plays when selected. If you click it a second time, directly on a field of information, you can change its location and value by typing in new information. Use the numeric keypad's period key to move between fields, and the Enter key to select the next event in the list. When you finish editing, hit the Return key. Events can be manually inserted anywhere in the track by choosing Insert... from the window's mini-menu, or by clicking the *insert (I) button* on the window's selector bar. Select an event, then type in its location, value, and duration.

You can find an event by its location with the window's mini-menu commands *Goto...* and *Goto Counter*. When you select Goto, you're presented with a box to type in the desired location. The event which occurs at that point or the next event thereafter appears at the top of an event list window or on the left side of a graphic editing window. A faster way is to use the numeric keypad's period key to move the counter to the location, then choose Goto Counter.

You can also find an event by its type, using the *Set View Filter...* mini-menu command. If you're trying to find a patch change, for example, just turn off the display of everything except patch changes. Then you don't have to scroll through all those notes looking for just the right patch change.

When you set the view filter, it applies to all editing windows, not just the active one.

Graphic editing

In addition to editing music numerically in event list windows, you can edit music graphically in *graphic editing windows*. A graphic editing window is a piano roll-type display with "rulers" for time, pitch, and controller data. Editing techniques conform to the conventions of paint and draw programs, like option-dragging to copy a note and dragging selection boxes over notes. To open a graphic editing window, open a event list window, then choose Graphic Editing from its mini-menu. When you close the window, the sequencer file will remember what kind of window it is.

Just below the title bar, there's an *information bar*. It's divided into three sections: the cursor location, the event information box, and the "snap-to" resolution. Below that is the *time ruler*. It represents a beat like a real ruler represents an inch. The *marker strip* is just

below the time ruler, displaying markers, meter and key changes, and loops. The *note grid* shows notes as horizontal bars, and the *continuous data grid* shows velocities, continuous controllers, pitch bend, and aftertouch as tiny, simple icons. You can reshape continuous data curves by choosing Reshape from the mini-menu and dragging in the grid. The *median strip* is between the note and continuous data grids. It shows patch changes, switch controllers, system exclusive events, and miscellaneous MIDI data.

The note grid is a graph of pitch plotted against time. Pitch corresponds to the piano keyboard on the left edge, and time corresponds to the time ruler. Only note events show up on the note grid. To change a note's pitch or location in time, click and drag it to a new position. As you drag pitch, the piano keys are highlighted. To change duration, click and drag a note's handle to lengthen and shorten it.

To magnify your view, zoom in on the note grid by clicking the *pitch zoom icons*, left of the median strip. It also zooms out so you can see more of the track at once. You can zoom in and out on the time ruler, too, with the *time zoom icons* to the ruler's left.

The *event information box* is found in the middle of the information bar. When you select an event, it appears here numerically, just as it would in an event list. If more than one event is selected, the last one is shown. If a region is selected, the event information information box shows the start and end points of the selection.

Selecting and editing regions

Most editing is performed on groups of events called regions. A region may be a single event, a series of events, or a discontiguous group (not in series). Region editing actions include transposing, quantizing, deflamming, changing velocity or duration, splitting a track into two parts, changing controller data, and altering pitch and rhythm.

There are several ways to select a series of events as a region. In the tracks window, *edit fields* appear just below the window's title bar. Clicking on the word "Start" changes the edit start point to the counter's current position, and clicking it again changes it to the sequence's beginning. The same goes for clicking the word "End", except when you click it a second time, it shows the location of the last recorded event. You can also click in the edit bar's numeric field, type in a new number, and scroll to the other fields with the numeric keypad's period key. By clicking on a track, clicking and dragging, or shift-clicking on any number of tracks, the regions between the edit points for selected tracks can be modified with commands in the Edit and Region menus.

Another way to select regions is within editing windows. Select a series of notes by clicking and dragging across them, or click

the first event in the region, then command-click (not shift-click, as you might expect) the last event. Shift-clicking lets you select discontiguous events without selecting the events between them. If you want to hear the selected region played in tempo, hold the Option key and click the speaker icon. In graphic editing windows, you can also drag within the time ruler to select all the events occurring in that time. You can't shift-click or command-click in the time ruler.

Once a region is selected, it can be transposed by selecting Transpose... from the Region menu or typing command-9. A small dialog box lets you type in or play two notes to indicate the interval that the selection is to be transposed. Command-0 (zero) chooses the Quantize... command, summoning the Quantize dialog box to set quantization parameters, including offset, sensitivity, and strength. Choosing Change Velocity... calls up a similar dialog box to set all velocities in the region the same, to add or subtract from the region's velocities, to limit minimum or maximum velocity values, to scale velocity by a percentage of current values, or to create crescendos or decrescendos in velocity.

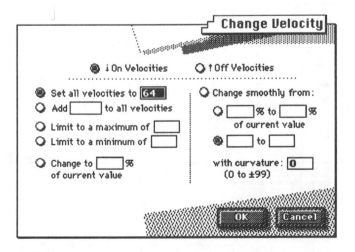

Vision

Vision is an advanced sequencer from Opcode Systems, built around an extensive environment for managing MIDI information. Its range of functions clearly make it one of the most comprehensive MIDI programs available for any computer. It has most features found in other sequencers, plus a few unique tricks of its own, like sophisticated MIDI processing, subsequences, remote control of sequencer functions, and the ability to play up to nine sequences simultaneously. Because it can link instruments in various ways, scale velocity, remap pitch and controllers, reroute channels, overflow voices, and split keyboards into multiple zones, Vision operates as a master information processor in a MIDI system. Edit track information, including notes, controllers, and in fact, all MIDI data, both from event list windows and graphically, piano roll-style. On-line help files make Vision easier to tackle.

Recording and playback are controlled from the *control bar* or from the Mac's keyboard. Any sequence in a file can be played to pressing its associated letter key. To play sequence A, type the letter A. To play B, type B. To stop, press the Return key, or click the Stop button. To pause, press the Space Bar or click the Pause button, which changes into a Continue button. To record a track, click the track's Record button and press Tab.

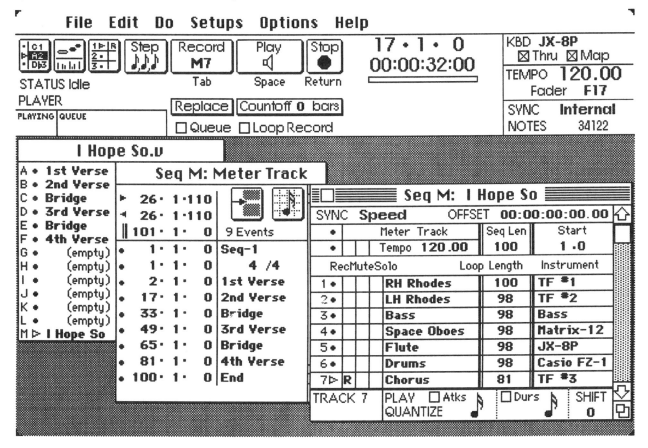

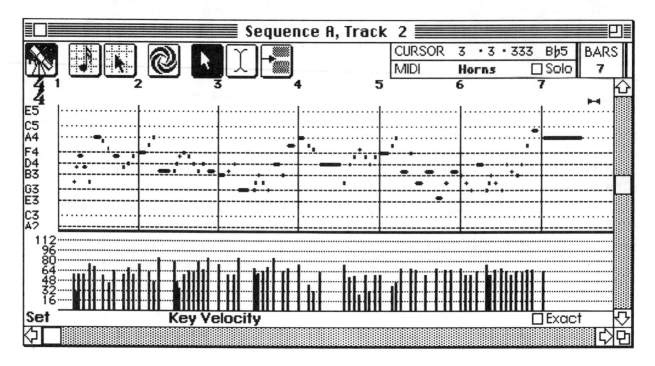

The *file window* on the left shows a list of sequences in a file. Up to 26 sequences may be recorded in a single file, one for each letter of the alphabet. To open a sequence's *sequence window*, double-click on its selection button, which Opcode calls a selector dot. A sequence window displays a list of the tracks in a sequence, along with information about its meter, tempo, length, playback quantization, and so on.

Along with tracks containing MIDI events, each sequence has meter and tempo tracks governing its time signature and playback speed. Tempo and meter tracks may be edited and new information inserted, just like a data track. You can insert text into any track, such as lyrics, a copyright notice, or performance notes.

Any track can be edited, one track at a time, by opening its *list editing window* or its *graphic editing window*. To open a list editing window, select a track and type option-D. To open a graphic window,

double-click the track's selector dot or select it and type option-E. (Vision uses the Option key a lot.) In a graphic editing window, you can summon a *strip chart* to view and edit velocities, event durations, patch changes, continuous controllers, etc. When you click on the words "Strip Chart" in a graphic editing window, it presents a pop-up menu to select which parameter you want to view graphically.

Anything that appears onscreen in boldface type can be changed. To summon a *help window* about any parameter in boldface, click it as you hold down the Shift, Option, and Command keys simultaneously. You can also get information about menu selections if you press the same keys as you choose a menu item.

There are a few concepts that are unique to Vision. Rather than going into too much detail about functions that should be obvious, like the basics of recording and editing tracks, let's examine features like mapping, remote control, faders, and the many ways of linking and playing sequences in Vision.

Maps

Vision can be customized to your own instrumental

Instrument Name	Mute	Solo	⌖	#b Map	Prog No	Chan	Veloc Fader	Fade Amt	8va	m2	Range		Voices
Emulator III					0-127	1	Off	100	0	0	A0	C8	
Proteus					0-127	2	Off	100	0	0	C-1	B1	
Mode: Layered						3	Off	100	0	0	C2	B3	
						4	Off	90	0	0	C4	C8	
DX7IIfd/E!					1-128	1	Off	100	0	0	A0	C8	
Korg M1					0-127	2	Off	100	0	0	A0	C8	
S1000HD					0-127	3	Off	100	0	0	A0	C8	
S1000PB					0-127	4	Off	100	0	0	A0	C8	
Matrix-12					0-127	5	Off	100	0	0	A0	C8	
Roland D50					0-127	6	Off	100	0	0	A0	C8	
LinnDrum	M		⌖	Map	0-127	10	Off	100	0	0	A0	C8	
Drums	M		⌖		0-127	10	Off	100	0	0	A0	C8	
Mode: Layered						11	Off	100	0	0	A0	C8	
Alesis HR16	M		⌖		1-128	11	Off	100	0	0	A0	C8	
TF1 A-C					1-128	12	Off	90	0	0	A0	C8	
TF1 D-G					1-128	13	Off	90	0	0	A0	C8	
TF1 H					1-128	14	Off	90	0	0	A0	C8	
Casio FZ-2M					1-128	15	Off	100	0	0	C0	C8	8
Mode: Overflow						16	Off	100	0	0	A0	C8	8

MIDI channels, each with its own parameters. Parameters on the left apply to all lines in an Instrument, and parameters on the right pertain to each line individually.

setup. An *Instrument* is either a single MIDI instrument or a combination of MIDI instruments played as one. (For the sake of clarity, let's refer to MIDI instruments as synthesizers.) The selection in a track's Instrument field determines which synthesizers the track plays. To assign an Instrument to a recorded track, click in the track's Instrument field for a pop-up menu listing the Instruments. You can also select the first ten Instruments in the list by holding the Command key and typing the numbers 1 through 0.

Selecting Instruments (option-I) from the Setup menu calls up a window to define MIDI channels, serial ports, layers, overflows, transpositions, and velocity scaling for each Instrument. The MIDI channel and port determines which synth receives that Instrument.

In the Instruments window, the settings for each MIDI channel are shown in a *line*. A line is one synth assigned to a MIDI channel. An Instrument may have one or more lines, and therefore, one or more

Vision gives any synth the ability to overflow notes to another, and lets you split any keyboard into multiple zones. If an Instrument has more than one line, its mode is shown below its name. It may be *layered*, sending the same data to different synthesizers, or it may *overflow*, making several synthesizers function as one big synth with plenty of voices. A layer may also be one synth doubling itself in different octaves. In a layer, you can vary which synths play on different parts of the the keyboard by limiting each line's range of notes, meaning that you can assign any number of splits. In overflow mode, when the number of notes played exceeds the maximum number of voices from one synth, additional notes spill over to another synth. Linking two eight-voice synthesizers together in overflow mode plays them like one 16-voice synthesizer.

A *transpose map* can be assigned to each Instrument. When you click in the Map field, a Transpose dialog box lets you assign notes from any key or scale to any other key or scale. You can make an A key play a C#, a major scale play minor, or a keyboard play in a different octave. Transpose maps are especially useful when a drum machine track has been recorded and you want it to play a different drum machine, or for assigning several drum machines to different areas of the keyboard. Click in the field to its left, Drum Instrument, to protect that Instrument from being transposed when you transpose other Instruments in the same sequence.

The velocity fader field controls the percentage of *velocity scaling* for each line. How is this useful? Yamaha synthesizers, for example, reach their maximum output at a MIDI velocity of 114, rather than 127. On most MIDI controllers, when you play a note as hard as you can, its velocity value is 127. By reducing the Fade Amount, playing a velocity of 127 on your controller sends less velocity to your Yamaha synth, so it doesn't distort. If you're playing a Yamaha controller, increase the Fade Amount to turn its maximum 114 velocity into a 127 velocity. On a scale of 1 to 200, numbers below 100 reduce velocity, and numbers above 100 increase it.

Input maps route incoming multi-channel MIDI data to appropriate Instruments. Use the *input map* to split keyboards, to record from more than one controller, and to dump sequences from another sequencer in real time. Different zones of any keyboard can be sent to different synthesizers, or used to start and transpose sequences instead of playing notes.

When a controller sends MIDI data to the computer, the input map routes that data to its appropriate destination. Instead of being routed through to an Instrument, certain

notes may be assigned to play and transpose sequences. There are four modes: transpose, trigger, continuous trigger, and gated trigger. When you press a key, *transpose* mode modulates all sequences that are playing to another key. In *trigger* mode, pressing a key starts a sequence and also transposes it. If you press another key, the sequence stops and starts again, transposed to the new note. If you don't want it to stop, use *continuous trigger* mode. In *gated* mode, a sequence plays only as long as a key is depressed. Transpose and trigger modes may be selected with combination keystrokes.

MIDIKeys and assignable faders

MIDIKeys is a feature that lets you control sequencer functions by pressing keys or switches on a MIDI controller. Any command you can give with the Mac keyboard, you can give with a MIDI message. You can set aside your keyboard's lower octave, so that one key starts playback, another stops it, another punches the record button, etc. So you don't lose part of your MIDI controller for playing music, any note or switch can serve as a Shift key. That way, playing a note doesn't trigger a function unless that MIDIShift is depressed as well.

Vision's 32 *faders* make it possible to do an automated MIDI mixdown. Faders can be assigned to change tempo, velocity scaling, and continuous controller values. Fader assignments may be saved in the Setup File (a set of defaults for all new sequences) or in a sequence file. Fader values are changed by scrolling or by typing numbers in the Fader window, or with an external MIDI controller like a footpedal.

Whenever a fader moves, a change is sent. If you move a fader when you're recording, its changes are duplicated when you play back. Using a fader to control MIDI controller #7 (volume), you can easily record level changes for each instrument as it plays. (For the scoop on continuous controllers, see the chapter on MIDI.)

To assign a fader to send a controller message, click on the fader number. This displays the fader definitions at the bottom of the Fader window. Click Send, then assign an instrument and controller number. To control a fader with a MIDI controller, click receive and make the assignments. You can use a fader to remap a MIDI controller to another by assigning a controller to move a fader, then telling that fader to control a different controller.

On the right side of the control bar, any fader can be assigned to be the *tempo fader*. Moving that fader changes the sequence's tempo, as seen in the Tempo display, ranging from 40 to 360 beats per minute. If you move the fader while recording the tempo track, those changes are recorded. The current tempo is always reflected by the position of the tempo fader.

Linking sequences

Sequences can be chained together to form a song, or for live performance, a playlist of songs. The easiest way to chain songs is in step time. Open a new sequence and click the Step button to begin chaining sequences. Then instead of playing a note or a chord, press the letter of the first sequence in the chain. The counter automatically advances to the end of the first sequence. Then press the letter keys for the other sequences in the order you want them to play. In this manner, a chain of sequences is recorded on a single track. Chained sequences are called *subsequences*, and they're independent of their source sequences.

When you open a list window to view the contents of a subsequence track, they appear as a series of subsequence events. If you entered A, A, B, A, C, that's what appears in the list. The selector dot on the left selects the subsequence event (A, B, C, etc.), and the dot to its right selects the subsequence itself. To see and edit the tracks in a subsequence, double-click on its subsequence selector dot. This opens its sequence window. You can then open edit windows for individual tracks.

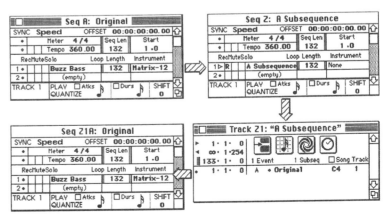

If a track contains a subsequence more than once, changing one changes them all. If you mute a track or change its Instrument, those changes are heard each time that subsequence plays. To change one occurrence without changing the others, select the subsequence, copy it, and paste it over itself. A number suffix is added to its letter name. If the original is A, the pasted version becomes A2 and the others become A1.

Like other events, subsequence events can be cut, copied, pasted, and inserted. To move a subsequence event to another part of the song, select it, copy it, and choose Delete Selected Time from the Edit menu. This makes the other subsequences move to close up the gap. Then select a new location and choose Insert Clipboard. The other subsequences move again to make room. If you change a subsequence's length or meter, first check Song Track on the right side of the subsequence event list. This insures that other subsequences move to accommodate changes.

You can preview an arrangement of sequences without actually recording subsequences by using *Queue* mode. Queue lets you line up sequences in any order so that as soon as one finishes playing, another begins. Normally, when you start a sequence while another is playing, the first sequence stops abruptly and the new one takes over. If Queue is checked in the Player display in the Control Bar, it waits its turn until the current sequence has played through. As you type letters to queue up subsequent sequences, they appear in the Player

STATUS Playing
PLAYER

PLAYING	QUEUE		
A	ABACBAC		☒ Queue

display in the lower left corner. As soon as they begin playing, they disappear from the display. As many as 16 sequences can in the queue at any moment.

It's possible to record with Queue turned on, but Vision doesn't actually record a new subsequence until the previous finishes playing. To record a chain of queued subsequences, don't press Stop until the last one starts to play. It's much easier to record subsequences by step recording.

With a feature called *players*, up to nine sequences can play at the same time without recording subsequences. To use players, just type a number key before you type a letter key to play a sequence. If you don't type a number first, starting a new sequence stops the previous one. By selecting a player first, the new sequence starts as the previous one continues unaffected. Typing a number before starting a sequence is your way of telling Vision, "Play this, but don't stop playing that." Of course, if a numeric field is selected, the number keys can't select a player. To see which sequences are assigned to each player, click on the Player display or choose Players from the Options menu.

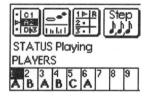

STATUS Playing
PLAYERS

1	2	3	4	5	6	7	8	9
A	B	A	B	C	A			

When two or more sequences are playing simultaneously, which one controls how fast they're playing? Displayed at the top of the sequence window, the *sync mode* defines whether a sequence plays at its own tempo or is slaved to the master tempo. There are three choices: Off, Speed, and Start. If the sync mode is *Off*, each sequence plays at its own independent tempo, governed by its tempo track. The master tempo, determined by the tempo of the first sequence played, controls the rate of playback in Speed and Start modes.

When you start a sequence with the sync set for *Speed*, the sequence plays immediately without waiting for the previous one to stop (unless Queue is checked in the control bar, in which case it waits). If the sync mode is *Start*, it waits until the next measure. Then the previous sequence stops playing and the next one plays. Even if you press a key to start a sequence a moment late, Vision has enough artificial awareness to jump in without missing a beat.

In Start mode, the next sequence starts as soon as the counter reaches its *start point*. By default, the start point is precisely on the first beat of the measure, but it can be relocated to any point in the first measure. Changing the start point accommodates pick-up notes in the first measure of a sequence.

Generated sequences

Generated sequences is a type of step time recording that lets you enter pitch and rhythm information separately, or play notes with a different rhythm or in a different order than they were recorded. There are only four tracks in a generated sequence: meter, tempo, rhythm, and notes, and the rhythm track is optional. Only note events, durations, patch changes, and subsequences are recorded in rhythm and note tracks. Velocities, controllers, and other data are filtered out.

With a generated sequence, you can record a series of pitches without regard to their rhythm, then superimpose a rhythm on top of it for playback. If *Rhythm Track* is selected as the rhythm mode, durations can be controlled by what's recorded on the rhythm track. Change the mode in the left side of the Rhythm field by clicking it and holding the mouse button to open a pop-up menu. In *Constant* mode, all notes play with equal duration, like they were recorded in step time without changing the duration. Duration is determined by the values given in the right side of the Rhythm field. If *Note Track* is selected, the notes play at the rhythm they were recorded, unless their durations are affected by the Duration mode. The Duration settings control how long a note is held within its rhythmic value — in other words, how legato or staccato it plays.

In the rhythm and note tracks, there's a box to change the *order* in which a generated sequence plays. A pop-up menu lets you choose from Forward, Random, Alternate, and Reverse. If Reverse is chosen, it plays backwards. If Random, notes and rhythms are played in a random order. If you choose Alternate, first it plays forward, then in reverse order without repeating the notes or rhythms on either end.

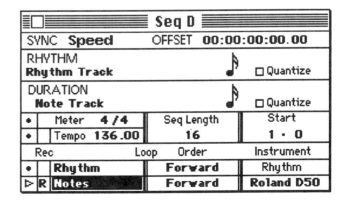

Librarians and Editors

Synthesizer patch librarians

Almost everyone with a synthesizer needs a patch librarian sooner or later. A librarian organizes and stores synth sounds, called *patches* or *programs*. A synthesizer has enough memory to store a finite number of patches, usually in a *bank* of 32, 64, 100, or 128 sounds. Each patch has its own location in the synth's battery-powered memory or in ROM, indicated by a patch number. Some synths let you expand onboard memory by adding a RAM cartridge or card, increasing the number of patches immediately available at the touch of a switch. If you have a patch librarian for your computer, you don't have to be limited to 64 sounds, or even 128, and you don't have to buy overpriced RAM cartridges. You can store literally thousands of synth patches on a single floppy disk. The number of patches is only limited by the amount of disk space. Think of how many sounds you can transfer to a hard disk or an optical disk!

All the information in a synthesizer's patch bank can be downloaded, via MIDI, to your Macintosh, where it appears as a list in a bank window, organized by patch numbers. A patch is just a list of parameters in the form of system exclusive messages. Transferring patches is simply a matter of exchanging system exclusive codes. If you can name patches on your synth, the names appear in the bank. Even if the synthesizer

doesn't display patch names, you can type in names on the Mac for the sake of organization. When a Mac user buys a new synth, he or she often buys a librarian to go along with it.

In the old days, before MIDI software, you could backup patch banks by dumping patch data onto cassette tape. Some synths still have jacks for connecting to a cassette recorder. There's no way to view patch names or rearrange their locations on tape. The process of dumping patches to tape is relatively slow and undependable, and setting correct audio levels is crucial to success. Locating individual patches on tape can be tedious. Sending patch data over MIDI cables to a computer is much faster and more dependable. If you have software that records system exclusive data, you don't even need a librarian to store patches, but it sure is handy for viewing and changing the contents of patch banks.

Once a bank of patches is loaded into a librarian, you can easily rearrange their locations in the bank. Let's say you have 64 sounds: eight strings, eight woodwinds, eight horns, eight basses, eight pianos, eight organs, eight percussion instruments, and eight sound effects, randomly scattered in your synthesizer's memory. Perhaps you'd rather organize them in groups, with string sounds as patches 1-8, woodwinds as 8-16, horns as

	Max's TX	
	Ch 12 Yamaha TX	
1	PIAN YAZ	**17** FUNK BASS2
2	BERN PIANO	**18** E.BASS 1
3	BRT ROADES	**19** E BASS 4
4	PIANO 1	**20** VIRGINBASS
5	ZEBOW	**21** DON HENLEY
6	LEAVE IT 2	**22** AGITATO 2
7	BERNTHO	**23** AGITATO 2
8	ALLEYWAYS	**24** STRINGS 1
9	BELLS SOP	**25** STRG-CHIME
10	BRASS 5THS	**26** MARIMBA
11	SAX BC	**27** WAY ABOUT
12	FAT HORNS	**28** YOUR WORLD
13	BUKLASH	**29** SYNTVAR3
14	VOX 1C	**30** JUST A TRY
15	SYNCHROS	**31** STORMY
16	RECORDERS	**32** PROPH

17-24, and so on. A patch librarian lets you copy and paste from one patch location to another within a bank, or if two or more bank windows are open onscreen, between banks. Sometimes it's as easy as clicking a patch name and dragging it to a new location. You can also open a new bank window and construct a patch bank from the contents of other banks. When you've assembled a bank in exactly the form you want it, it can be uploaded from the computer back to your synthesizer, where it's stored permanently, or at least until you want to reorganize it again or add new sounds.

Another advantage of librarians is that it's easy to exchange patches with other synthesists. If they don't own a compatible librarian, use your librarian software to transfer sounds from their synths to your Mac. New patches in librarian format are commercially available from many third party sources. One company offers 6000 Yamaha DX7 sounds on floppy disk. You can also save and distribute your own original patches with a librarian.

It's also possible to send individual sounds to your synthesizer's *patch buffer* or to a patch location. Usually, when you load a patch into a synth, it goes into a section of RAM called the patch buffer, where it's temporarily stored until you load another patch. In the buffer, patch parameters can be changed, without affecting the version that's stored in memory. Sending a patch to the patch buffer lets you preview sounds one at a time, without changing anything in the patch bank. With a librarian, sending a single patch to a synth may be as simple as clicking on its name. Stepping through a list with the Tab, Return, or arrow cursor keys lets you listen to all the sounds in a whole bank very quickly. Unless you save a patch into the synth's memory, it disappears whenever you send a new patch.

If you have two different librarians for the same synthesizer, transfer sounds from one format to another by first sending a patch or a bank to the synth. Then open the other librarian and send it back to the computer.

The **Opcode Patch Librarian** is the most popular synthesizer librarian for the Mac. It was among the earliest Macintosh MIDI software, and versions are now available for an impressive variety of instruments. If you have a popular synth, it's likely that Opcode makes a librarian for it. A different librarian is necessary for each model of synthesizer. If you have a Korg M-1, you need the M-1 librarian. If you have an Oberheim Matrix-1000, you need the Matrix-1000 librarian. It is possible to combine Opcode librarians, so that M-1 and Matrix-1000 banks appear onscreen at the same time.

In addition to *banks* that organize sounds by patch number, Patch Librarians create alphabetized lists of patches called *libraries*. Library files of any length are made up of sounds copied from patch banks. Organize a library of mallet percussion sounds and another of saxophones, then copy and organize individual sounds into a custom patch bank. If you try to copy two different patches with the same name into a library, you're given the opportunity to change the name of one of them. If you indicate No Duplicates In Library, then try to paste two identical patches with different names,

you're also given an opportunity to rename one of them.

Opcode Patch Librarians include a feature called *Patch Factory*. Patch Factory creates new patches by randomly altering the parameters of existing patches. Admittedly, most patches created in this fashion are useless, but occasionally you find one that can be fine-tuned into something new and exciting. Some librarians offer a choice of patch generation algorithms. All have the *Shuffler* algorithm. Shuffler combines parameters from an entire bank of patches into a new bank. If you don't want to specify which patches are used as source material for a generated bank, they can be randomly selected from a library and organized into a bank with the *Library Sampler* function. *Shade Two* takes two selected patches and produces a full bank or a library that gradually blends parameters from one patch into the other, resulting in a smooth gradation of instrumental characteristics. Even the patch names change gradually from one to the other. The *Constrained Random* algorithm randomly combines two patches within the bounds of the upper and lower limits of each parameter.

OB Lib				
Ch 3	Xpander (Single)	28 items in library		
NY SURF	FUNKREED	Q-SWEEP	SCIFI FX	
BUZZBASS	G-BASS	Q-SWEEP2	SPACEOBO	
BWOW GY	G-BASS 2	Q-WOBBLE	STACCATO	
CHUUU'	GYSTRNGS	QU'RAN	SUSDRON2	
CHUUU2	OMINOUS	RANDOM	SUSDRONE	
CLARINET	PPTT'...	REEDS	SWOOP 1	
FUNKBASS	PPTT2...	S-WOBBLE	WIND	

There are several ways to preview sounds by playing them from the librarian, without using a synthesizer keyboard. One way is to use *MouseKeys*. The MouseKeys window is an onscreen keyboard that sends note information over MIDI when you click the

actions performed in the librarian. It's like a one-track sequencer that records system exclusive, but has no means of editing.

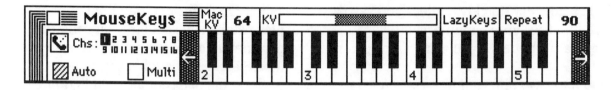

keys. It has buttons to select the play channel or channels, serial port, keyboard transposition, range of velocity, and rate of repetition. *LazyKeys* plays whenever the cursor is over the keyboard, without clicking. The Option key works as a sustain pedal for playing chords.

If you enable *Testing Sounds* from the Edit menu, the Macintosh keyboard can also play a synthesizer. The 21 letter keys on the left play three octaves of a major scale, starting with middle C play by the Z key. Pressing Shift or Caps Lock transposes everything down three octaves, for a total of six octaves played from the Mac keyboard. Note velocities are set in the MouseKeys window.

Two more ways to preview sounds are to open and play a MIDI File or record a new sequence with the Play menu. By choosing *Play on Select*, the sequence plays whenever you click a patch name. Selecting *Capture To MIDI File* sends all MIDI information into a buffer which can be saved to disk and later reopened. Normally, all data is captured, including patch parameters, patch transfer requests, notes played, and anything else that sends MIDI messages, but you can filter out everything except patch dumps and parameter changes. Capture To MIDI File lets you create a macro to recreate a series of

Sometimes it's inconvenient to quit another program to send sounds to your synthesizer, especially when you're sequencing. That's why some patch librarians can be accessed from desk accessories. As long as there's an Opcode Patch Librarian on the same disk, it can be opened with the **Opcode PatchLib DA**. You can send patches and banks from the computer to the synth, but you can't send them back the other way.

A more complete librarian in a desk accessory is the **Zero One Librarian**. Its main window is called the *controller* window. It's used to open and save files, send and receive banks, and open other windows. *Patch file* windows display banks of patches, and let you send, receive, copy, and rename single patches. *Tone file* windows send and receive tones that make up linear arithmetic patches.

A few companies offer patch library programs for just a handful of popular synths. Blank Software makes Sound File, a patch and sequence librarian for the Ensoniq ESQ-1 and SQ-80. Passport MIDI Voice Librarians are available for the original Yamaha DX7, Casio CZ-101, and their offshoots. Other librarians are combined with patch editors into editor/librarians.

Synthesizer patch editors

Back in the old days, synthesizer patch parameters were changed with knobs or sliders on the synth's front panel. You could see the settings of each parameter by the positions of the knobs and switches. In the past few years, synthesizer user interfaces have grown visually simpler, but conceptually more difficult. All those knobs have been reduced to as few as one control for selecting a parameter and another for changing its value. Using fewer front panel controls makes synths cheaper to build, and admittedly, many of today's synths are so complex it would take a wall of front panel controls to access every parameter. Partially as a result of synthesizer user interfaces becoming more complicated to use, fewer synthesists bother to program their own sounds.

Fortunately for computer users, there are patch editors to make the task easier than ever. A patch editor displays all the parameters in graphic form. Every parameter can be changed in its own field, and parameters like envelopes and velocity curves can be graphically reshaped. Most editors are combined with other programs, like patch librarians. In addition to synth editors, there are editors for MIDI-controlled mixers and effects processors. A patch editor is one of the best things about MIDI, giving synthesists creative sound designing capabilities that were once available only on the Synclavier and the Fairlight CMI.

Opcode makes a variety of patch editors integrated into their **Editor/Librarian**

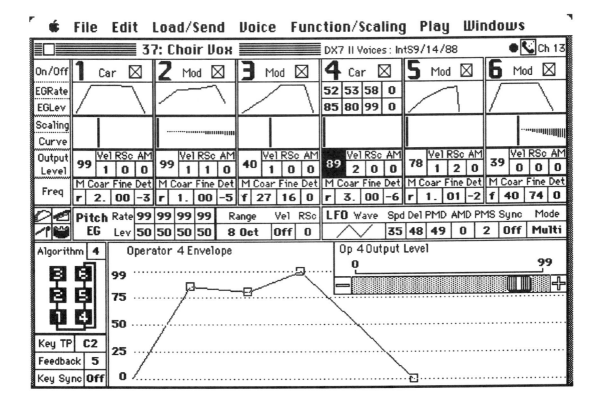

software, which combine editors and librarians in the same program. To edit a patch stored in a librarian window, select it and click the Edit button in the window's upper right, or type command-E. This opens the *editor window* and changes the menu bar commands. With the editor open, you can change patches with the Voice menu.

Usually, every parameter is listed in the editor window. Clicking on an envelope displays it numerically and as a graph. Change its shape by typing new values or by clicking and dragging its handles. Most parameter values, when you click them, are displayed in a scroll bar box. Scrolling in this box shows you the complete range of values from which to choose. After you've made changes, you can temporarily revert to the original patch with the *Compare/ UnCompare* command in the Edit menu. If you want to change only some parameters to their original settings, you can copy from the stored patch and paste to your edited version. Sometimes there are menu selections to open separate windows for changing groups of parameters, like performance functions.

Any changes you make are immediately transmitted to your synthesizer, as if the editor was a real control panel. If *Play on Parameter Change* is enabled, a recorded sequence plays every time you alter any parameter value. You can even record a macro of parameters being changed by capturing a MIDI File with the Play menu. This MIDI File can then be pasted into a sequence for real time parameter changes in a sequence.

Of course, the editing capabilities of any editor is dependent on the synth itself. The **Roland D-50 Editor/Librarian** lets you edit partials, patches, EQ, and effects, and it features a pop-up menu for selecting PCM sounds. The **Oberheim Matrix-6 Editor/ Librarian** displays onscreen patchcords to represent matrix modulation paths. The **Kawai K-1 Editor/Librarian** graphically displays note ranges, velocity curves, key scaling, and vibrato.

Many editor programs are specific not just to a particular synth, but to a whole line of similar synths. Opcode's **Yamaha DX7II Editor/Librarian**, for example, works with all 6-operator Yamahas: the DX7IIFD, DX7IID, DX7S, TX802, TX7, the original DX7, and any configuration of TF1 modules in the TX816. With it, you can transfer patches from one synth model to another. The **Yamaha DX11 Editor/Librarian** has the added ability to convert 6-operator patches in Opcode format into 4-operator patches for the DX11, TX81Z, DX21, DX27, and DX100. In addition to the patch editor, some Opcode programs have separate editors for performances, micro-tunings, fractional scalings, drum setups, and other capabilities that are particular to certain synthesizers.

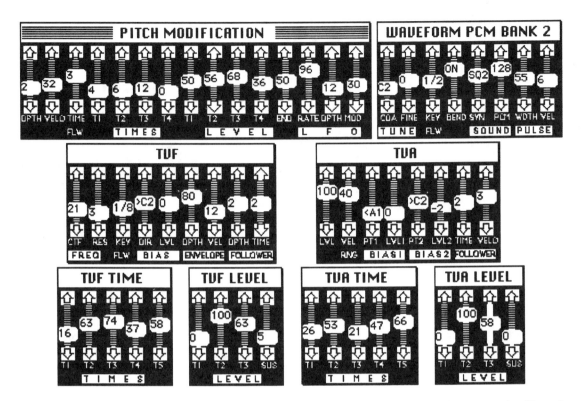

Zero One patch editors are available as desk accesories, so you can use them while you're doing something else with your computer. The **Zero One D-50 Editor** and **D-10 Editor** work a lot like Zero One's patch librarian DAs.

A small *controller* window opens other edit windows, like *graphic editing* windows for altering the structure, TVA settings, TVF settings, pitch envelopes, structures, and output mode. Other edit windows include MIDI setup, *patch ballparking* for setting up a rough patch to begin editing, and *patch generation*, which interpolates or copies parameters between two patches. Partials are displayed and edited in their own windows, and the *rhythm set-up* window maps and mixes percussion sounds. There's even a *step recorder* that remembers your last hundred changes, so you can undo the last several changes you made.

Other Macintosh editors and editor/ librarians are made by Beaverton Digital, Dr.T's, Sonus, Digidesign, Blank Software, Digital Music Services, and others, for a variety of MIDI instruments and devices.

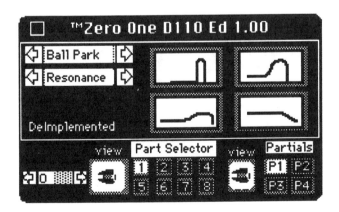

Software for samplers

Samplers are specialized computers that allow us to digitally record, or sample, any sound, and then control the musical pitch of that sound's playback with a MIDI control source, like a keyboard or a sequencer. The process of sampling is by nature imperfect, so the recording process is only the first step in a captured sound's journey to becoming a musically useful sample. First it has to be edited, processed, and otherwise massaged into something that comes as close as possible to the original sound (if that's your goal). It's also desirable to make samples as short as possible, so that more samples fit into the sampler's memory.

yours and yours alone. Unfortunately, recording and editing flawless samples is seldom simple. You have to record the sound at the right level, chop off the silence at both ends, probably loop it, map its pitch range, shape its envelope, normalize it, equalize it, filter it, then assign its audio output, velocity range, modulation, MIDI channel, and overall loudness.

All the signal processing that goes along with creating samples can be a lot of hard work. A program like Digidesign's **Sound Designer** or Blank's **Alchemy** simplifies the process of processing samples by making it possible to actually see an accurate visual representation of sound suspended in time. What's more, you can edit this image of full-fidelity sound much as you edit text in a word processor. Select slices of sound to cut, copy, replace, and otherwise modify, and merge one file into another. Zoom in on a single wave or zoom out to see a complete envelope. Do all the truncating, looping, and maybe even

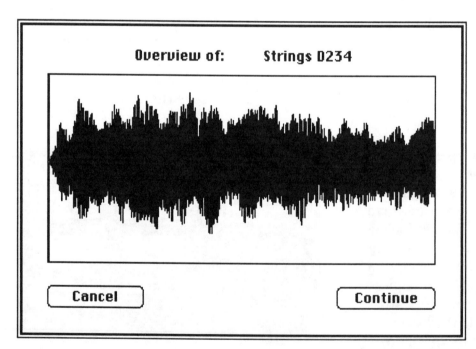

Sample editors exist to make life easier for people who create the samples that get played on samplers. With a sampler, you can craft unique musical sounds that are

mapping and processing, from the computer screen where you can see what you're doing. Import samples from one sampler and export them to another.

The figure image contains:
Overview of: Strings D234
[Cancel]   [Continue]

Sample creation software, as opposed to sample editing software, uses the Macintosh to digitally synthesize sound data, then transfers it to your sampler via MIDI, SCSI, or serial port. Instead of digitizing real sounds, the computer's processing power is harnessed to digitally fabricate new sounds. Such an approach makes it possible to work with complex synthesis algorithms that aren't built into any synthesizer. Digidesign's **Softsynth** is an advanced FM and additive synthesis program, and **Turbosynth** lets you build waveforms from the ground up using a variety of sophisticated algorithms accessed from a straightforward interface.

When you transfer sample data from your computer to your sampler, how does it know where to go? Every sample in a sampler is assigned a number which tags its location in the sampler's memory. When sample data is sent to the sampler, where you send it may determine its playback pitch and its location on the keyboard, depending on how it's mapped. When a sample editing program asks the sampler to send over a sound, you have to tell it where to look in the sampler's memory by typing in the sound number. Sample data is converted to the software's format when it's sent to the computer, and back to the sampler's format when it's sent back to the sampler.

Sample editing

Sound is audio information that's converted by our ears into nervous impulses which stimulate our brains. A sampler turns audio information into digital data, converting it to a series of numbers. Like other musical data, these numbers can be changed in all sorts of ways to suit our needs. By importing this information into our computers, we can make changes visually. Editing samples increases efficiency and gives us lots of new sounds to work with, like fragments of spoken words and tones that fade from one instrument into another.

There are a lot of ways you can improve a sample after it's been recorded. Truncate so it takes as little memory as possible. Loop it so that when you hold a note it sustains rather than dies out. Process it so that certain frequencies are emphasized, or it plays backwards, or it blends into another sampled instrument. The various functions of a sample editor let you make these improvements by dealing with sound visually.

Sampling, like any audio recording, is a trade-off between too much signal and too much noise. If you make a recording and the level is too low, the result is poor fidelity with too much hiss due to a poor signal-to-noise ratio. If you record at too high a level, the result is clipping, a familiar form of audio distortion. With a sample editor, you can easily see where clipping occurs. Conversely, if the sample's peak amplitude never reaches a full 100% (the maximum level before clipping), it isn't as noise-free as it could be. When mapped with other samples, it may not be as loud as the others. You can easily increase its peak amplitude to exactly 100% by performing an operation called *normalization*.

Before you begin sampling, you usually have to guess how much sampling time you need. After it's recorded, you can *truncate* it, cutting out the dead air just before and after the sound itself. If there's unwanted noise before the desired start point or after the end point, truncating removes it. Truncating the beginning insures that when you play a sample, it triggers immediately. When a sound is truncated, you can recover the memory that had been used to record the discarded portions.

Most musical sounds are too long to fit many into a sampler's memory. This is why we usually record very short sounds, then *loop* them so that when you play a note, a portion repeats as long as you hold down the key. This kind of loop is a *sustain loop*. Some samplers also play a different loop, called a *release loop*, which repeats another portion of the waveform when the key is released. If a sound is long, looping makes it unnecessary to record the whole thing, thus conserving memory.

Samples are looped by defining where the loop begins and ends. The portion between these points is what gets repeated. Ideally, the loop points should be very similar parts of the waveform. To avoid audible "bumps" because of slight changes in pitch, timbre, or amplitude, the connection between these points should be seamless. Matching up loop points can be very tricky. That's where

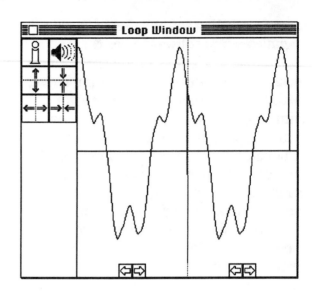

a sample editor comes in. You can zoom in on individual cycles to look for loop points that match, then preview the loop over the Mac's sound circuit before sending it to your sampler.

Most loops play from beginning to end and then repeat. An *alternating* or *reversing loop* plays from beginning to end, then backwards from the end to the beginning before repeating, rather like a bow on a violin string. With a *crossfade loop*, the beginning and end points overlap, making a smoother transition.

Some samplers let you *splice* part of one sample to another. With a sample editor, you can combine sound files to create new sound files. By splicing two samples together, you can create a sound that begins as a trumpet and turns into a guitar, or one that starts with a whimper and ends with a bang. Like looping, you must be very careful that the end of the first sound precisely matches the beginning of the second sound. Otherwise, there's an audible click at the splice point. Again, crossfading helps smooth the transition from one sample to another.

Sample editors usually have some form of *digital signal processing* functions. Equalization and time compression are two kinds of processing. A sample editor gives you the means to filter sounds digitally, with cutoff slopes and parameter controls that would be impossible, or at least very expensive, in the analog audio world. You can specify huge amounts of boost or cut at bandwidths as narrow as 1 Hz. Choose from lowpass, highpass, bandpass, and notch filtering, as well as peak/shelf parametric equalization. See a visual preview of the equalization curve before you apply it to a sample.

Some sample editors can create a three-dimensional display called a *Fast Fourier Transform* or *FFT*. An FFT shows you the spectral dynamics of individual harmonics as a mesh, a graph, or a chart. In an FFT frequency analysis, sound files are sliced up into frequency bands and the changing amplitude of each harmonic is plotted against time. You can define the number of bands and the length of time displayed.

Sound Designer

Sound Designer, introduced by Digidesign in 1985, is a sample editor that's had time to mature. Sound Designer transfers data from a sampler to the Macintosh and back through a MIDI interface connected to a serial port, or if your sampler has RS-422 or SCSI ports, directly through them, without the need for a MIDI interface.

Sound Designer translates sample data into 16-bit sound files that the Macintosh can understand. Once translated, sound data may be graphically manipulated in a multitude of manners, including cut and paste editing, onscreen looping, and signal

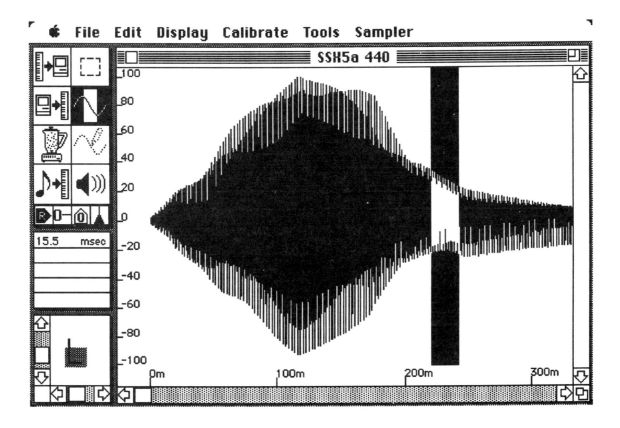

processing. Usual Macintosh click and drag procedures apply for making selections. To prevent pops from occurring in cut and paste edits, the *Smoothing* command creates quick crossfades at the edit points. Use the *zoom box* to magnify a selected portion, or see the whole waveform in the *overview* window. You can also change your perspective with the *scale box*, which graphically expands and compresses time and amplitude. Create loops by placing markers for the start and end points, then zoom in on the loop splice in the *loop window* (command-L). The instantaneous amplitudes of both loop points are displayed as percentages of full amplitude.

Sound Designer is packaged in several versions. Originally, it was model-specific, with versions for several samplers, including E-mu's Emulator II and Emax, Ensoniq Mirage, and Sequential Prophet-2000. Each had a screen for controlling the sampler's front panel functions, like changing filter frequency and defining keyboard maps. To transfer sample data between samplers, you had to have a different version for each sampler. Then came **Sound Designer Universal**, with the ability to import and export sample data from an impressive variety of popular samplers, including instruments that support the Sample Dump Standard.

Click on the *mixer* icon to summon a dialog box of digital signal processing possibilities. The *mix* function combines two sound files into one, so you can layer sounds without cutting the number of voices your sampler plays. *Merge* creates smooth crossfades from one sound file to another. To perform *digital equalization*, choose from lowpass, highpass, peaking, notching, high shelving, and low shelving filters.

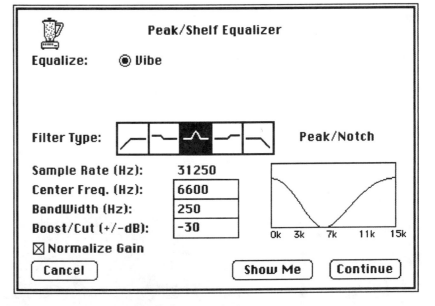

Sound files can be previewed over the Mac's speaker. Just click the speaker icon to play a sound file. Hold down the mouse button to hear a sustain loop, or option-click to hear a release loop. Once a sampled sound is custom-tailored to your needs, send it back to the sampler to be played. Clicking the *preview* icon sends sample data to the sampler's first memory location, or specify its destination with one of the *transfer* icons.

Sound Designer II is optimized for use with multitrack hard disk recording systems. With all the features of Sound Designer Universal, it adds MIDI Time Code synchronization, time compression, seven-band stereo equalization, and a variety of advanced processing tools. **Sound Designer II SK** links several samplers into an integrated network, converting sample rates to exchange sample data between instruments.

Alchemy

Blank's 16-bit stereo sample editor Alchemy is designed to support a network of samplers connected to the computer via MIDI, SCSI, and RS-422. It links most popular samplers together with DAN, its *Distributed Audio Network*, and is capable of transferring sampler data from one type of sampler to another. To do this, it automatically resamples a sound file to match the sampling rate of its destination. An *instrument setup window* lets you enter a sampler ID, communications, printer, or SCSI port, and MIDI setup for each sampler in the network, and this information is remembered. By converting samples to Alchemy sound files, one sampler's sound library can be ported over to any other sampler.

Alchemy converts sound files to a variety of formats for compatibility with other programs, including Sound Designer, Audio IFF, Sound Lab, Drum File, Dyaxis, and Apple SND resource formats. That means you can turn high-quality samples into sound resources for the Mac's audio circuit.

Keyboard ranges are defined by clicking and dragging across an onscreen keyboard. Multisample maps are saved as part of a sound file. This feature is extremely convenient because it saves sets of samples as if they were sampler presets.

Alchemy's *overview display* lets you view a whole sound file, with loop points, selected region, and cursor location indicated. Mono or stereo sound files showing one or both channels can be viewed in as many as eight different windows per sound file. Any number of sound files can be onscreen simultaneously. When a portion is selected, the waveform display resizes itself. Location is shown by fractions of seconds, samples, or SMPTE frame, with amplitude shown in decibels or as a percentage of maximum.

Selected regions can be *looped* with a single command. To simplify looping, zero crossings and crossfades can be found automatically. Selections can be cut, copied, pasted, and mixed with other selections. Everything outside the selected region can be *truncated* with a single command. A selected portion's gain can be adjusted and faded, and its phase can be inverted. The *waveform draw mode* lets you draw or edit waveforms with a pencil tool.

Harmonic content can be analyzed in the *harmonic spectrum display* and seen as a series of up to 16,000 harmonic bands. It's possible to perform digital filtering effects and graphic manipulation of individual harmonic amplitudes. Harmonics can be cut, copied, cleared, and pasted. Once new harmonic data is entered, it actually resynthesizes new waveforms.

Alchemy is currently available in two versions. **Alchemy Apprentice** has all the functions normally needed to edit samples from many samplers. **Alchemy 2.0** adds compatibility with Digidesign's **Sound Accelerator** and plays files directly from disk for hard disk recording systems. It also features enhanced signal processing functions, including time compression and pitch shifting.

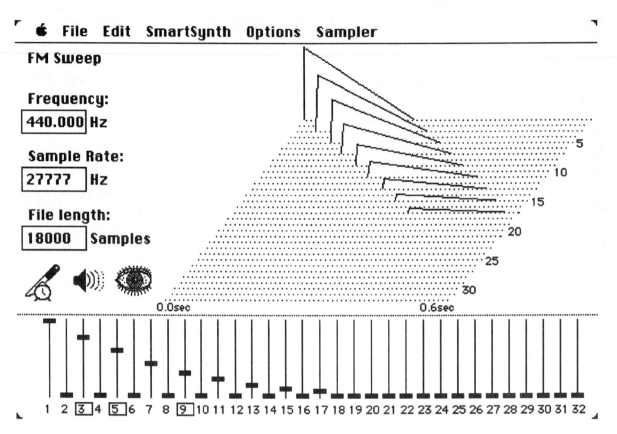

Softsynth

Digidesign's Softsynth creates sounds for samplers by means of additive and FM synthesis. Creating sounds by combining sine waves is considerably easier if you have a graphic image of the sound you're synthesizing. Up to 32 partials (or harmonics) are defined by harmonic number. You specify their waveforms, frequency ratios, and amplitudes, then mix them into a composite waveform. Partials can be routed to frequency modulate one another. Representations of each partial and of the composite waveform can be viewed onscreen and played by the Mac as you make changes. When it's ready, a Softsynth sound is transferred directly to your sampler, or you can open it up in Turbosynth, Sound Designer, or Alchemy for additional processing.

On the main screen, the fundamental frequency, sampling rate, and length in samples are given for each sound file. A series of faders at the bottom show the relative levels of the mixed partials. To view a single partial, click on its harmonic number. To see the composite waveform again, click on the mixer icon. A large three-dimensional graph plots harmonic number, time, and amplitude, resulting in a quasi-FFT display. Whenever you make changes in harmonic content, click the *eye icon* to draw an updated graph. Clicking on the *speaker icon* plays the updated sound and redraws the graph.

Softsynth has 32 oscillators. Each oscillator produces one partial from a choice of five waveforms, increasing in complexity from sine wave to noise. Each partial has its own complex pitch and amplitude envelopes. To shape an envelope, click anywhere on its line and a handle appears. Drag the handle to its desired position. Use the *eraser tool* to remove handles.

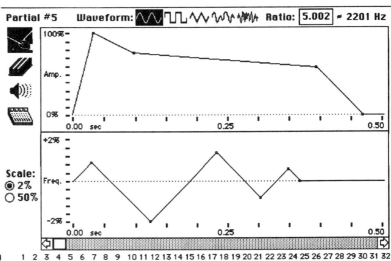

The frequency of each partial is defined by its ratio to the fundamental frequency. By default, the ratios are whole number multiples of the fundamental, but you can fine-tune them by 1/1000ths of a whole number. The frequency ratio doesn't necessarily have anything to do with the harmonic number. Any partial can have any harmonic ratio. This means that if the lower 16 partials are used to create a sound, the upper 16 partials can be used to double it. If the doubling is slightly offset in pitch or time, chorusing and delay effects are achieved.

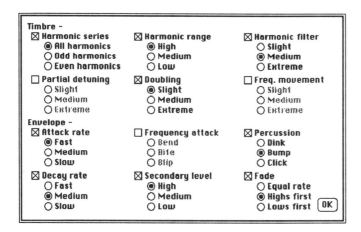

There are three approaches to synthesizing with Softsynth. You can work with each partial individually and mix partials together for additive synthesis, routing selected carriers to selected modulators for FM synthesis. You can also set up a *time slice*, defining a series of harmonic events that occur in the duration of an envelope. Any sound file can be converted to a time

slice representation. The third method is called *Smartsynth*, in which you specify general parameters to give the computer a rough idea of what you want, and then see what it comes up with.

Turbosynth

Turbosynth is a do-it-yourself wavetable synthesis program. It lets you create new sounds as simple or as complex as you wish, then transfer them to your sampler. Turbosynth offers many tools for synthesizing and reshaping sound. Create onscreen *oscillators* generating waveforms you define, or use sounds imported from other sampler programs like Sound Designer or Softsynth. Turbosynth lets you create sounds that can't be created any other way.

Turbosynth's *tool palette* offers several modules, which can be configured on the screen and connected in various ways via virtual patchcords, in the manner of a block diagram. Outputs are routed to inputs, with each module contributing its talents along the way, until audio paths are routed into a mixer and to the output. There are also

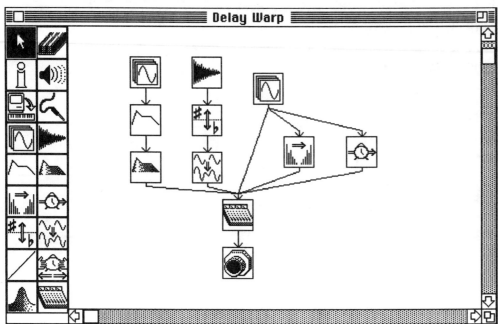

pitch and another distorts time. A *modulator* module combines two different sources for frequency, amplitude, and pitch modulation. There are more modules for time delay, resonance, looping, and mixing sound sources. The *waveshaper* gives you more tools to reshape

tools for selecting, erasing, previewing on the Mac's sound circuit, transferring to a sampler, and calling up an information box to specify length, sample rate, and frequency. Working with Turbosynth is very much like modular synthesis in the late 1960s and early 1970s, but the sound sources and processing possibilities are much, much more sophisticated.

The oscillator module provides user-drawn waves, randomly generated waves, a palette of presets, and a library of sampled waves. It gives you the tools to subtly reshape waves without changing them drastically, by inverting them, scrunching them up, stretching them out, and shoving them around graphically. Complete Sound Designer and Softsynth files can be used as sound source modules.

There are modules to shape envelopes, adjust filters, and specify spectral inversions. All three give you a palette of presets and include a random generator and reshaping tools. One module shifts

waveforms after they've been processed by other modules.

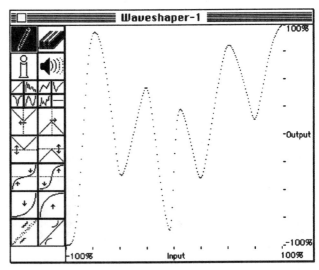

Turbosynth opens sound files from other programs, and it saves files in various forms. A configuration's output can be saved as a sound file. A waveform, or just the looped portion, can also be saved a sound file. Any configuration of modules can be converted to a single sample module for use as a sound source.

Mastering the Macintosh

Every kind of hardware or software has its own *user interface*.

A user interface is a means of interaction — a set of features and actions employed to operate something. An automobile's interface is its steering wheel, accelerator pedal, brake pedal, clutch, gearshift, speedometer, fuel gauge, and the like. Using a book's interface involves opening its cover, turning pages, and receiving information in the form of printed words and graphics.

A user interface is how we interact with a computer: we tell it what to do, and it provides us with information. The Macintosh user interface features a typewriter-style keyboard with a numeric keypad, a rolling, handheld box called a *mouse*, and an almost black-on-white monitor screen that displays interactive symbols, multiple choice menus, and two-dimensional boxes called *windows* that can be resized, scrolled, stacked, opened, and closed. Different Mac programs have a consistent user interface that makes them easier to learn. Apple Computer has provided software developers with published guidelines for many aspects of the Mac's interface. When you learn one Mac program, others are immediately familiar.

The Mac's graphical interface is based more on pictures than words. Instead of typing memorized commands into an almost empty monitor screen and moving an onscreen cursor with computer keys, you point at images appearing in windows with the Mac's one-button mouse. (Often you can also move the cursor with arrow keys.) Visually, the interface of many Mac programs is a metaphor for the surface of a

desk. Files, folders, documents, desk accessories, and other objects may be strewn across the desktop. A folder may be opened to reveal the files inside. Commands are chosen from lists called *menus*. Windows may be filled with small symbols called *icons*, representing objects and actions.

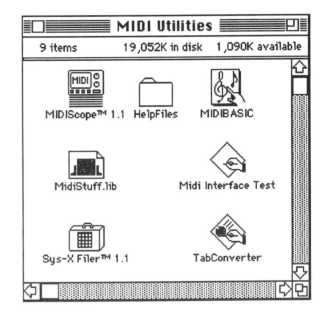

The variety of icons is just about infinite. An icon might be a little tape recorder representing a sequencer program, a tiny sheet of score paper representing a song file, a folder representing a file sub-directory, a tool for placing notes on a musical staff, or any image that reacts when you point to it. Mac users accomplish necessary tasks by pointing at icons, objects, pictures, words, areas, boxes, and buttons. The primary advantage of a "point-and-click" method of operation is that it's logical and easy to learn. When it takes too long to move the cursor across the screen with the mouse, most Mac programs are flexible enough to let you give commands from the keyboard alone, using combination keystrokes or function keys.

Part of the reason it's so easy to learn Mac programs is that there are alternate ways of giving all kinds of commands. If you want to close something, you might click the close box, or choose Close from the File menu, or hold down the Command key and type a W. You might scroll through a list with the arrow cursor keys or by clicking on an arrow on the screen with the mouse, by dragging a scroll box, or by typing the first letters in your selection. If there's a logical way to do something, you'll probably stumble across it, without ever consulting a user's manual. Besides, anyone can figure out how to point at things with a mouse.

Most of the time, just pointing at something doesn't really do much. You have to press and release the mouse button as well, an operation called *clicking*. This yields an immediate result, determined not just by where you click, but also how you click. If you point at an image and click it, it may become highlighted (black and white are reversed) to signify that it's *selected*. Selecting something indicates that it's ready to by modified. If you quickly click twice on something, that's called *double-clicking*. Double-clicking starts something, opens something, or selects something that a single click doesn't.

There are several other variations on clicking. If you move the cursor across the screen as you hold down the mouse button, you're *clicking and dragging*. When you're using a graphics tool like a pen or a paint brush, clicking and dragging is how you press it to the paper, so to speak. Clicking and dragging can move objects around on the screen, and it's also used to select multiple items and draw *selection boxes* around objects. By dragging the cursor

over an area, perhaps a group of musical notes, you make a selection that starts at one point and ends at another, highlighting everything in between. A variation called *shift-clicking* involves clicking the beginning, holding down the Shift key, and clicking the end of the selection. Sometimes you can click an object, hold down the Shift key, and select other objects, without selecting everything in between. If you select something as you hold down the Command key (the one with an Apple on it), that's *command-clicking*. If it's the Option key being held, that's *option-clicking*. Then there's command-shift-clicking, option-shift-clicking, option-command-shift-clicking, ad infinitum.

Many choices are made by clicking onscreen *buttons*. A button is simply a spot to click, drawn to look like some kind of pushbutton, and often serving the same kind of purpose. Buttons are highlighted at the moment you click them. Buttons let you make choices like "Yes", "No", or "Cancel", or they may open files or windows or simply turn something on and off. In a sequencer, for example, buttons are used to play, record, rewind, select, solo, and mute tracks. Buttons may select a range of values, like MIDI channels or velocity levels. If a button is surrounded by a thick-thin double line, pressing the Enter or Return key has the same effect as clicking the button.

Buttons appear in windows and in *dialog boxes*. A dialog box is an interactive window that lets you respond to the computer. Unlike a normal window, a dialog box can't be moved or resized, and the computer may refuse to do anything else until you respond to it. It's where you make choices and supply data, resulting in an effect of some kind. One of the choices may be a Cancel button, which closes the box and says, in effect, "never mind".

In addition to buttons, windows and dialog boxes may contain numeric or text *fields*, blank spaces where you enter information, usually by typing. An *insertion point*, frequently a blinking vertical line, shows where your typing will appear. You can tell when a field expects your input; it contains a blinking cursor or the entire field is highlighted in black. If there's a series of fields, you can usually move the insertion point from one to another with the Tab key.

```
┌─────────────────────────────────────────────────────────────────┐
│  LaserWriter  "LaserWriter"              5.2      ┌────────────┐  │
│                                                   │     OK     │  │
│  Copies:[1]         Pages:◉ All  ○ From:[   ] To:[   ]  └──────┘  │
│                                                   ┌────────────┐  │
│  Cover Page:   ◉ No ○ First Page  ○ Last Page     │   Cancel   │  │
│                                                   ┌────────────┐  │
│  Paper Source: ◉ Paper Cassette  ○ Manual Feed    │    Help    │  │
└─────────────────────────────────────────────────────────────────┘
```

A good example of fields and buttons in a dialog box is the box that appears when you print a document. When you choose Print from the File menu, a dialog box lets you specify paper size, number of pages, number of copies, and printing resolution, and then start up and stop the printer. Some dialog boxes show a scrollable list of choices, and when you click an item in the list, it becomes highlighted. When one choice leads to another, you may see several dialog boxes in succession.

Some Macintosh programs, especially music programs, have numeric fields that scroll to higher or lower values when clicked in the upper and lower halves. Some of them scroll faster as you drag the cursor away from the field, which is handy for scrolling through a large range of values. A lot of MIDI programs let you enter information into a field by sending a

MIDI event, such as playing a note or moving a continuous controller, like a modulation wheel or sustain pedal.

Menus, palettes, and windows

At the top of the Mac screen is the *menu bar*, a vertical strip listing command headings. Many commands are selected from *pull-down menus* accessed from the menu bar. To choose a command, click on its heading in the menu bar, then drag down to the command and release the mouse button. Commands are how we tell computers what to do. They're used to create and manipulate files, programs, and disks, to modify selections, to change the appearance of the screen, to print pages, and for dozens of similar functions. Sometimes, a menu has *sub-menus*, menus that pop up from main menu selections. Some menus are called *tear-off menus* because when you click and drag them away from the menu bar, the whole menu moves to wherever you drag it. A few programs have windows with *mini-menus* that pop up from menu bars to affect selections within those windows.

Some programs let you choose functions from a bunch of icons on a *palette bar* or *tool palette*, usually off to the side. Some have tear-off palette bars. Palette bars are good for quickly selecting tools, symbols, patterns, and various functions, just by clicking the appropriate icon. Such a bar may contain music symbols, graphics tools, fill patterns, etc. When you click a tool's icon, the cursor becomes that tool, ready to carry out its function.

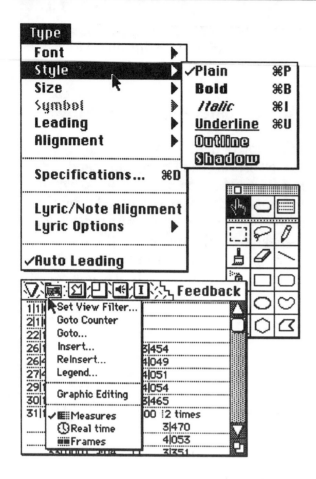

Windows are onscreen boxes that contain images. Most windows conform to a certain set of features that make them useful. A standard Mac window has a title bar at the top, resize boxes in the right corners, a close box in the upper left corner, and possibly scroll bars on the right and bottom edges. A window can usually be moved around by clicking and dragging on its *title bar*. Close it and send it away by clicking in its *close box*.

Your view of a window's contents is changed with *scroll bars*. Scroll bars have three elements: a gray column, a square "thumb" which travels along the column, and an arrow at each end. The thumb's location on the column indicates the location of your view of the document. If

you're looking at a text file that's three screenfuls long, positioning the thumb in the middle of the right-hand scroll bar shows you the middle screenful. You can scroll to a new view by clicking and dragging the thumb to a new location on the bar. Scroll a screenful at a time by clicking directly on the gray column. Click on an arrow to scroll just a little, or click an arrow and hold the mouse button to scroll continuously.

The computer keyboard

In addition to the letter, number, and symbol keys found on typewriter keyboards, Mac keyboards have special purpose keys. Some of these keys, like the Option, Command, and Control keys, are used in combination with other keys. Older Macs don't have a Control key, but most Mac programs don't use it anyway. The arrow keys to the right of the Space Bar change the position of the cursor, so they're called *cursor keys*. Some keyboards have *function keys*. A function key sends a pre-assigned command, like Save or Print, when you press it.

More often, commands are given from the keyboard with combination keystrokes. By holding the Command key as you press the letter S, most programs perform a Save, storing the file on disk in its present form. Pressing Command and N opens a new file. Command-O opens documents, command-W closes them, and command-P prints them, depending on the application. Command-period (.) often substitutes for clicking Cancel, or to cancel an operation in progress, like printing or playback. The precise function of combination keystrokes varies between programs, but there is a certain amount of standardization. If combination keystrokes have the same effect as selecting commands from menus, they're called keyboard equivalents.

There are utilities that let you set up any keystroke or combination as a function key. With a macro program such as QuicKeys or MacroMaker, you can define your own customized user interface. Such keystrokes can be equivalent to selecting any menu item, clicking a particular spot, opening a certain file, running an application, and so on. Their function is user-definable. Some macro programs actually record a series of actions as you perform them, and others let you chain individual actions in series.

The Finder and MultiFinder

The **Finder**, also called the Desktop, is an application that "finds your way around" on disks. When you first boot up (turn on) the Mac, you can't use the computer until the

Finder opens. Whenever you quit an application, you're sent back to the Finder. It's a key part of the Mac's operating system.

The Finder is an easy-to-use disk utility program that uses the graphic metaphor of documents in folders on a desk. It allows you to open other applications and perform basic utility functions. In the Finder, you can name, delete, and arrange files and folders, copy files from one disk to another, initialize and copy disks, and shut down the computer. To ensure that data is properly stored on disk, you should always exit to the Finder and shut down before you switch off your Mac.

Five different kinds of icons appear in the Finder: disks, folders, applications, files or documents, and the trash can. Disk icons appear in the upper right corner of the screen. Double-clicking a disk opens its

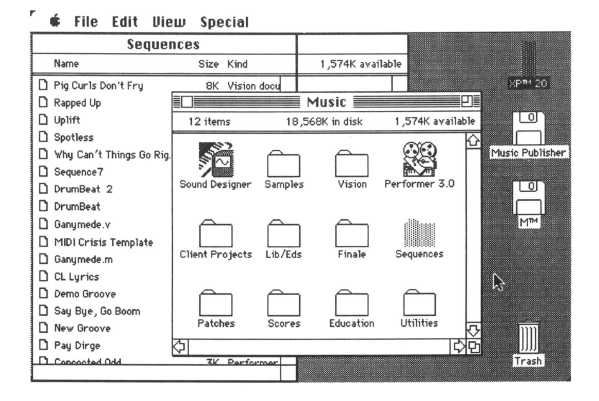

window, displaying folders, documents, and applications. Applications and files are opened by double-clicking their icons. If they're contained within a folder, you have to open the folder's window to see them.

Place an application or a file in a folder by clicking and dragging its icon directly over the folder. When the folder becomes highlighted, the icon is placed in it. A new folder is created by selecting New Folder from the File menu, or by typing its keyboard equivalent, command-N. With a new folder already highlighted, select it to type its new name.

If you select a file or a folder and drag its icon over the *trash can* icon, it's deleted from the disk by choosing Empty Trash from the Special menu. If it's locked, you can usually throw it away by holding the Option key as you drag it into the trash. If you try to throw away an application, you're asked if you're sure you want to do that. You can bypass this warning, also by holding Option as you drag the icon into the trash. When you quit the Finder by shutting down or opening another application, the trash is automatically emptied. When you're finished using a disk, dragging its icon into the trash can ejects it and removes its image from the screen.

There are several ways of displaying folders and their contents. They can appear as full-sized icons, small icons, or in a list. The list can be arranged alphabetically, by date, by size, or by kind, depending on your choice in the View menu. If displayed as a list, useful information is shown along with a tiny generic icon, like its size and the time and date it was most recently changed. This information, along with the time and

date of its creation and a text block typed in by its user, can also be seen in an information window by selecting a file and choosing *Get Info...* (command-I) from the File menu. Applications, files, and folders can be locked in the information window, to prevent you from casually throwing them into the trash.

Applications and files can be selected and dragged into a different folder, which removes them from their previous folder. They can be copied onto another disk by dragging them over the new disk's icon, which doesn't delete the original. The contents of an entire disk can be copied onto a different disk by dragging one disk's icon over another.

Normally, the Finder opens when you power up the Mac. In the Finder, there's a selection called *Set Startup...* in the Special menu. By choosing Set Startup..., then selecting an application, whenever you restart your computer, the selected application opens first, rather than the Finder.

MultiFinder is a multi-tasking alternative to the Finder. With MultiFinder, you can have several applications open onscreen at the same time. One of the applications is always MultiFinder itself, which means that you can always perform Finder-type operations like deleting files and opening other applications. It also lets you work on a document while printing or downloading another. Cutting and pasting between applications is easier. Using MultiFinder in combination with Apple's MIDI Manager and PatchBay, MIDI applications can share and exchange data in real time. To use MultiFinder, you need plenty of memory, typically a megabyte for every application in use. If memory runs short, the computer could crash, and every change made since the last time you saved would be lost.

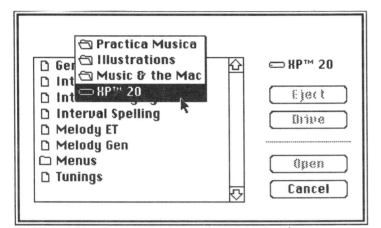

Using files

Folders containing files and applications may be within other folders, which may also be located in folders. This hierarchy of arranging files in folders is called the *Hierarchical File System*, or HFS. HFS helps gets things organized. Mass storage demands the use of HFS. Without it, all the files on a hard disk appear in a single directory, limiting their number.

To run an application within a folder from the Finder, open the folder, then open the application. If the folder is in another folder, open it first. You can open documents from within an application without returning to the Finder. When you select Open... , a *file dialog* box appears with a scrolling window containing a list of folders or documents that can be opened. Above the list is the name of its directory, either a disk or a folder. The obvious way to open a file or folder is to scroll to its name, click it

once, then click the Open button. You can also double-click its name, or select it and press the Enter or Return key. Two faster, mouseless methods of opening a file are to type the first letters in its name, or scroll with the up and down arrow keys, then press Return or Enter.

Opening a folder from the file dialog changes the directory name to the name of the folder, and its contents are listed in the scrolling window. To view the contents of other folders, you have to step through the hierarchy. When you click on the directory title, it turns into a list of folders on the same disk or within the same folder. Hold down the mouse button and choose a higher level to get out of the current folder. Another way is to hold the Command key and use the up arrow key to move up through the hierarchy, one step at a time, and the down arrow key to move down. To save something to a different disk, insert the disk and its name appears as the directory name. If a disk is already on-line, click the Drive button to switch disk directories or simply press Tab.

File dialogs also appear when you first save something to disk, so you can specify into which disk or folder it goes. This type of dialog box has a field for naming the file as well, and sometimes buttons to specify its format.

The Edit menu

Most applications, including the Finder, have an Edit menu just to the right of the File menu. The Edit menu makes it possible to cut and copy a selection, storing it in a section of memory called the Clipboard, and paste it to another location. Select something to be copied or cut, choose the command, then move the insertion point and choose Paste. Sometimes the Edit menu also includes a choice for clearing a selection, deleting it without placing it on the Clipboard. Some applications even let you view the contents of the Clipboard.

If you make a mistake, you can correct it by choosing *Undo* from the Edit menu. This takes back your previous action, provided you haven't clicked the mouse or performed another action since then. If you accidentally delete a sequencer track that took hours to record and edit, Undo can save the day. Unfortunately, it can't get back something that's been thrown in the trash can when the trash is emptied. Usually, when you undo something, the Undo command turns to Redo, so you can take back your Undo command. Sometimes Undo only applies to deletions, replacing whatever was cut, cleared, or erased. A few programs have multiple levels of Undo, so you can perform a series of edits, then take back each step, one at a time.

System resources

Every startup disk has a folder called the *System folder*, which contains the Finder, the System, the printer drivers, and other operating system files. The size of the System file itself depends on the *resources* it contains. Resources are things like fonts, desk accessories, icons, and sounds which are contained in the System. Some resources may be manipulated, adding and removing them from the System to suit your needs. It may contain as many or as few resources as you wish, within limits. By changing its resources, your computer's operating system can be customized.

Fonts are a familiar resource to Mac users. There are two kinds of fonts: display fonts, also called screen fonts, and printer fonts, also called laser fonts or PostScript fonts. A display font is a representation of a typeface that appears onscreen. You can change the appearance of text, usually by selecting it and choosing a different typeface from the Font menu. When you print a document with a dot-matrix printer like an Apple ImageWriter, the printer uses the display font to print it at the same bit-map resolution as the screen. When you print with a PostScript printer like a LaserWriter, you need printer fonts for maximum resolution. Instead of being installed in the System, printer fonts are simply dragged into the System folder. To use a printer font, its corresponding display font must be in the System so it appears in the Font menu.

Desk accessories are equally familiar. Desk accessories, or DAs, are small applications that can run while full-sized applications are open. DAs give you multitasking without the memory requirements of MultiFinder.

The System file comes with several useful DAs like the Alarm Clock, Calculator, Chooser, Key Caps, and Scrapbook. You can add new DAs and remove the ones you don't need with an Apple utility program called the **Font/ Desk Accessory Mover**, or F/DAM for short.

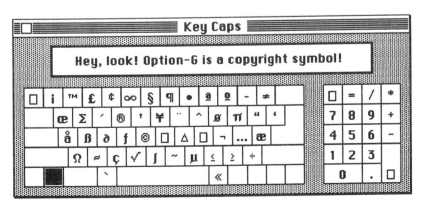

A few desk accessories are indispensable. The Control Panel lets you change sound generator volume, time and date, background pattern in the Finder, mouse tracking speed, settings for CDEVs and some INITs, and other details which are stored in the Mac's battery-backed parameter RAM. Another useful DA is Key Caps, which can display every character in any font. If you use more than one printer, the Chooser is used to select printers and AppleTalk network devices connected to the Mac's serial ports. Find File helps you locate a lost file if you type in part of its name. Text

processor DAs let you create, save, and open text files without quitting what you're working on. For musicians, there are DA patch librarians to send new sounds from your Mac to your synthesizer without quitting. Because the number of fonts and DAs is limited, you may need a font/DA utility like Suitcase II or Master Juggler, which give you access to a much larger number.

Apple's Font/Desk Accessory Mover is found on the System Tools disk that accompanies your Macintosh. Use it to add and delete fonts and DAs. When you run F/DAM, you're presented with a list of all the display fonts present in your System. Select a font by clicking on its name to display a brief example of its appearance. If you click the Desk Accessory button, it becomes a list of all your installed DAs. To remove a font or a DA, select it, then click the Remove button. To add a font or DA to your System file, open the file containing it, select it, then click the Copy button. You can click and drag to select a series of fonts or DAs, or you can shift-click to make discontiguous selections. Complete instructions for using Font/Desk Accessory Mover can be seen by clicking its Help button.

Deleting fonts and DAs is useful for "slimming down" your System to free up disk space. If your startup disk is a floppy, you need all the space you can get. At least one DA is required, so F/DAM will refuse to remove the last one. All fonts can be removed except for four required system fonts: Monaco 9 point, Geneva 9 point, Geneva 12 point, and Chicago 12 point.

INITs are another kind of system resource. They are loaded into memory when you start up your computer and run in the background until it's switched off. INITs include things like macro programs, screen savers, print spoolers, and virus detectors. Be careful that you have enough RAM to support the INITs in your System, or you may encounter memory problems when you run large applications.

Another system resource that should be mentioned is Apple's *Macintalk*. Macintalk is a system file that's required by program that makes the Mac speak. Talking Hypercard applications, games, kid's programs, and desk accessories like the Talking Moose can't work without Macintalk in the System folder.

Printing

Music scoring software exists to print music on paper. For that you need a printer. There are three kinds of printers that are most at home with the Macintosh: a dot-matrix Apple ImageWriter, a QuickDraw-based printer like the Apple LaserWriter IISC or the Hewlett-Packard DeskWriter, and a PostScript printer, most often a laser printer. An ImageWriter uses an inked fabric ribbon and prints at the same resolution as the Mac screen: 72 dpi (dots per inch). What you see on the screen, you get on paper, jagged lines and all. Other dot matrix printers without the

Just what is PostScript, anyway?

PostScript is a page description language used by some computer programs and output devices such as laser printers. Licensed to various manufacturers by Adobe, its developer, it has helped revolutionize the printing industry. PostScript tells a processor how to draw text and graphics, including music symbols, on a page. It describes images in a high-level computer language, not unlike English, as a series of instructions. A curve, for example, is described by its mathematical formula rather than as an arrangement of pixels. A *PostScript font* is a set of complex calculations for drawing every letter in a particular typeface.

The resolution of a PostScript image is limited only by the output device. An image can be as sharp as its printer is capable. The same PostScript document prints out on a LaserWriter at 300 dpi and on a Linotronic 300 at 2540 dpi. Images may be in black-and-white or color, again depending on the output device.

Some computers use a version called Display PostScript for monitor output, insuring that onscreen images look almost exactly the same as when they're printed. Just like the version for printers, the coarseness of Display PostScript is dependent on the resolution of the display screen.

Ultimately, printers and monitors do generate images as an assembly of bit-mapped dots. For finer resolution, some devices have higher dot density (measured in dots per inch) than others. Inside or attached to every PostScript output device, there's a dedicated image processor called an interpreter. Its job is to convert instructions from a PostScript program into a bit-mapped pattern of dots at whatever resolution the output device can handle.

ability to print 72 dpi bit-mapped graphics may not accurately reproduce what's onscreen, if they can print it at all. QuickDraw-based printers print high-resolution text by scaling down large fonts. PostScript printers usually have the best resolution, typically 300 dpi or better. Superior resolution results in smoother curves, less jagged angles, and better definition of text and images.

When printing on an ImageWriter, there are at least three degrees of print resolution. Draft printing prints very quickly in a simple, computerized-looking font. Music doesn't usually print in draft mode. Better resolution prints something as it appears onscreen. High quality resolution actually prints at 144 dpi, twice the resolution of the Mac screen. For high quality text, font dimensions are taken from an installed display font twice the size that's indicated, scaled by half. If twice as big isn't installed, the driver uses the largest font size available and scales it. A printer that uses QuickDraw, like GCC's Personal Laser Printer, uses the largest font size it can find and scales it down. If you use a QuickDraw printer, you want very large font sizes installed for the best print quality.

To use any printer, an appropriate printer driver should be installed by placing it in the System folder. The Macintosh System disk comes with drivers for the ImageWriter and LaserWriter, and other printer drivers are available. To avoid trouble, the version of the driver should match the version of the System. Most applications have a Page Setup… command in the File menu to tell your document about your printer.

It's possible to print the entire contents of the Mac screen, or take a "snapshot" of the screen and save it as a paint-program document. To do a *screen dump* to an ImageWriter, press Caps Lock, then shift-command-4. If you don't press Caps Lock, you print the contents of the currently active window. To create a paint document of the screen, press shift-command-3, or use the Camera DA. There are also utilities for doing a screen dump directly to a laser printer.

The *Chooser* is a desk accessory that lets you select which printer driver your computer uses to print. Your choice, of course, depends on which printer your computer's attached to. To change drivers, just click the new driver's icon and if a list of connect printers shows up, click the one you want to use. The Chooser also lets you turn AppleTalk on and off, and type in your user name.

Print spoolers are a real convenience. They allocate a certain amount of RAM as a print buffer. When you give the Print command, the printer data is loaded into this buffer. Then you can go back to work while your document is being printed. Large, complex documents take up lots of memory, so the use of a print spooler may be restricted by the amount of RAM in your computer.

Copy protection

It's an unfortunate fact of life that the majority of music software is copy-protected. In most cases, this means that you can't normally create a backup copy of an application disk. Copy protection prevents people from indiscriminately distributing software that's not paid for.

Most software works when you use a *key disk*, inserting the original floppy when you open a program before it will run.

A lot of professional music software uses a method which makes it impossible to copy to another floppy, but gives you a limited number of *hard disk installs*. Once installed, you can run a program without using a key disk. When you first run a protected

Some non-copy-protected applications don't fit on a single floppy, but have to be installed to a hard disk from a series of floppies. The only copy protection on some software is a serial number embedded in its code. If you give copies to your friends, your serial number points to who it came from. Some programs even ask your name the first time you run them, which is subsequently displayed every time you run them. Other software that isn't copy-protected may a specialized peripheral like Music Publisher's Presto keypad.

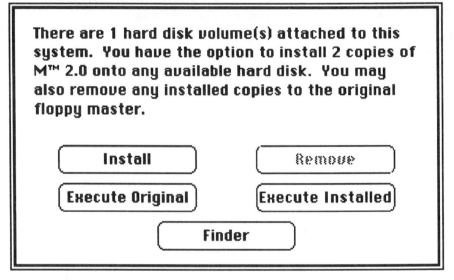

application from its original disk, the program detects if there's a mass storage device attached to your Mac. A window appears to install an application or remove it from the hard disk, recovering an install. Installing a program creates an invisible document that's needed to run it. If it's not installed on your hard disk, you can still use the key disk method. The risk in installing an application is that if the hard disk crashes or you forget and throw the application into the trash, you lose the install. Also, if you use a de-fragmentation program to rearrange the data on your hard disk, remove all installed applications first. Some programs come with separate utilities for installing to a hard disk.

Macintosh Hardware

All personal computers have at least four functions: input,

output, processing, and storage. Every Macintosh includes all the hardware it needs to fulfill these functions. A computer's potential computing power is determined by its hardware. Hardware is the main difference between more than ten existing models of the Macintosh.

Two means of user *input* are common to every Mac. The keyboard is used to type text and to issue commands. The mouse is used to select text and onscreen graphics, to choose commands, and to click buttons or whatever else needs clicking.

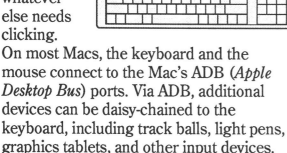

On most Macs, the keyboard and the mouse connect to the Mac's ADB (*Apple Desktop Bus*) ports. Via ADB, additional devices can be daisy-chained to the keyboard, including track balls, light pens, graphics tablets, and other input devices.

Two *RS-422 serial ports* provide additional sources of input. One is marked as a printer port and the other as a communications port, though most software that uses serial ports can use either. With a modem connected to the communications port, your computer can receive information from other computers over telephone lines.

MIDI interfaces also connect to the Mac's serial ports, so you can enter musical information from MIDI instruments. Some devices, like certain samplers, connect directly to the serial port. The SCSI port offers another means of input, receiving information from external devices like samplers and scanners.

The display monitor is the Mac's primary means of *output* in the form of bit-mapped text and graphical images. The Mac screen supplies visual information to its user. Its standard display resolution is 72 dpi (dots per inch), or 5184 square pixels per square inch. This is the same resolution as the Apple ImageWriter dot-matrix printer. The printer, communications, and SCSI ports all provide output. Connecting a printer or a plotter lets you display information on paper. Connecting a modem lets you send information to other computers. A MIDI interface sends data to musical instruments. The sound port provides audio information in the form of beeps, bongs, synthesized music, samples, and computer-generated speech.

The *processor*, also called the central processing unit or CPU, is the heart of any computer-based device, including desktop computers. It's the part that manipulates information, performing calculations and converting numbers into text, graphical images, and other useful forms. The processor needs instructions to know what to do. These instructions come from ROM chips and input devices.

The SE, the Portable, and all Macs made prior to the Mac II contain a Motorola 68000 microprocessor. Though its internal data path is 32 bits wide, it communicates with other circuits via a 16-bit bus. In the Mac, its clock speed is around 8 megaHertz. The Mac II contains a 68020, which has a true 32-bit external bus and twice the speed of the 68000 in other Macs. The 68030 found in most current models is even faster, with a built-in Paged Memory Management Unit to simplify multitasking, and data caches for the most recently executed instructions. Both the 68020 and 68030 are capable of clock speeds up to 33 megaHertz.

The remaining function of hardware is *storage*. There's nothing better than a computer for storing and retriving information. Data is stored temporarily in RAM, permanently in ROM and on optical disks, or semi-permanently on floppy disk, hard disk, magneto-optical disk, and tape backup.

Random Access Memory, or *RAM*, is the computer's main memory, the workspace where information is temporarily stored. Random access means that the processor instantly retrieves data from any memory location without having to look for it. RAM is very fast, but its contents are lost when the power is switched off. At any particular moment, RAM may contain an application, a file, a few resources like DAs and fonts, a disk directory, and the contents of the Clipboard. With large amounts of RAM, you can run more and larger files with more and larger applications.

Read Only Memory, or *ROM*, contains instructions for the microprocessor, permanently stored on one or more static memory chips. It tells the Mac what to do when it's switched on. It also stores most of the instructions for controlling the disk drive and the display monitor and for dealing with input. It contains the Hierarchical File System, the Macintosh Toolbox, QuickDraw and Color QuickDraw routines, and drivers for the various output ports and any coprocessors. The processor retrieves information from ROM just as quickly as RAM.

Files and applications are stored on various kinds of *disks*. Most desktop computers have a drive for reading an writing to floppy disk. Macs use single-sided, double-sided, or high-density 3.5-inch disks with a storage capacity of approximately 400K, 800K or 1400K. Two floppy drives are convenient for copying from one floppy disk to another, and practically necessary if you don't have mass storage. Hard disks and other mass storage devices connect to the Mac's *SCSI* (pronounced *scuzzy*) port. Up to seven SCSI devices can be chained.

Some mass storage drives have removable disks or cartridges for storing large amounts of data on a portable magnetic medium. These are great for storing sampler sound files. Digital information can also be stored on optical disks like CD-ROMs (compact disc with read only memory) and WORM (write once, read many) disks, and well as newer, eraseable optical disks. Apple's CD-ROM drive for the Macintosh can also play standard audio compact discs in stereo.

The Macintosh family

The original Apple Macintosh entered the world on the afternoon of January 24, 1984, a date that any self-respecting Mac pioneer should be able to recall at the drop of a proverbial hat. It had 128 kilobytes of RAM (that's one-eighth of a megabyte), a 400K floppy drive that used a new kind of single-sided 3.5-inch disks housed in plastic shells with metal shutters, a pointing device called a mouse, and something called a "user-friendly graphical interface" that made it comprehensible to the teaming masses. It looked like no computer ever built before. For $2495, the **Macintosh 128K** was the first mass-produced computer to use the Motorola 68000 32/16-bit processor, followed by the Commodore Amiga and the Atari ST.

Back in those days, when software was scarce and slow in coming, the Macintosh withstood a lot of unfavorable (and unfair) criticism in the press. Most computer folks didn't take it seriously. For a full year, all Macs had the same 9-inch monochrome screen, the same keyboard, the same mouse, the same sound hardware, the same clock/calendar circuit, ad infinitum. With no expansion slots, everything was standard, so everything was compatible.

When affordable RAM chips became easily available, the **512K** "Fat Mac" was introduced, also for $2495. The original Macintosh dropped to $1995. Upgrading an older Mac was a simple matter of soldering

in new RAM chips. With half a megabyte of memory — four times that of the earlier Mac — the Mac 512K could run more sophisticated programs.

A year after the Mac 128K's introduction, the **Macintosh Plus** appeared, sporting a keyboard with a numeric keypad, a double-sided 800K 3.5-inch drive, the first Macintosh SCSI port, a revised 128K ROM, and a full megabyte of expandable memory. Along with the Plus, Apple introduced the **512Ke** (Enhanced), a 512K with th ROM set and a double-sided drive. An upgrade from the 512 to 512Ke was offered for around three hundred dollars, and is still available.

The SCSI port was of special significance, because it allowed the Mac to connect to a new world of high-speed peripherals, making it realistically possible to compete with established business computers. SCSI stands for small computer systems interface. SCSI was an emerging standard developed not by Apple, but by a group of computer makers. The Mac was one of the first computers to integrate it.

On Mac Pluses and all later models, the printer and modem ports are round, mini-8 serial ports without the power pin needed by earlier MIDI interfaces, sound digitizers, and other hardware. The makers of a few of these older devices offer upgrades to adapt their hardware to newer Macs. To use an older Mac with a newer MIDI interface, all you need is an adapter cable.

Macs made before the Plus use something called the *Macintosh File System*. MFS is a method of organizing files on a disk, burned into the computer's ROM. Later

The SE is available with two internal floppy drives or with an internal hard disk and a single floppy drive. Newer SEs contain Apple's 1.4-megabyte (1400K) FDHD drive which reads and writes to disks formatted for the Mac, MS-DOS, OS/2, and ProDOS.

Mac ROMs, including the 512Ke, Plus, SE, and II, feature the *Hierarchical File System.* HFS lets you organize files in folders and folders in other folders, in a hierarchy. Older Macs don't recognize HFS disks unless the System folder on the startup disk contains a system file called HD20. If you own a Mac 128K or an older 512K, a lot of newer software won't run on your computer, especially graphics applications. Likewise, an HFS machine can't run some older Mac programs.

In 1987, both the Macintosh SE and the Macintosh II were unveiled. The 512Ke was discontinued and the Plus became the entry-level machine, where it's been ever since. The **Mac SE** (SCSI-Enhanced) has an SE expansion slot, a bit more speed than a Plus, and a built-in cooling fan. A choice of two keyboards and a redesigned mouse connect via the Apple Desktop Bus, which was introduced at the same time as the SE and II. Nineteen circuits in the Mac Plus were reduced to just one chip on the SE.

The SE, the II, and subsequent Macs run on both 120 volts and 240 volts, eliminating the need for a power transformer when you travel abroad.

With a true 32-bit 68020 processor running at twice the speed of 68000-based Macs, the **Macintosh II** also has a 68881 floating-point coprocessor for faster numeric computations. The II has twice as many SIMM locations as a compact Mac, so it can hold twice as much RAM. There are six 96-pin Nubus expansion slots and a 50-pin internal SCSI connector for internal hard drives, but no port for an external floppy drive. The Mac II doesn't have a built-in display, and requires one or more expansion cards to drive a monitor. It contains the Apple Sound Chip, a stereo circuit with a sampling rate of 44.1 kHz. The II was the first color Macintosh, with ROM support for 16.8 million colors. Though it runs software that earlier Macs can't, a lot of pre-1988 Mac software doesn't run on the II.

The **SE/30** is more powerful than the II, but it looks almost exactly like an SE — same small footprint, same monochrome display, but with a 32-bit 68030 processor running at four times the speed of the SE. Its 68882 coprocessor crunches numbers up to 25 times faster. It has one 1.4M FDHD drive and a port for connecting a second floppy drive. There's also one high-speed 030 Direct slot with a 120-pin Euro-DIN connector to plug in an accelerator card, a DSP (digital signal processing) card, or a video card for a large external monitor. The SE/30's 256K ROM is on a snap-in SIMM for easy replacement. It contains Color QuickDraw, so it runs just about any Macintosh software. The SE/30 is the only compact Mac with the Apple Sound Chip.

The **IIx** looks like a II, but contains all the same enhancements as the SE/30, plus six Nubus expansion slots instead of an 030 Direct slot. There's room for a larger internal hard drive and an optional second FDHD drive. Like the II, it lacks an external floppy port. At 24 pounds without a keyboard or monitor, the Mac IIx CPU weighs more than any compact Mac.

The **Mac IIcx** looks like a sawed-off Mac IIx. It has only three Nubus slots, and it does have a port for an external floppy drive. Like the IIx and SE/30, it has a 68030 processor, a 68882 coprocessor, and an FDHD drive. The IIcx is the most portable of the modular Macs.

With a 68030 processor running at 25 MHz, the **Macintosh IIci** is the fastest Mac made by Apple. It features three Nubus slots and a built-in 8-bit color video controller, so connecting a monitor doesn't take up one of the slots. The IIci also has a direct 120-pin slot for a high-speed RAM cache card.

Answering the demand for a laptop version of the Macintosh, the **Mac Portable** has a rechargeable, battery-operated power supply and an active matrix liquid crystal display screen. Like older Macs, it's based on the Motorola 68000, so its data buses are 16-bit rather than 32-bit, but it runs at twice the speed of other 68000-based Macs.

The Portable has a power manager chip to conserve battery life. It comes with one megabyte of RAM, and a 40-megabyte hard disk is available as an option.

Whenever you buy a computer or any piece of music technology, you're running the risk that a new model will come along to make yours obsolete. What new Macs does the future have in store? An entry-level computer resembling the original Mac SE is slated to eventually replace the venerable Plus. A 68030 laptop version is probably inevitable. Motorola's 68040 will probably find its way into future Macs. Only time will tell, but Apple will certainly take new models where no Mac has gone before.

Keeping up with upgrades

As computer technology advances, the design and capabilities of musical equipment (including desktop computers) are subject to change. During the life of the Mac, Apple and other companies have offered upgrades to give older models the power of newer ones. Among the most useful hardware upgrades are ROMs with new operating systems, faster processors, and increased memory to handle

multitasking and larger, more demanding applications.

Since the introduction of the original Macintosh in 1984, ROMs have been changed to support HFS, AppleTalk, and newer hardware, SCSI and ADB ports have been added, and the serial ports have been redesigned. The capacity of floppy drives has grown. The number of internal parts has been reduced, and the keyboard and mouse have been redesigned. Larger, more capable Mac configurations have become available, with stereo sound, expansion slots, and color monitors. All current Macs except the Plus and SE have the Apple Sound Chip, with twice the performance of the older Mac sound generator.

It's possible to buy certain hardware upgrades from Apple, like kits to turn a Mac 128K or 512K into a 512Ke or a Plus, an SE into an SE/30, a II into a IIx, or a IIcx into a IIci. You can upgrade a 68020-based Mac II to run software intended for 68030 machines simply by adding a 68851 PPMU chip. Depending on the cost, upgrading your Mac isn't always a smart idea. It's often cheaper to sell an old Mac and buy a new one than to upgrade to a newer model.

Memory expansion

Macintosh applications are becoming more memory-hungry than ever. Fortunately, it's rather simple to boost the RAM in any current model simply by replacing the SIMMs. A *SIMM* is a *single in-line memory module*, a small, plug-in circuit board containing dynamic random access memory (DRAM) chips. SIMMs with the memory chips soldered on are called surface-mount SIMMs. These are desirable because they have a low profile and take less space than socketed SIMMs. SIMMs with chips in sockets are taller, which may prevent installing an expansion card on an SE or a hard drive on a II.

The SE and the Plus have sockets for four SIMMs, two banks with two sockets each. The SE/30 and all the IIs have two banks with four sockets each. Both banks don't have to be filled, but you can't have an incomplete bank. Each bank must contain SIMMs of the same size.

Most Macs are sold with a single megabyte of memory in the form of four 256K SIMMs. They may be replaced by one megabyte SIMMs or the newer four megabyte SIMMs. Replacing all four SIMMs with 1M versions adds up to four megabytes of RAM. If you replace two 256K SIMMs with 1M SIMMs, leaving the other two in place, the result is two and a half megabytes. If your Mac has eight sockets, you can leave all four 256K SIMMs in place and add up to four 1M SIMMs, for a total of five megabytes. If all eight SIMM sockets contain 4M SIMMs, the computer has 32 megabytes of main memory, 256 times as much as the original Mac. Even larger capacity memory chips no doubt lie in the future.

SIMMs are fairly easy to remove and install, but if you feel uncomfortable popping open your computer and mucking around in its guts, get a service technician to do the job. That way, if it doesn't work, you don't have to pay extra to make it right. Can you survive overnight without your trusty Mac by your side?

Mass storage

Adding any mass storage device to your Mac greatly increases your status as a power user. For the Mac, mass storage includes magnetic media like hard disks, removable hard disks, removable cartridges, megafloppies, Bernoulli disks, and tape, including DAT, and optical media like CD-ROMs, WORMs, and erasable optical discs. Drives for these devices connect to the Mac via the SCSI port. The technology of mass storage is subject to change in the next few years, and the storage device you buy today may be considered obsolete down the road. Magnetic drives are faster than optical drives, but they're more prone to damage. Optical media are written to and read by lasers. Optical discs can store a lot more data than magnetic disks (note the difference in spelling), but optical drives are generally more expensive.

For most people, a *hard disk* is the usual choice for everyday data storage. Hard disks are fast, pretty dependable, and relatively economical. The cost of hard disks has fallen dramatically in the last few years, as their speed and storage capacity have increased, ranging from 20 to as much as 1000 megabytes. With a hard disk, you can boot up your computer and have immediate access to dozens of applications and files. All your fonts, desk accessories,

INITs, and other resources are always online. SCSI hard disks are accessed much faster than floppy disks, so loading and saving times are decreased. A hard disk can be internal, within your computer's case, or an external peripheral that connects with a SCSI cable.

Unfortunately, they're not very rugged. Hard disks are not permanent storage, because they can be fairly easily damaged and data can be destroyed. Avoid dropping a hard disk. (As I was writing this chapter, my hard disk fell right off the table. Kids, don't try this at home.) If your hard disk crashes, you can lose everything. For this reason, it's a good idea to acquire a good backup utility to regularly backup your hard disk on some other magnetic medium, typically a series of floppies or a tape backup drive, or to an optical medium like a WORM or an EO for archiving. I've got some bad news about copy-protection: If you have music applications that have been properly installed onto your hard disk, there's no way to keep from losing an install in event of a hard disk crash.

The advantages of a removable storage medium are that you can tuck it safely away or take it with you wherever you go, provided there's an appropriate drive at your destination. Removable-medium drives are more expensive, but once you've invested in the drive, it costs less to buy more storage space.

Removable hard disks range in capacity from around 30 to 200 megabytes. The drive itself is a chassis for the disk pack, which contains both the disk and the read/write mechanism. Removable hard drives are as fast or faster than fixed hard drives, but considerably more expensive.

You can pack up a removable hard disk and take it to another location, but to read it, you need a drive like the one that wrote it.

Removable *SyQuest cartridges* are less expensive, because the read/write mechanism is in the chassis rather than in the cartridge. They're also more vulnerable to damage. The media is smaller than removable hard disks, and they all have a capacity of 42 megabytes. Different vendors repackage the drives they purchase from SyQuest. Since all SyQuest drives are identical, their cartridges are interchangable, inscreasing the odds of finding another drive to read it.

Bernoulli boxes are drives for high-density 5.25-inch disks that store from 20 to 44 megabytes. They're not as fast as hard drives, but they have a well-established reputation for reliability, and drives aren't hard to find. *Megafloppies* are essentially similar, but slower and less expensive. They use disks that hold from 20 to 40 megabytes. Megafloppy drives aren't standardized, and they're not considered as dependable as Bernoullis.

Optical drives are considerably slower than magnetic drives, but they're still faster than floppy drives. Optical discs permanently store relatively huge amounts of information. A single *CD-ROM* disc stores over 550MB, and like any removable medium, you can have as many CD-ROM discs as you can afford. One company is developing a CD-ROM jukebox capable of holding 240 discs.

Though CD-ROM discs aren't expensive to manufacture, the drives are still fairly costly, but prices are expected to drop considerably in the next couple years. They have two disadvantages: they're painfully slow at present, and you can't store, alter, or erase information on them (unless you're into large-scale manufacturing). Used mainly as a medium for software distribution, you can buy CD-ROMs containing entire reference libraries or high-quality sampler sound libraries in sampler editor format.

Erasable optical (EO) discs, like the ones used for the NeXT computer, hold a lot of promise. Storing around 600 megabytes, they're double-sided and can be flipped over like an LP. These so-called "floptical" discs are partially magnetic, because the drive's laser changes the polarity of the surface. Reversing the polarity erases stored information. Erasable opticals have the fastest drives of all the optical discs, but they're the most expensive at present.

WORM drives are also expensive, but they're slower than EO drives. Most useful for permanent storage and archiving, you can write to a WORM disc repeatedly until it's full, but you can't erase or change anything once it's stored. A single disc holds 200 or 400 megabytes, depending on whether it's single- or double-sided. Sony makes a WORM jukebox system that stores around 160 gigabytes.

Display monitors

Macintosh display screens are found in many sizes, all the way up to a 37-inch model from Mitsubishi. Along with the video card required to drive it, a big-screen monochrome, gray-scale, or color monitor probably costs more than a typical monitor for most computers. All Macs except the IIci require a video card plugged into an expansion slot to use an external monitor.

On an SE or SE/30, an external monitor probably prevents you from installing an accelerator board or a *Sound Accelerator.*

When you get a larger display for most kinds of computers, you increase the size of the *pixels*. Pixels are those tiny square bits on a bit-mapped screen. A Mac monitor maintains approximately 72 dpi resolution no matter what size it is to maintain WYSIWYG (what-you-see-is-what-you-get). When you move up to a larger monitor, your onscreen desktop just gets bigger. There's room for more windows, bigger windows, and more open applications and documents. Full-page and two-page displays are great for desktop publishing and music scoring. On the downside, sometimes it's an awfully long way from the bottom of the screen to the menu bar. If you have a Mac with an onboard monitor, most external monitor drivers let you use both monitors at the same time. You can even drag images between screens.

Irrespective of size, there are three kinds of Macintosh monitors: monochrome, gray-scale, and color. A *monochrome* display has pixels that are either black or white. Shades of gray are accomplished with patterns of black and white pixels. Portable Macs have built-in monochrome monitors. In addition to balck and white, *gray-scale* monitors have pixels that display shades of gray, making them much more clear and photographic in appearance. Gray-scale monitors differ by how many levels of gray they display, all the way up to 256 shades. The number of shades a single pixel is capable of displaying is determined by bit resolution. Gray-scale video cards are available in 4-bit, 8-bit, 16-bit and 32-bit versions. *Color* monitor drivers also differ in bit resolution. With a large monitor and a

32-bit driver, you can display 16.8 million different colors simultaneously with more clarity than a 35mm movie screen.

Accelerators

The performance of any Macintosh can be significantly improved by installing an accelerator to replace the Mac's factory-installed processor. On modular Macs, an accelerator board replaces the original processor instead of plugging into a Nubus slot, which would slow down data transfer. On SEs and SE/30s, accelerators plug right into the expansion slot. For the Plus and older Macs without slots, clip-on expansion cards are available.

Accelerator boards contain a 68000, 68020, or 68030 processor running at higher speeds than normal Mac processors. They usually have a floating-point coprocessor, instruction and data caches, and sockets for high-speed RAM chips. The advantages are faster execution of instructions, faster calculation of real numbers, and a wider data path. In other words, an accelerator speeds up everything: how fast a program loads, how fast a file is opened, how fast the screen redraws, and so on. Unless you're experienced at such matters, you may want to rely on a service technician to install an accelerator board.

Add-on audio hardware

The **Sound Accelerator** is Digidesign's 16-bit accelerator board for processing digitally recorded sound. In a modular Mac, it goes into one of the Nubus slots. In an SE or an SE/30, it fills the expansion slot. When you're working with sampler software, Sound Accelerator plays full-fidelity, stereo samples directly from the Macintosh, without having to transfer them to your sampler. Thanks to its Motorola 56001 digital signal processor, it performs DSP functions, if not in real time, then very, very quickly. This means that when you change something about a sound file, you can hear your change almost instantly. For editing recordings on digital tape machines, digital outputs are available as an option. Best of all, it works with a variety of software, including everything mentioned in the chapter on sample editors.

To record equally high-quality samples into the Macintosh without a sampling instrument, there's Digidesign's **AD-IN** box. Essentially a two-channel, analog-to-digital converter with a pair of clipping indicators and gain controls, it records sound directly to the Mac's hard disk. Teamed with a Sound Accelerator and editing software like Sound Designer II or Alchemy, AD-IN turns the Mac into a hard disk recording system called **Sound Tools**. With Sound Tools, it's possible to cut and paste real recorded music and easily perform complex digital signal processing functions. Create and edit a playlist to hear alternate versions of a recording, like rearranging the verses in a song, for instance. Recorded events can be synchronized to SMPTE with a MIDI Time Code converter.

Another Macintosh-based hard disk recording system is the **IMS Dyaxis**. The Dyaxis is an audio processor that handles A-to-D conversion for recording and D-to-A conversion for playback. It has variable sampling rates, topping out at 48 kHz. With a Dyaxis and sample editing software, you have, in essence, a 16-bit stereo sampler that can record an entire album side if your hard disk has the capacity. Part of the system is a dedicated Dyaxis hard drive. A SMPTE reader/writer is also available as an option.

MIDI interfaces and synchronizers

To get MIDI signals into and out of the Macintosh, it needs a MIDI interface or adapter connected to one of its RS-422 ports. Most interfaces connect to a single serial port and provide 16 channels of MIDI. By connecting a MIDI interface to each port, you have 32 channels of MIDI. Some interfaces provide up to 64 channels. A few interfaces have built-in SMPTE-to-MIDI Time Code converters to synchronize sequences and event lists to tape or film. These often have powerful MIDI processing functions as well. Some MIDI interfaces connect to an external time code reader/generator like the Opcode Timecode Machine to give them sync-to-tape capabilities.

MIDI interfaces don't have to be complicated. The simplest have a MIDI In jack, a MIDI out jack, and a serial port cable. The **Apple MIDI Interface** is a basic one-in, one-out unit. Passport's interface is similar, and it connects to Passport's optional FSK synchronizer. The Altech interfaces are economical and popular. Their **1 x 3 MIDI Interface** is a plastic tube with a single MIDI input and three MIDI Out ports for three separate MIDI sends. Altech also makes a **2 x 6** model, a box that connects to both serial ports, with assignable MIDI

Out jacks. Three outputs can be assigned to each serial port or all six to a single port. Two inputs let you connect two MIDI keyboards or other controllers. Alternately, you can connect a controller and a MIDI Time Code converter so you can record while synched to tape. Another two-in, six-out unit is the **MacFace**, from Sonus. It has LEDs to indicate MIDI activity on each of the Mac's serial ports, and serves as a MIDI thru box even when the computer is turned off. Opcode's two-input, six-output MIDI interface is the **Studio Plus Two**. It connects to both serial ports and fits perfectly under a portable Mac. It has bypass switches so you can use your modem or printer without disconnecting the MIDI interface. Opcode also makes a one-in, three-out model called the **Professional Plus**.

Opcode's top-of-the-line model is the **Studio 3**. It's a combination MIDI interface, SMPTE-to-MTC synchronizer, and click-to-MIDI trigger with two MIDI Ins and six assignable MIDI outs. It reads and writes four SMPTE formats. Like the Studio Plus Two, the Studio 3 has switches to patch other serial devices through.

There's also an optional foot controller unit with two switches and a pedal for controlling tempo and remote functions of their sequencer Vision.

Passport makes the **MIDI Transport**, a two-in, four-out interface that reads and writes SMPTE, converts SMPTE to MTC or direct time lock, and converts FSK signals to MIDI Song Pointer messages. The MIDI Transport connects to both serial ports and is designed to sit under the Mac.

The original, all-in-one MIDI interface, MIDI processor, SMPTE reader/generator, SMPTE-to-direct time lock, and SMPTE-to-MTC converter is the Southworth **JamBox/4+**. It has four inputs and four outputs that can be configured in a multitude of ways. Any combination of inputs can be routed to any combination of outputs, with 16 separate channels on each MIDI Out. You can merge, filter, and rechannelize MIDI data, assigning it to any output. MIDI processing and synchronization functions are controlled by a desk accessory that installs a menu in the menu bar. The JamBox/4+ connects to either of the Mac's serial ports, and features a high-speed MIDI mode for software that supports it.

If you already have a MIDI interface, it's possible to add sync-to-tape capability with a free-standing MIDI synchronizer like the Southworth **JamBox/2** or the Opcode **Timecode Machine**. Both devices read and write SMPTE and convert SMPTE to MIDI Time Code. Along with the ability to merge two MIDI inputs to a single output, the JamBox/2 offers sync-to-click synchronization and stores tempo maps for sequencers that don't record tempo changes. The Timecode Machine also converts SMPTE to the direct time lock used by some sequencers.

Appendix: Company Contacts

Adobe Systems
1585 Charleston Road
Mountain View, CA 94039
(415) 961-4400

Alesis
3630 Holdrege Avenue
Los Angeles, CA 90016
(213) 467-8000

Altech Systems
831 Kings Highway, Suite 200
Shreveport, LA 71104
(318) 226-1702

Apple Computer
20525 Mariani Avenue
Cupertino, CA 95014
(408) 996-1010

Apriori
859 Hollywood Way, Suite 401
Burbank, CA 91510
(818) 955-9638

Ars Nova
P.O. Box 40629
Santa Barbara, CA 93140
(805) 564-2518

Baudville
5380 52nd Street SE
Grand Rapids, MI 49508
(616) 698-0888

Beaverton Digital
1485 North Bundy Drive
Los Angeles, CA 90049
(213) 471-7190

Blank Software
1477 Folsum Street
San Francisco, CA 94103
(415) 863-9224

Bogas Productions
520 Cashew Court
San Ramon, CA 94583
(415) 332-6427
(415) 829-2444

Casio
570 Mt. Pleasant Avenue
Dover, NJ 07801

Coda Music Software
1401 East 79th Street, Suite 1
Bloomington, MN 55425
(612) 854-1288

Compusonics
2345 Yale Street
Palo Alto, CA 94306
(415) 494-1184

CTM Development
av. Cardinal-Mermillod 18
CH-1227 Carouge (GE)
Geneva, Switzerland

Digidesign
1360 Willow Road, Suite 101
Menlo Park, CA 94025
(415) 327-8811

Digital Music Services
23010 Lake Forest Drive, Suite
D334
Laguna Hills, CA 92653
(714) 951-1159

Dr.T's Music Software
220 Boylston Street, Suite 206
Chestnut Hill, MA 02167
(617) 244-6954

Electronic Arts
1820 Gateway Drive
San Mateo, CA 94404
(415) 571-7171

Electronic Musician
6400 Hollis Street, #12
Emeryville, CA 94608
(415) 653-3307

E-mu Systems
1600 Green Hills Road
Scotts Valley, CA 95066
(408) 438-1921

Farallon Computing
2201 Dwight Way
Berkeley, CA 94704
(415) 849-2331
OR
Farallon Computing
2150 Kittredge Street
Berkeley, CA 94704
(415) 549-7283

GEnie
401 North Washington Street
Rockville, MD 20850
(301) 340-4494

GPI Publications
20085 Stvens Creek Blvd.
Cupertino, CA 95014

Great Wave Software
5353 Scotts Valley Drive
Scotts Valley, CA 95066
(408) 438-1990

H.B. Imaging
560 South State Street, Suite
G1
Orem, Utah 84058
(801) 225-7222

Hip Software
117 Harvard Street, Suite 3
Cambridge, MA 02139

Intergrated Media Systems
1370 Willow Road, Suite 201
Menlo Park, CA 94025
(415) 326-7030

Intelligent Music
116 North Lake Avenue
Albany, NY 12206
(518) 434-4110

International MIDI Association
5316 West 57th Street
Los Angeles, CA 90056
(213) 649-6434

Julian Systems
2280 Bates Avenue, Suite J
Concord, CA 94520
(415) 686-4400

KAT
43 Meadow Road
Longmeadow, MA 01106
(413) 567-1395

Kawai America Corp.
2055 East University Drive
Compton, CA 90220
(213) 631-1771

Keyboard Magazine
20085 Stevens Creek
Cupertino, CA 95014
(408) 446-1105

Keyboard Technologies
16137 Sherman Way, Suite 169
Van Nuys, CA 91406
(818) 891-6999

Kinko's Academic Courseware
Exchange
4141 State Street
Santa Barbara, CA 93110
(805) 967-0192

Korg U.S.A.
89 Frost Street
Westbury, NY 11590
(516) 333-9100

Kurzweil Music Systems
411 Waverly Oaks Road
Waltham, MA 02154
(617) 893-5900

MacMIDI Distributing
18 Haviland Street
Boston, MA 02115
(617) 266-2886

MacroMind
1028 West Wolfram Street
Chicago, IL 60657
(312) 871-0987

Mark of the Unicorn
222 Third Street
Cambridge, MA 02142
(617) 576-2760

Oberheim ECC
2015 Davie Avenue
Commerce, CA 90040
(213) 725-7870

Opcode Systems
1024 Hamilton Court
Menlo Park, CA 94025
(415) 321-8977

Optical Media International
485 Alberto Way, Suite 115
Los Gatos, CA 95032
(408) 395-4332

Passport Designs
625 Miramontes Street
Half Moon Bay, CA 94019
(415) 726-0280

Primera Software
650 Cragmont
Berkeley, CA 94708
(800) 248-0403

Resonate
P.O. Box 996
Menlo Park, CA 94026
(415) 323-5022

Roland Corp. US
7200 Dominion Circle
Los Angeles, CA 90040
(213) 685-5141

Sonus
21430 Strathern Street, Suite H
Canoga Park, CA 91304
(818) 702-0992

Southworth Music Systems
91 Ann Lee Road
Harvard, MA 01451
(508) 772-9471

Studio Master Computer Systems
229 Sunny Isles Boulevard
North Miami Beach, FL 33160
(305) 945-9774

Words & Deeds
4480 Sunnycrest Drive
Los Angeles, CA 90065
(213) 255-2887

Yamaha Music Corporation
6600 Orangethorpe Avenue
Buena Park, CA 90622
(714) 522-9011

Glossary

accidental - a prefix or suffix modifying a note's pitch, including sharp, flat, natural, double-sharp, and double-flat

additive synthesis - the construction of complex waveforms by combining simple waveforms of various amplitudes and frequencies

ADSR - 1) four stages of an envelope: attack, decay, sustain, and release; 2) a common four-stage envelope generator

aftertouch - pressure-sensitivity; the ability of a keyboard to produce controller data in response to how hard a key is pressed after it's struck

algorithm - 1) a digital set of instructions for performing a function; 2) the configuration of operators in an FM synthesizer

algorithmic composition - a form of improvisation in which a computer makes musical decisions, usually within parameters defined by the performer

amplitude - 1) the strength or intensity of a sound or signal; 2) the measure of a current's deviation from its zero value

analog - 1) a term describing a circuit, device, or system which responds to continuously-variable parameters; 2) generated by hardware rather than by software

analog-to-digital converter - a circuit which periodically samples a continuously-variable voltage and generates a digital representation of its value; also called an A-to-D or A/D converter

attack - the beginning of a sound

bank - a group of digital storage locations; a section of memory

basic channel - the MIDI channel on which a multitimbral instrument receives patch changes and mode messages

beat - a metronomic division which indicates rhythmic pulse, most often represented by a quarter note's duration

bit - a binary digit; a digitally-stored number with a value of either 0 or 1

break point - 1) a graphical handle on an envelope's line segment, used to reshape the envelope; 2) the note above or below which an instrument's output or envelope parameters are boosted or cut, controlled by keyboard scaling or rate scaling

byte - a digital unit of information comprised of an eight-bit word

carrier - a signal which is modulated; modulation destination

channel message - a MIDI command or data which is sent over a specific MIDI channel

click - 1) to position an onscreen cursor, then press and release the mouse button; 2) an audible metronomic pulse, usually played at a rate of once per beat

clock - a periodic signal used to indicate tempo and synchronize playback

continuous controller - 1) a device such as a wheel or slider which sends MIDI data whose values can be varied in real time; 2) a MIDI message sent by manipulating a manual controller such as a thumbwheel, slider, lever, pedal, or switch

controller - 1) a MIDI instrument played by a performer and capable of producing musical information, especially note data; 2) a continuous controller

cut and paste - an editing operation in which data is moved from one location to another via the Macintosh clipboard

data byte - an eight-bit word which specifies a numeric value

decay - a portion of an envelope in which a signal level decreases in value

default - a parameter value which exists when hardware is turned on or an application is run

digital-to-analog converter - a circuit which generates a digital representation of a continuously-variable signal; also called an D-to-A or D/A converter or DAC

edit - to change or modify existing information

editor - a type of MIDI software used to change sound data parameters

envelope - a graph of changes in a sound's loudness characteristics; a waveform with dynamic variations in amplitude or signal level; also called contour

envelope generator - a circuit or function which generates a changing control signal in discrete stages, often applied to give shape to events in time; also called contour generator

equalization - a selective alteration of an audio signal's frequency spectrum or bandwidth; also called EQ

filter - a circuit or function which alters a signal's frequency spectrum by attenuating or accentuating certain portions

FM synthesis - a method of generating complex waveforms by modulating the frequency of audio waveforms (carriers) with other waveforms (modulators); frequency modulation

font - typeface or family of related typefaces

frame rate - in film or video, the frequency at which single frames are shown, usually equal to 24, 25, or 30 frames per second

fundamental frequency - a sound's primary frequency; the first harmonic

harmonic - a simple component of a complex waveform that's a whole-number multiple of the fundamental frequency; a partial

Hertz - cycles per second, the standard unit of frequency; abbreviated Hz

interval - the difference in pitch between two musical tones

layering - a mode in which two or more sounds are played simultaneously with the same note on message

LFO - low-frequency oscillator; a circuit or function which generates repeating signals in the sub-audio range, most often used as a modulation source for vibrato

librarian - a type of MIDI software which stores and organizes sound data for MIDI instruments

loop - 1) to repeat a recorded passage a number of times; 2) to repeat a portion of a digital sample, extending its duration while conserving memory; 3) repetition defined by a start point and end point in time

MIDI - musical instrument digital interface; a means of communicating musical information among computers and microprocessor-based devices

MIDI Time Code - a format which indicates location in real time by sending quarter frame messages at a rate of 120 per second; abbreviated MTC

mode - a condition which determines how something may function

modulation - a perceptible change in a sound or signal's character in response to a control signal, such as vibrato or tremolo

monophonic - capable of playing only one note at a time; single-voiced

multitimbral - a term describing an instrument which is capable of producing a number of dissimilar sounds simultaneously, often receiving information on more than one MIDI channel

operator - a software-generated pairing of an oscillator and an envelope generator used in FM synthesis

oscillator - a circuit or software which generates audio signals

parallel interface - a connection between devices which transfers one or more bytes of information simultaneously

parameter - a variable characteristic or value

partial - a component of a complex sound with a frequency higher than the fundamental frequency; overtone

patch - a collection of parameters which defines a synthesized sound; also called a program and sometimes a voice

patch change - a command which loads a configuration of parameters into main memory; also called a program change

pitch bend - an action which momentarily raises or lowers oscillator frequency, usually under manual control

polyphonic - capable of playing more than one note at a time; multi-voiced

punch - to replace selected musical information on a tape or sequencer track by recording between two specific points in time, without altering the information that occurs before the punch in point or after the punch out point

quantization - an editing operation that moves the beginning of each note to the nearest fraction or multiple of a beat

RAM - random-access memory; a computer's main memory in which information is temporarily stored

real time - the actual time in which something takes place, such as a live musical performance

release - an envelope generator's final stage, in which its signal usually returns to a zero value, and which occurs when a note off signal is received

resynthesis - the process of digitally replicating a sound by generating a model of its spectral profile

ROM - read-only memory; information permanently stored in memory circuits, often containing instructions or other unalterable data

sample - 1) to digitally encode an analog signal; 2) a digitally-recorded sound; 3) a single digital representation of an audio signal, usually occurring hundreds or thousands of times per second

sampler - an electronic musical instrument which samples, manipulates, and plays back sounds under MIDI control

scoring software - an application used to transcribe music in traditional notation

semitone - the chromatic interval between two adjacent notes; a half step

sequencer - an application or device that records MIDI data, usually emulating a multitrack tape recorder

serial - a connection between devices which transfers information one bit after another

sine - a pure, simple waveform comprised of a single frequency with no overtones; a single partial in a complex waveform

SMPTE - a type of time code adopted by the Society of Motion Picture and Television Engineers, used to indicate location in time and synchronize playback

song file - a computer document which contains musical information such as a musical score, sequence, or song

song position pointer - a MIDI message which indicates location in a sequence by counting how many MIDI clocks have passed since its beginning

split - to divide a keyboard or another MIDI controller by pitch range, so that each section controls a different instrument or sound

status byte - an eight-bit word which identifies what kind of message it is and where it's going

step time - a means of recording musical data one event at a time, as opposed to real time

subtractive synthesis - the process of producing sounds by filtering complex waveforms; commonly called analog synthesis

sustain - an envelope stage with a constant level

synchronization - a means by which instruments and/or recordings play in tandem, and whose playback rate is controlled by a common time code; also called sync

system exclusive - a MIDI message addressed to a specific type of instrument, and whose format is defined by the instrument's manufacturer

system message - a MIDI message which isn't channel-specific

tempo - the rate at which music is played

timbre - tone color, which is dependent on harmonic content and distinguishes one sound from another

transpose - to change pitch or key signature

truncate - to remove recorded data before or after a sample

velocity - the force with which a note is played or released, which produces a MIDI value between 0 and 127

vibrato - sub-audio variation in pitch, used to add expression to musical performance

waveform - the shape or instantaneous amplitude of an individual wave; the transient characterisctics of a single cycle

wavetable - a set of digitally-recorded or digitally-generated waveforms used as a source of instrumental sounds; also called a lookup table

zone - a specific division of keys or notes which controls a particular sound or transmits on a particular MIDI channel; a section of a musical keyboard with multiple split points

Index